Race Against the Court

RACE AGAINST THE COURT

The Supreme Court and Minorities
in Contemporary America

Girardeau A. Spann

NEW YORK UNIVERSITY PRESS
NEW YORK AND LONDON

NEW YORK UNIVERSITY PRESS
New York and London

Library of Congress Cataloging-in-Publication Data

Spann, Girardeau A., 1948–
    Race against the court : Supreme Court and minorities in contemporary America /
Girardeau A. Spann.
        p.   cm.
    Includes bibliographical references and index.
    ISBN 0-8147-7963-8
    1. Afro-Americans—Civil rights. 2. United States. Supreme Court. I. Title.
KF4757.S65 1993
342.73′0873—dc20   92-31342
[347.302873]   CIP

New York University Press books are printed on acid-free paper, and
their binding materials are chosen for strength and durability.

Manufactured in the United States of America

c 10 9 8 7 6 5 4 3 2 1

Contents

v

Acknowledgments

I would like to thank Anita Allen, Derrick Bell, Gregg Bloche, Richard Chused, Richard Delgado, Steven Goldberg, Tom Krattenmaker, Elizabeth Patterson, Gary Peller, Barry Pollack, Mitt Regan, Louis Seidman, and Mark Tushnet for their help in developing the ideas expressed in this book. In addition, I benefitted from the comments of faculty, students, and staff members who participated in the workshop series at Columbia Law School and at the University of Michigan Law School, where I delivered portions of the thesis that is developed herein.

I am extremely grateful to my editor Niko Pfund and to the New York University Press for their help and cooperation in the publication of this book. In addition, the MICHIGAN LAW REVIEW was kind enough to publish portions of the manuscript that ultimately evolved into this book in *Pure Politics*, 88 MICH. L. REV. 1971 (1990). Support for the book was generously provided by a research grant from the Georgetown University Law Center.

Race Against the Court

Introduction

The present Supreme Court has been noticeably unreceptive to legal claims asserted by racial minorities. Although it is always possible to articulate nonracial motives for the Court's civil rights decisions, the popular perception is that a politically conservative majority wishing to cut back on the protection of minority interests at majority expense now dominates the Supreme Court. In reviewing the work of the Court during its infamous 1988–89 term, U.S. LAW WEEK reported that "[a] series of civil rights decisions by a conservative majority of the U.S. Supreme Court making it easier to challenge affirmative action programs and more difficult to establish claims of employment discrimination highlighted the 1988–89 term's labor and employment cases."[1] LAW WEEK went on to cite seven decisions handed down that Term alone that adversely affected minority interests.[2] Many of those decisions, as well as some of the other conservative civil rights decisions issued by the Court since 1985, were subsequently overruled by Congress in the Civil Rights Act of 1991.[3] These legislative reversals, however, came only after a bitter political debate that was characterized most strongly by the racially divisive political opposition mounted against the proposed legislation by the Bush Administration.[4] Since the 1988–89 Term, Justices Brennan and Marshall have resigned from the Supreme Court and have been replaced by Justices Souter and Thomas, both of whom are significantly more conservative than their predecessors in matters relating to civil rights. As a result, the common perception is that the new Supreme Court will be even less receptive to the claims of racial minorities in the foreseeable future.

One could argue, of course, that what we are witnessing is the proper operation of a complex and sophisticated governmental process; that the Court, consistent with a refined understanding of its constitutional function, is exhibiting a proper sensitivity to the evolving content of our fundamental social values; that the same social sensitivities that once permitted the Court to condemn segregation and permit miscegenation now compel the Court to retard the rate at which minority gains can be extracted from an increasingly disgruntled majority. The problem is that it is not supposed to work that way.

Under the traditional model of judicial review, the Court is supposed to be above the inevitable shifts that occur in the prevailing political climate. Exercising the skills of reasoned deliberation, within the constraints of principled adjudication, the Supreme Court is expected to insulate minority rights from the majoritarian efforts at exploitation to which those rights would otherwise be vulnerable. The easy resonance of LAW WEEK's political account of the 1988–89 Term reveals that no one really takes the countermajoritarian aspects of the traditional model very seriously. The Supreme Court has never been able to sustain significant independence from the demands of ordinary politics in the past, and it is unlikely that the Court will ever be able to do so in the future. What eludes consensus, however, is an assessment of just how far the actual performance of the Court diverges from the ideal of the traditional model, and just how much significance that divergence properly ought to command. This book postulates that the discrepancy between actual and model Supreme Court performance is sufficient to preclude the existence of any meaningful difference between Supreme Court adjudication and ordinary politics.

There is a fundamental flaw in any model of judicial review that posits the Court as a check on majoritarian excesses. The viability of such a model depends upon a qualitative distinction between the way in which the Court ascertains the contours of minority rights and the way in which minority interests are assimilated into the political process. However, the constraints within which the Supreme Court is required to operate make it vulnerable to the same political considerations that govern majoritarian responses to minority interests. Moreover, the process of principled decisionmaking on which the Court relies to ensure the integrity of its constitutional exposition is incapable of preventing the Court from becoming a surrogate for majority interests. Ultimately, the societal pressures that prompt the representative branches to sacrifice minority rights to majority interests will prompt the Supreme Court to do so as well. Indeed, far from serving the countermajoritarian function envisioned by the traditional model of judicial review, the Supreme Court is better understood as serving the veiled majoritarian function of promoting popular preferences at the expense of minority interests. So viewed, the gesture of judicial review becomes simply a less-immediate form of majoritarianism. The only significant difference that exists between political and judicial dispositions of minority interests is that judicial majoritarianism functions with undetected effectiveness precisely because it transpires behind the veil of judicial review.

A rational minority response to the majoritarianism inherent in Supreme Court adjudication would be to avoid the Supreme Court and to concentrate on ordinary politics as the means for advancing minority interests. Racial minorities have now accumulated sufficient political power to participate meaningfully in the political process, and historically, minority interests have fared better before the representative branches of government than before the Supreme Court. However, Supreme Court involvement in the process of ordinary politics cannot be avoided. Minorities must not only rely on the Court to implement minority political gains, but those gains must be defended before the Supreme Court when they are made the focus of legal challenges.

The inevitability of Supreme Court review is likely to have an adverse effect on minority interests because the Supreme Court has been structured to operate in a manner that is inherently conservative. Life tenure and judicial independence cause the Court to function as a political force for preservation of the status quo. However, because racial minorities in the United States are disadvantaged by the socioeconomic status quo, the Court's inherent conservatism impairs minority efforts to achieve racial equality. The Court has manifested its inherent conservatism in subtle, yet effective, ways. *Brown v. Board of Education*,[5] the case most often lauded as the icon of judicial sensitivity to minority interests, has had the ironic effect of luring racial minorities into a dependency relationship with the Court that has impeded minority efforts to acquire political power. In addition, the Court has centralized the law of affirmative action in a way that forces minorities to compete for societal resources on a national level, where it is difficult for them to prevail politically, rather than on a local level, where they have an opportunity to achieve political and economic self-determination. Finally, the rhetoric that the Court uses in writing its civil rights decisions legitimates a series of demeaning and counterproductive assumptions about the status of racial minorities in the United States. Although this revisionist understanding of the Supreme Court has only limited instrumental value in the face of the Supreme Court's potent political power, its epistemological value may nevertheless permit racial minorities to transcend their vulnerability to Supreme Court protection.

Part I of this book discusses the phenomenon of veiled majoritarianism and suggests that the social function that the Supreme Court has been structured to serve consigns the Court to the role of perpetually endorsing majoritarian preferences. Chapter 1 discusses the traditional model of judicial review, and emphasizes the ways in which that model is dependent upon the assumption that the Supreme Court can resolve disputes in a way that is qualitatively different from how those disputes would be resolved by the political branches. Chapter 2 discusses the subtle majoritarian nature of the Court and argues that neither the formal nor the operational safeguards on which we customarily rely to insulate the Court from popular political preferences can operate effectively.

Chapter 3 demonstrates that on some occasions the Supreme Court expressly incorporates majoritarian preferences into the meanings of the legal principles that it applies, while on other occasions the Court acquiesces in majoritarian preferences through deferential standards of judicial review. Chapter 4 argues that even when this is not the case, majoritarian preferences will ultimately dominate judicial selection of the legal principles that are deemed applicable to a particular case. Chapter 5 argues that once a governing legal principle is selected, majoritarian preferences will also dominate the process of applying that principle, because those preferences will control the manner in which the ambiguities inherent in all legal principles are resolved.

Part II discusses the manner in which the Supreme Court perpetuates the subordination of racial minorities. Chapter 6 discusses the inability of racial minorities to escape the influence of the Supreme Court by retreating to the sphere of ordinary politics, and it describes why the structure of the Supreme Court makes it inherently conservative. Chapter 7 discusses *Brown v. Board of Education*[6] and the manner in which that case has fostered the continued dependence of racial minorities on the Supreme Court. Chapter 8 discusses the law of affirmative action in order to demonstrate how the Supreme Court has centralized the law in a way that stymies minority efforts at political and economic self-determination. Chapter 9 illustrates how the Supreme Court has utilized the process of legitimation to perpetuate a perception of racial inferiority in the minds of the majority and of racial minorities themselves. Finally, Chapter 10 concludes that the only hope that racial minorities have of escaping the protections of the Supreme Court is through the route of epistemological maturation.

Although the thesis of the present book is that the Supreme Court functions to perpetuate the subordination of racial minorities in the United States, the argument that I wish to make is a structural argument rather than a conspiratorial one. I do not intend to suggest that Supreme Court justices commence their deliberations by asking themselves how they can best ensure that racial minorities never achieve political, economic, or social parity with whites in the United States. Although some justices may on some occasions be consciously racist, it is not in this sort of racism that the subordinating power of the Supreme Court resides. Rather, my argument is that, for structural reasons, the institutional role that the Court is destined to play within our constitutional scheme of government is the role of assuring the continued subordination of racial minority interests. I believe that this subordinating function is inevitable; that it will be served irrespective of the Court's composition at any particular point in time; and that it will persist irrespective of the conscious motives of the individual justices. Moreover, my argument does not imply that the Court will always rule against minority interests. On the contrary, the most potent method of perpetuating minority subordination in the United States has proven to be through the intermittent issuance of highly visible minority victories.

I have used the terms "racial minority" and "racial minority interests" in an unelaborated manner that might cause some to suspect that I consider all racial minorities to be fungible, or that I deem racial minority interests to be homogeneous and monolithic. This, of course, is not the case. Racial minorities differ significantly from one another, and within particular minority groups views about what best serves the interests of the group can vary significantly. My use of these terms is not intended to be reductionist, but rather aspirational. For me, the concept of race is a promising abstraction possessing an untapped potential to serve as an organizing principle in both political and epistemological endeavors. As such, its linguistic imprecision is simply inapposite. Stated more concretely, my direct experience with racial minority status is limited to my background as someone who is black. Although many of the illustrations and statistics that I use relate to blacks, I have chosen to write about racial minorities in generic terms, rather than simply to write about blacks. I have done so in order to highlight my normative view that racial minority status should supersede particular racial group identifications. The hierarchy of concerns that such a view engenders will foster the development of consensus within, and promote the formation of coalitions among, racial minority groups.

Some of the comments that I received on drafts of the manuscript, from supporters and critics alike, caused me to realize how difficult it is to present an idea in a way that will permit it to be evaluated free from the context out of which it has emerged. These comments contained helpful observations concerning my case analysis, my use of the literature, my compliance or noncompliance with certain analytical conventions, and my utilization of particular rhetorical techniques. However, I was sometimes unable to prompt much reaction to the thesis itself. It was as if the thesis had been subsumed by the attributes of presentation. That is not what I intend. I have attempted to articulate a vision of the Supreme Court and its relationship to racial minorities that I find to be compelling. My hope is that readers will confront that vision and not be distracted by their agreement or disagreement with my method of presentation.

Finally, I recognize that my revisionist conception of the Supreme Court is vigorously at odds with the traditional countermajoritarian conception, and that it will be resisted by both political conservatives and Warren Court liberals alike. My argument is *not* that I am right and that they are wrong. Consistent with my postmodern sympathies, I do not believe that the Supreme Court possesses a true or essential nature that can make one characterization of the Court more correct than another. Rather, I believe that at the present time my revisionist conception is more *valuable* than the traditional conception, especially for racial minorities and for members of the white majority who are concerned about racial inequality. Adherence to the traditional, countermajoritarian model of the Supreme Court may have been expedient in the era of officially mandated segregation that existed when *Brown* was decided. Indeed, adherence to that model may have been necessary for the United States to evolve beyond its obsession with *de jure* segregation. Today however, when the challenge for racial minorities is to overcome the more subtle forms of discrimination that actually masquerade as race neutrality, I believe that adherence to a veiled majoritarian conception of the Court is instrumentally more realistic and epistemologically more sound.

PART ONE

Veiled Majoritarianism

CHAPTER I

The Traditional Model of Judicial Review

Under the traditional model of judicial review, which is traceable to John Marshall's seminal decision in *Marbury v. Madison*, the function of the Supreme Court is to protect the rights of minorities who are unable to protect themselves effectively in the pluralist political process. Racial minorities have typically been thought to be among those who require Supreme Court protection because their "discrete and insular" character precludes their effective participation in the political process. Although a variety of substantive process, and hybrid theories of judicial review have evolved as an elaboration upon the traditional *Marbury* model, all theories share the belief that the Supreme Court possesses the capacity to act in a manner that is countermajoritarian. That is, the Court is able to perform the function assigned to it in a manner that is both different from and better than the manner in which that function could be performed by a representative branch of government. In order for this countermajoritarian assumption to hold, the Supreme Court must be free from domination by the representative branches. This freedom is secured in the Constitution through two types of formal safeguards, namely, life tenure and salary protection, which although easy to evade, nevertheless serve the symbolic function of emphasizing the need for judicial independence from majoritarian control. In addition to the formal safeguards, the process of principled adjudication provides an operational safeguard to ensure judicial independence. By demanding that case outcomes be determined by legal principles rather than popular preferences, the process of principled adjudication enables the Supreme Court to protect minority rights from the transitory majorities that would abrogate those rights for reasons of political expediency. It is apparent that the viability of the traditional model is only as sound as the countermajoritarian assumption upon which it rests.

The Traditional Model

The system of government envisioned by the framers was designed to operate in a manner that was essentially political. Influenced by the Enlightenment, the framers of the Constitution understood the dangers of self-interest and faction. In a democracy, individuals and groups motivated by a desire to maximize their own welfare could be expected to form coalitions whose aggregate power would permit them to abrogate the liberty and property interests of those who, because of their exclusion from the coalition, lacked the political power to protect themselves. The framers sought to protect these political minorities from the tyranny of the majority by establishing a system of government in which the natural inclination toward self-interested factionalism could be used in a controlled manner to check itself.[1]

The primary mechanisms on which the framers relied were structural. They adopted a democratic form of government, designed around James Madison's conception of republicanism, in which power was broadly dispersed in the hope of permitting the formation of only transitory, shifting majorities. Because today's majority perpetrators might be tomorrow's minority victims, the danger of retaliation created an incentive for factions to treat each other with deference. Accordingly, the Constitution diffused power horizontally within the federal government through the doctrine of separated governmental powers and vertically between the state and federal governments through the doctrine of federalism. Moreover, the establishment of distinct constituencies for the President and each house of the bicameral legislature, staggered terms of limited but different duration for each of the representative bodies, and indirect election of a President who possessed the power to veto legislative enactments all combined to minimize the concentration of power that factionalism requires in order to flourish.[2] Because the concurrence of diverse power centers was difficult to secure, all governmental actions—including tyrannical actions—were less likely to ensue. In addition, the allocation of jurisdiction over most significant substantive matters to the states promoted a level of decentralization that was conducive not only to the emergence of qualified governmental leaders, but to optimum levels of citizen participation and civic virtue that would help to neutralize the threat of self-interest.[3]

It is likely that the framers contemplated judicial review as an additional safeguard against the dangers of faction. Although there is some debate about whether the framers intended to give the Supreme Court the power to invalidate the acts of coordinate branches,[4] the prevailing contemporary view appears to be that the framers did intend to grant the Court the power to engage in such judicial review.[5] The framers, however, may well have contemplated a fairly mechanical type of judicial review that entailed very little judicial discretion.[6] The flavor of such review is captured by Justice Roberts' famous statement in *United States v. Butler*:

It is sometimes said that the court assumes a power to overrule or control the action of the people's representatives. This is a misconception. [When] an act of Congress is appropriately challenged in the courts as not conforming to the constitutional mandate the judicial branch of the Government has only one duty,— to lay the article of the Constitution which is invoked beside the statute which is challenged and to decide whether the latter squares with the former.[7]

Many people question whether such nondiscretionary review is realistically possible.[8] Indeed, there is doubt about whether Justice Roberts intended the mechanistic sentiments often attributed to him.[9] Skepticism about the Supreme Court's ability to engage in such mechanical review has led commentators to undertake the herculean task of developing theories of judicial review that comport with democratic principles.[10]

Contemporary judicial review now seems to be firmly established. But in the beginning, the protections for minority rights were primarily structural. Moreover, the manner in which those protections were to operate was expected to be political. The strength of this proposition is evidenced by the fact that the Constitution was drafted and ratified without a bill of rights that could guide legislative deliberations and serve as a basis for judicial review. Although the desirability of a bill of rights was forcefully asserted during the ratification debates,[11] forceful opposition was also articulated on the grounds that the structural safeguards made a bill of rights not only superfluous but also counterproductive. THE FEDERALIST NO. 84 argued:

[B]ills of rights [a]re not only unnecessary in the proposed Constitution, but would even be dangerous. They would contain various exceptions to powers not granted; and, on this very account, would afford a colorable pretext to claim more than were granted. For why declare that things shall not be done which there is no power to do? [I]t is evident that it would furnish, to men disposed to usurp, a plausible pretence for claiming that power. They might urge with a semblance of reason, that the Constitution ought not to be charged with the absurdity of providing against the abuse of an authority which was not given, [and therefore by] clear implication[, a] power to prescribe proper regulations concerning [the area of power exempted by the bill of rights] was intended to be vested in the national government.[12]

Over time, the structural safeguards began to erode. Ultimately, the New Deal desire for economic recovery prompted the political bodies to adopt, and the Supreme Court eventually to endorse, the effective nullification of the framers' primary precautions. The creation of administrative agencies, established with the conscious goal of increasing governmental efficiency, seriously diluted separation of powers protections while vesting the bulk of governmental power in the executive branch. The Supreme Court has permitted administrative agencies to exercise legislative power[13] and adjudicatory power,[14] in addition to the executive power granted to the President under the Constitution. In part to increase agency efficiency, the Court has also upheld the constitutionality of independent agencies that operate largely free of presidential control.[15] Moreover, in matters affecting foreign affairs, the powers of the President and the foreign affairs agencies are essentially plenary.[16] In addition, belief in the need for national solutions to national economic problems eliminated all meaningful subject-matter restrictions on the scope of federal power. In upholding the limitations imposed on private agricultural production by the Agricultural Adjustment Act—one of the pieces of New Deal legislation designed to ameliorate the economic hardships of the depression—the Supreme Court held, in *Wickard v. Filburn*, that the power to regulate interstate commerce under art. I, sec. 8, cl. 3 of the Constitution permitted Congress to regulate the production of an Ohio farmer who grew wheat for his own consumption.[17] Prior to the New Deal, such private production was viewed as inherently local, which the doctrine of federalism placed beyond the reach of regulation by the federal government. *Wickard* has now come to stand for the proposition that the scope of federal regulatory power is virtually limitless.[18]

As the framers' structural safeguards diminished in importance, the significance of Supreme Court protection increased. John Marshall laid the foundation for this enhanced judicial role in *Marbury v. Madison*, where he characterized judicial review as essential to the protection of individual rights from majoritarian abrogation.[19] John Marshall stated that "[t]he very essence of civil liberty consists in the right of every individual to claim the protection of the laws whenever he receives an injury" and that "[t]he province of the court is, solely, to decide on the rights of individuals."[20] Although Marshall stated that the protection of individual

rights was important enough to require invalidation of the acts of coordinate branches that abrogated those rights,[21] in retrospect, Marshall's
actions seem ironically to have been motivated by political considerations.
Rather than being protected, Marbury's rights appear actually to have been
sacrificed for partisan political gain. By denying Marbury his commission,
Marshall was able to divert attention from his true objective, which was
to establish a power of judicial review that would enable the recently
defeated Federalist party to retain political power through its hold over
the life-tenured judiciary.[22] This detail, however, has not deprived the
decision of its symbolic significance as the harbinger of modern judicial
review. The *Marbury*-based model of judicial review has both endured
and flourished over time, and the Supreme Court has now designated itself
the ultimate guarantor of constitutional rights.[23] Although racial minorities
were almost certainly not among the political minorities whose protection
the framers had in mind, enactment of the Reconstruction amendments
gave racial minorities specific new constitutional rights that could be exercised against the majority. The thirteenth, fourteenth, and fifteenth
amendments to the United States Constitution were enacted during the
Reconstruction period following the Civil War in order to give certain
rights to the newly freed former slaves and to authorize the enactment of
congressional legislation that might be needed to enforce those rights. The
thirteenth amendment, ratified in 1865, prohibited slavery. The fourteenth
amendment, ratified in 1868, gave all persons, including former black
slaves, the rights of national and state citizenship, and guaranteed to such
persons due process and the equal protection of the laws. The fifteenth
amendment, ratified in 1870, gave blacks the right to vote.[24] This, in turn,
enhanced the significance of judicial review as a means of protecting racial
minority interests. As a result, we have now come to vest the Supreme
Court, rather than the political process, with the primary responsibility
for protecting the interests of racial minorities from disregard by the majoritarian branches of government.

Under the *Marbury* model of judicial review, the Supreme Court is
constitutionally obligated to nullify actions of the majoritarian branches
that impermissibly interfere with rights guaranteed to minorities by the
Constitution. This judicial function is captured most crisply in the representation-reinforcement model of judicial review, which has been described, developed, and popularized by Professor Ely. Under the representation-reinforcement model, Supreme Court intervention in the
political process to invalidate substantive outcomes is justified when it
appears that the process has been distorted by discounting the interests

of "discrete and insular" minorities who are underrepresented in that process.[25] In order to perform this function, however, the Court must possess the capacity to operate in a countermajoritarian manner. To the extent that the Court is subservient to majoritarian desires, it cannot effectively protect minority interests from majoritarian abrogation. Accordingly, consistent with the traditional model, judicial independence is promoted by both formal and operational safeguards.[26]

Formal Safeguards

Formally, the Court's insulation from political pressure is established through life tenure and salary protection.[27] These safeguards are designed to facilitate judicial independence in two ways. First, they are designed to prevent domination of the judicial process by the representative branches of government, precisely because the majoritarian accountability of those branches might prompt them to pressure judges into deciding particular cases in ways that benefit the majority at the expense of a politically powerless individual or minority group. Although it is difficult to imagine the representative branches having a significant interest in the outcome of most private litigation, many public law cases do raise significant policy or structural concerns in which the representative branches might be interested. This is especially true of those cases that reach the Supreme Court.[28] To the extent that representative branches do become concerned about the outcome of particular cases, life tenure and salary protection are designed to assure judges that they will not be fired or punished financially for disregarding the wishes of the representative branches.[29] Second, the safeguards are designed to insulate the judiciary from direct popular pressure by freeing judges from the need to worry about reappointment. No matter how much popular resistance their decisions may engender, judges will not be subjected to retaliation by the majoritarian branches of government. Life tenure and salary protection, therefore, are designed to protect judges from both direct and indirect forms of majoritarian control. The life-tenure and salary-protection concerns are also reflected in the bill of attainder provision of the Constitution.[30] Although the Supreme Court has limited the reach of the bill of attainder provision to penal enactments, the functional definition of a bill of attainder is simply an enactment that benefits the majority by allocating the costs associated with that benefit to identifiable individuals or groups who lack the political power to prevent majoritarian exploitation of their interests.[31] Accordingly, the bill of attainder provision is of obvious significance to minorities seeking to protect themselves from the tyranny of the majority. Although the bill of attainder prohibition is addressed to Congress, its bite depends upon its judicial enforceability. In theory at least, life tenure and salary protection give the Court the countermajoritarian capacity to resist the popular pressures that caused Congress to enact a bill of attainder to begin with.

Realistically, it is unlikely that the formal safeguards of life tenure and salary protection in and of themselves do much to ensure judicial independence. Congress could circumvent those safeguards and impose political pressure on the Court in any number of ways. Congress could cancel the Court's term for political reasons, as it did with respect to the Court's June and December Terms in 1802.[32] Congress could also cut the Court's budget, or refuse to appoint needed additional judges as it did in the mid-1970s, when the Democratic Congress repeatedly declined to create new federal judgeships until a Democratic President was elected to appoint the new judges.[33] To some extent at least, Congress could also restrict the Court's jurisdiction in order to coerce certain outcomes. The Constitution authorizes Congress to regulate the appellate jurisdiction of the Supreme Court.[34] In the past Congress has threatened politically motivated use of this power in a way that may well have influenced the Court's subsequent constitutional exposition.[35]

Congress could even manipulate the Court's personnel in order to affect Supreme Court adjudications. The most famous effort at personnel manipulation involves President Franklin D. Roosevelt's "court-packing" plan. After the Supreme Court had invalidated several pieces of New Deal legislation on constitutional grounds, President Roosevelt proposed legislation that would expand the number of justices on the Supreme Court. The proposal called for one additional justice to be appointed, up to a maximum of fifteen, for each justice over the age of seventy. In 1937, at the time that the proposal was made, six sitting justices were over the age of seventy. Although the legislation was nominally offered to ease the caseload of the older justices, it is widely recognized to have been a politically motivated effort to "stack" the Court with justices that would be receptive to future New Deal legislation. The court-packing plan generated significant opposition. However, Senate Majority Leader Joseph Robinson might have been able to amass enough political support to secure enactment if he had not died of a heart attack shortly before the proposed legislation was voted on.[36]

In addition to the many methods that Congress could use to influence Supreme Court adjudications, the President could impose pressure on the

Court by declining to give effect to its judgments. Thomas Jefferson threatened not to comply with Supreme Court directives affecting questions that he believed the Constitution delegated to the President rather than to the Court.[37] President Lincoln also argued that the *Dred Scott* decision of the Supreme Court invalidating the Missouri Compromise[38] should be limited to the parties before the Court and should not be followed as a political rule by the representative branches.[39] In addition, President Franklin D. Roosevelt was prepared to ignore any Supreme Court order that invalidated federal abrogation of "gold clauses" in federal obligations, thereby interfering with his New Deal economic recovery objectives. Although Roosevelt's actions were probably not known to the Court at the time that it upheld the government's power to abrogate gold clauses, subsequently acquired knowledge of the President's intentions may have affected the Court's behavior in later cases.[40]

The President could also simply threaten to defy the Court's orders. The perceived unwillingness of President Andrew Jackson to enforce judgments of the Supreme Court favorable to the Cherokee Indian Tribe appears to have affected the manner in which the Court chose to act in at least one case. In 1827, the Cherokee Tribe declared itself an independent nation with complete sovereignty over its tribal lands—lands the United States viewed as falling within the geographical boundaries of the State of Georgia. In 1830, President Jackson responded to this declaration, and the political controversy that ensued, by asserting that the Cherokee must leave Georgia and move west in order to avoid the force of Georgia sovereignty. Toward this end, Jackson signed congressional legislation setting aside land in the territory west of the Mississippi River for the Cherokee Tribe.

As it became evident that the sovereignty dispute between Georgia and the Cherokee Tribe would end up before the United States Supreme Court, Georgia governmental officials openly vowed to disregard any Supreme Court judgment that questioned State authority to exercise sovereignty over Cherokee lands. Moreover, President Jackson was perceived to be sympathetic to this position. The resolve of the Georgia officials was demonstrated when the State of Georgia proceeded to execute an individual convicted of murder on Cherokee lands despite issuance by the United States Supreme Court of a stay of execution pending Supreme Court review. When the Court was formally petitioned to restrain enforcement of Georgia law over the Cherokee Tribe in *Cherokee Nation v. State of Georgia*,[41] the Court refused to reach the merits of the case. While expressing sympathy for the plight of the Cherokee, the Court ruled that it lacked jurisdiction to consider the case.[42]

Although it is difficult to view life tenure and salary protection as having much instrumental effect in promoting judicial independence, they nevertheless convey a symbolic message. By constitutionalizing the concept of judicial independence, life tenure and salary protection probably promote a conception of acceptable governmental conduct that inhibits the representative branches from imposing inordinately high levels of political pressure on the Court. In addition, the symbolic value of the judicial safeguards may well enhance the courage of the Court to resist whatever pressures do come to be exerted upon it.

Operational Safeguards

In addition to the symbolic protections of life tenure and salary protection, the operational safeguard on which we rely most heavily to promote judicial independence is the judicial tradition of principled adjudication. Because the representative branches are subservient to pluralist political preferences, they cannot be relied upon to render principled decisions. Although principle may play a significant role in the way that representative-branch decisions are made, the role of principle is largely rhetorical. No one demands that members of the political branches genuinely believe in the principles that they espouse while advocating their favored positions, and no one suspects that those principles genuinely account for how those positions came to be adopted by the politicians who espouse them. The Supreme Court, however, is expected to make decisions that are genuinely principled.

The Court has a relative institutional advantage over the representative branches with respect to matters of principle because of both the conventions surrounding judicial decisionmaking and the procedural context out of which judicial decisions emerge. Historically, common law courts were expected to perform their governmental function by inducing general principles from judicial precedents and then deducing from those principles proper resolutions of the particular cases with which they were confronted. At times, the process was thought to be a scientific one in which legal rules possessed transcendent validity like the laws of physics or chemistry. Moreover, a properly functioning judicial process was thought to possess unimpeachable reliability, approaching that of the scientific method.[43] Although current claims for the adjudicatory process are more modest, fidelity to the tenets of principled decisionmaking remains an essential component of acceptable judicial behavior. Judges are selected in part on the basis of their aptitude and temperament for "reasoned elaboration,"[44] and the legitimacy of judicial actions is determined by the adequacy of the principled accounts that judges offer for their adjudications.

In addition to the tradition of principle in which the Court is steeped, adjudication occurs in a context that is conducive to principled decision-making. The doctrine of stare decisis under which the Court operates[45] is essentially an equality principle that requires like cases to be treated alike. Consistent with this doctrine, a judge tempted to deviate from the governing principle in resolving a particular case would be forced to hesitate before doing so for fear that an unprincipled decision today might bind the judge to reach a result that he or she would not desire in some future case. The procedural due process constraints that apply to the judiciary also promote principled decisionmaking. The stringent "record" requirements that the due process clause imposes for adjudications focus the Court's attention on factors that are relevant to the governing principle and divert the Court's attention from extraneous political factors that have no proper bearing on the principled resolution of a case. In this regard, due process is the procedural complement to the bill of attainder provision. The due process clause provides procedural safeguards to individuals and minorities whose lack of political power makes pluralist political safeguards unavailable to them. That is why hearings and on-the-record decisions are essential in an adjudicatory context but are optional in a legislative context.[46] In addition, judges tend to be lawyers, which gives them more familiarity with and appreciation of the process of principled decisionmaking than a nonlawyer legislator or executive official is likely to possess. Finally, most adjudication proceeds at a leisurely pace in which the luxury of thorough briefing and meticulous contemplation is more available than it often is in the legislative process.[47]

In sum, the traditional model of judicial review accords the Court a relative institutional advantage over the other branches of government in protecting the interests of minorities from abrogation by the majority. The formal safeguards of life tenure and salary protection emphasize the importance of this countermajoritarian function of the Court, and the operational safeguard of principled adjudication is responsible for its implementation. Because judicial decisions emanate from governing principles, they can be arrived at independent of majoritarian preference. Moreover, the doctrine of stare decisis, the due process clause, and other contextual factors help ensure that even the inevitable ambiguities embedded in governing principles will be resolved in a manner that is free from majoritarian control. Under the traditional model of judicial review, it is this countermajoritarian capacity of the Court that makes it a viable guardian of minority interests in our pluralist political society.

The Majoritarian Court

Despite the aspirations of the traditional model, the Supreme Court is ultimately unable to protect minorities from the tyranny of the majority. In fact, the Court is institutionally incapable of doing anything other than reflecting the very majoritarian preferences that the traditional model requires the Court to resist. Because Supreme Court justices are socialized by the same majority that determines their fitness for judicial office, they will arrive at the bench already inculcated with majoritarian values. And none of the traditional safeguards can reliably prevent those values from controlling judicial decisions. The formal safeguards of life tenure and salary protection, which are designed to insulate the judiciary from external political pressures, are not designed to guard against the majoritarianism inherent in a judge's own assimilation of dominant social values. Moreover, the operational safeguards surrounding the process of principled adjudication are not sufficient to permit reliable judicial protection of minority interests, because they cannot constrain the exercise of judicial discretion through which majoritarian preferences achieve their expression in the judicial process. In many instances, the governing substantive principles of law incorporate majoritarian values in a way that leaves the Court with no choice but to acquiesce in majoritarian desires with respect to the disposition of minority interests. And even when the governing principles are subject to judicial implementation, they cannot perform the insulating function that the traditional model demands of them because the principles themselves are too imprecise to neutralize the effects of majoritarian socialization. As a result, when the Court is called upon to protect minority interests, it is consigned to operate as little more than a covert agent of the majority.

The Socialized Judiciary

Judges do not assume office *tabula rasa*. Rather, the judicial selection process ensures that judges will be chosen from the ranks of those who have completed a socialization process that all but ensures their sympathy toward majoritarian values. This socialization process also makes it likely that judges will have internalized many of the beliefs and predispositions concerning racial minorities that can cause the majority to discount minority interests. Accordingly, one would expect the Supreme Court to reflect majoritarian preferences unless the safeguards surrounding judicial review could be shown to neutralize a judge's initial majoritarian inclinations.

The process of individual attitude formation is, of course, a complex one about which little can be said with certainty. In the absence of better psychological and sociological evidence concerning the effect of socialization on judicial decisionmaking, however, it seems safe to make one initial assumption. If all other factors are held constant, judges are as likely as members of the representative branches to be majoritarian. If judges were simply selected from the population at random, their personal attitudes would, by hypothesis, reflect the attitudes of the population at large. The percentage of judges favoring given positions would correspond to the percentage of the general population favoring those positions. Moreover, with respect to the resolution of any particular social issue, more people will hold the majority position concerning proper disposition of that issue than will hold any other position. As a statistical matter, therefore, a randomly selected judge is more likely to espouse the majoritarian position concerning an issue than any other position. Judicial safeguards or attitude changes accompanying the assumption of judicial office might prevent a judge's initial majoritarian sympathies from ultimately controlling case outcomes. But all things being equal, the personal attitudes of a hypothetical judge appointed through a random selection process are more likely than not to mirror the attitudes of the majority.

Statistically it is also true that some randomly selected judges would not share the attitudes and values of the majority. However, it is unclear how this could constitute an improvement of the situation. If judicial attitudes do not reflect the values of the majority, they must reflect the values of the individual judges who hold them, or of some interest group with which those judges identify. Although majoritarian control over the interests of racial minorities may be undesirable, control exercised by a particular judge or interest group is certainly worse. It cannot claim even the degree of legitimacy that majoritarian authorization might be thought

to offer. If judicial custody of minority interests is to be justified, it will have to be through features of the judicial process that protect minority interests from the personal attitudes and values of the judiciary, whatever their source.

Judges, of course, are not selected at random. However, the judicial selection procedures that we customarily utilize may exacerbate matters by effectively making judges *more* majoritarian than if they were selected at random. For reasons of checks and balances, federal judges are selected through a process that is intentionally political. They are appointed by the most majoritarian official in the government and confirmed by the upper house of the legislature after public hearings in which their political preferences are thoroughly explored. Although judicial temperament and legal competence play some role in the appointment and confirmation process, the acceptability of a candidate's political inclinations is likely to be dispositive at both stages.[1]

The political nature of our judicial selection procedures has the effect of reducing the range of attitudes that will be reflected in our judicial population. Only mainstream political preferences will survive the appointment and confirmation process. Proponents of peripheral political positions such as Marxism or anarchism are unlikely ever to become judges. More significantly, representatives of politically inactive constituencies such as aliens or the poor are also effectively excluded from consideration. Because racial minorities are disproportionately likely to fall into this latter category of exclusion, innate judicial sensitivity to minority views cannot realistically be expected. In addition, these tacit rules of exclusion are enforced with added vigilance when appointment and confirmation to the Supreme Court is involved, making the range of views that are directly represented on that Court extremely narrow.

Even minority judges will be firmly middle class. Only two black justices have ever served on the Supreme Court—Thurgood Marshall and Clarence Thomas.[2] Although both had backgrounds in which they experienced invidious acts of racial discrimination,[3] they had both become established government lawyers before being appointed to the Court. Justice Marshall had been both a United States Court of Appeals Judge and the Solicitor General of the United States before being appointed to the Supreme Court,[4] and Justice Thomas had been the head of the Equal Employment Opportunity Commission and a United States Court of Appeals Judge before his appointment to the Court.[5] Indeed, Justice Thomas, who was appointed by conservative President George Bush, was appointed precisely because of his traditional values and conservative political views, which placed him at odds with many black leaders.[6]

Although the views of a large percentage of the population may be represented on the Supreme Court, this percentage is still likely to encompass a narrow segment of the entire political spectrum. Because a large percentage of the population holds political beliefs that fall within a relatively narrow range, it is not surprising that the Court's members, who are appointed by an elected President and confirmed by an elected Senate, also hold views that fall within that narrow range. The failure of the Senate to confirm President Reagan's appointment of Robert Bork to the Supreme Court is an example of the process successfully preventing someone perceived to hold beliefs outside of the mainstream of American political thought from sitting on the Court.[7] Accordingly, rather than overcoming the problem of statistical majoritarianism that would characterize a judiciary selected from the population at random, our politically sensitive judicial selection process aggravates the problem by contracting the size of the majority that matters for the purposes of judicial selection. The judges who are successfully able to survive the judicial selection process will not only have been inculcated with majoritarian values, but theirs will be the values of an elite "majority" that is unlikely to include most members of racial minorities.

Because judges are well socialized before they assume office, they will also have internalized the biases and predispositions that enable the majoritarian branches to view undervaluation of minority interests as acceptable governmental behavior. The framers expected that the majority would seek to advance its own interests at the expense of politically less-powerful minorities.[8] It is true that in extreme cases, this tendency may result from malice or xenophobic dislike of minority groups. In the more typical case, however, the majoritarian tendency to discount minority interests will result from more subtle causes. Where racial minorities are involved, the majority will undervalue minority interests because of misinformation conveyed through cultural stereotypes, or because of an inability to appreciate adverse consequences upon interests with which the majority is culturally unable to empathize, or through mere inadvertence when the majority simply fails to consider the effect that its actions might have on minority interests.[9] Professor Lawrence has argued that racial attitudes and prejudices can operate in ways that are so subtle that majoritarian discrimination often occurs at an unconscious level. Indeed the majority culture can transmit prejudices so subtly and effectively that even members of the racial minority being disadvantaged can come to adopt them.[10] Whatever the precise factors are that cause the majority to undervalue the interests of minorities, judges who have been socialized by the majority culture will have been influenced by them too. Accordingly, judges will come to the task of protecting minority interests possessed by the very predispositions that they are asked to guard against.

Because it is unrealistic to expect judges to have personal attitudes and values that are significantly different from the attitudes and values of the majority, the safeguard of judicial review cannot be expected to protect minority interests from exploitation unless there is something in the judicial process that guards against the influence of majoritarian preferences. The traditional model of judicial review assumes that the formal safeguards of life tenure and salary protection, as well as the operative safeguards attendant to the process of principled adjudication, can accomplish this task. Contrary to this assumption, however, neither set of safeguards is likely to be effective.

Inadequacy of the Formal Safeguards

The formal safeguards of life tenure and salary protection are not adequate to ensure judicial protection of minority interests from majoritarian abrogation. The ability of the formal safeguards to protect the judiciary from political pressures that may be exerted on it by the representative branches or the electorate is questionable. It is also beside the point, because the formal safeguards do not purport to offer any protection from the personal attitudes and values of individual judges. Not even the symbolic value of the formal safeguards can have any prophylactic effect against majoritarian inclinations of which the judges themselves are not consciously aware.

As indicated above, the formal safeguards of life tenure and salary protection do not accord the judiciary meaningful protection from political pressures that may be exerted by the representative branches, because those safeguards are easily circumvented.[11] In theory, life tenure should provide more meaningful insulation from the majoritarian preferences of the electorate because it precludes the need for judges to seek majority approval of their actions. Empirically, however, it appears that whatever insulation life tenure actually provides is likely to be illusory. Professor Tushnet has noted that members of Congress have effective job security that rivals the security of life tenure; incumbents are all but assured of reelection.[12] Since World War II, 90 percent of all incumbent members of Congress running for reelection have been returned to office. Over time, margins of victory have become larger, the number of close races has become fewer, and the number of "safe" districts has increased substantially. By 1986, 98.4 percent of the incumbents seeking reelection were able to reclaim their seats.[13]

Tushnet argues that factors such as a candidate's personal voter appeal, the availability of staff support in implementing long term reelection strategies, and ease in attracting media attention give incumbents a distinct electoral advantage.[14] In addition, the provision of constituent services, such as assistance in dealing with the regulatory bureaucracy that governs a constituent's business, is what generates voter loyalty.[15] A candidate's voting record does not appear to be significant. In fact, only 10 percent of the voters even know how their representatives vote on particular issues.[16] As a result, Tushnet concludes that the electoral incentive from which life tenure is designed to protect federal judges does not appear to have enough of an effect on the formulation of political positions to make life tenure a relevant judicial safeguard.[17] Moreover, although judges do not run for reelection, they may seek higher judicial or executive office, which does make them subject to whatever majoritarian pressures the President and the confirming Senate can bring to bear.[18] In sum, life tenure probably provides little benefit by way of insulation from majoritarian preferences because, ironically, the type of majoritarian political pressure that life tenure is concerned with avoiding does little to affect the conduct of government officials. Our representative democracy simply does not work as well as political theory would predict.[19]

Professor Tushnet's data concerns the House of Representatives, and it is possible that different conclusions might be suggested from analogous data concerning the Senate. The Senate does not appear to have as high a percentage of safe seats as the House, nor has the number of safe seats in the Senate demonstrated a general increase over time. In House elections from 1956 to 1974, the proportion of incumbents winning at least 60 percent of the major party vote ranged from 58.5 percent to 77.8 percent. In the Senate, from 1946 to 1974, the range fluctuated from a low of 35.4 percent to a high of 48.8 percent.[20] Even if all of Tushnet's conclusions proved to be erroneous, however, life tenure would nevertheless remain irrelevant to the problem posed by a judge's personal attitudes.[21]

If life tenure and salary protection functioned precisely as the framers intended, they would still be nonresponsive to the primary factor that causes the judiciary to reflect majoritarian preferences. Judges are majoritarian because their personal values and attitudes are the product of elite majoritarian socialization. To the extent that life tenure and salary protection are designed to immunize the judiciary from political pressures exerted by the representative branches, those safeguards are simply irrelevant. A judge's personal attitudes will continue to operate even if the majoritarian branches exert no influence whatsoever. To the extent that the safeguards are designed to immunize judges from the majoritarian electorate, they are invoked too late to be of much assistance. The preferences of the majority will have been incorporated into a judge's own preferences long before the judge is sworn into office. Even assuming that life tenure and salary protection are completely effective in neutralizing judicial apprehensions of majority retaliation for judicial behavior, they offer no method for a judge to gauge the degree to which his or her own attitudes have been influenced by majoritarian values. Ironically, any protections that these safeguards may offer ultimately serve only to protect majoritarian judicial values from the minority political pressures to which they might occasionally be exposed.

The technical inadequacies of life tenure and salary protection would be inconsequential if the primary value of the formal safeguards were symbolic. If the formal safeguards functioned as aspirational reminders cautioning judges to guard against the majoritarian inclinations with which they have been inculcated as a result of their socialization, the safeguards might merit appreciation. However, not even such symbolic value is responsive to the primary cause of judicial majoritarianism. If Professor Lawrence is correct that much of the discrimination that is inflicted upon racial minorities results from unconscious prejudices,[22] the aspirational value of the formal safeguards cannot be more than marginal. It may permit judges to compensate for those incorporated majoritarian preferences of which they are aware, but it cannot inspire judges to neutralize those preferences that operate beneath the level of their conscious perception. Even judicial efforts to compensate for known or suspected prejudices will be suspect because they will be colored by the same majoritarian values that gave rise to the need for compensatory adjustments to begin with.[23]

For the reasons mentioned, the formal safeguards cannot be relied upon to ensure that judges will operate free of the influence of majoritarian preference when they endeavor to protect minority interests. By default, only the operative safeguards that surround the judicial process of principled decisionmaking can be counted on to serve the necessary insulating function. In theory, the principled decisionmaking process can guard against judicially incorporated majoritarian attitudes and values because the effectiveness of its insulating function does not depend upon a judge's conscious awareness of his or her majoritarian predispositions. The process of principled decisionmaking, however, rests upon other assumptions about the constraining effect of legal principles that ultimately prove difficult to accept.

Inadequacy of the Operational Safeguards

The operative safeguard upon which the legal system relies most heavily in order to ensure judicial protection of minority interests is the process of principled adjudication. The procedural requirements of adjudicatory due process are thought to create an environment conducive to the principled disposition of legal claims, and the substantive constraints of stare decisis are thought to prevent judges from allowing personal prejudices to control their decisions. There are three reasons for skepticism about the effectiveness of principled adjudication in achieving the desired degree of judicial insulation from majoritarian preferences. First, governing legal principles often derive their meaning through explicit or implicit reference to majoritarian preferences. Second, the bare injunction to engage in a process of principled decisionmaking does not identify for a judge which of the competing principles that plausibly could control resolution of a legal claim actually should control. Rather, identification of the governing principle entails an act of judicial discretion in which the personal, statistically majoritarian values of the judge are necessarily implicated. Third, even if a governing principle could be selected with the requisite degree of neutrality and disregard for majoritarian preferences, it is unlikely that the principle would be sufficiently determinate to generate only one outcome. Any principle broad enough to secure general acceptance as controlling in a controversial case would be subject to deconstruction. That is, ambiguities inherent in any formulation of such a broad principle could be uncovered that would permit the principle to generate contradictory results. Again, the only way in which a judge could select among the potentially available outcomes would be through an act of discretion that would implicate the judge's own socialized preferences. Because of these three sources of vulnerability, the process of principled adjudication—even if it occurs in a context in which due process and stare decisis have endeavored to exclude from consideration all improper majoritarian influences—cannot ensure judicial protection of the interests of racial minorities from majoritarian abrogation.

CHAPTER 3

Infiltration of Principles

Many legal principles expressly incorporate majoritarian preferences into their substantive contents. As a result, such principles cannot be relied upon to insulate judicial decisionmaking from the desires of the majority. On the contrary, the principles themselves ensure that the will of the majority is what ultimately controls any minority claims that are subject to those principles. Surprisingly, the Supreme Court has expressly incorporated majoritarian preferences into constitutional principles, as it did in *McCleskey v. Kemp*, even where the effect has been to permit the majority to define the content of racial minority rights. More subtly, the Supreme Court often incorporates majoritarian preferences into governing legal standards indirectly, through deferential standards of judicial review and through justiciability doctrines. Whenever the scope of review or a justiciability doctrine precludes the Court from giving final operative content to a governing legal principle, the Court is again permitting the content of that principle to be determined by the majoritarian body whose actions are under review.

Incorporation of Majoritarian Preferences

The Supreme Court has often interpreted legal principles to mean whatever the majority says that they mean. This, of course, deprives those principles of any capacity to shield judicial decisionmaking from majority domination. Instead, the principles themselves guarantee that majoritarian preferences will ultimately govern the minority claims that are subject to those principles. The clearest example of a principle that expressly incorporates the will of the majority is the principle of federalism, which the Supreme Court, in *Garcia v. San Antonio Metropolitan Transit Authority*,[1] held to contain no judicially enforceable standards. The Court held that although federalism limitations *are* imposed by the Constitution on the scope of congressional power under the commerce clause, the content of those limitations is to be determined by Congress itself and not by the courts.[2] The Court's justification for judicial deference to the preferences of a representative branch was that the states, who are the direct beneficiaries of federalism restrictions, are adequately represented in the Senate, thereby precluding the need for judicial enforcement of the principle of federalism.[3] Expressed differently, states are not "minorities" whose interests require protection from majoritarian abrogation because states have sufficient power to protect their own interests in the pluralist political process. Taken on its own terms, the *Garcia* decision may well be unobjectionable. However, the Court has also incorporated majoritarian desires into governing legal principles where the interests being adversely affected *are* minority interests.

In *McCleskey v. Kemp*,[4] the Court rejected equal protection and eighth amendment cruel-and-unusual-punishment challenges to the imposition of capital punishment under a Georgia statute. The challenge was based upon statistical evidence, which was undisputed for purposes of the Court's disposition, establishing that defendants convicted of murder were 4.3 times more likely to receive the death penalty if their victims were white than if their victims were black—a difference that is statistically significant. In addition, blacks convicted of murder were overall 1.1 times more likely to be sentenced to death than white convicts. Accordingly, blacks convicted of murdering white victims were the most likely class of defendants to receive the death penalty. The raw data also showed that, prior to adjustment for nonracial factors, the death penalty was imposed in 22 percent of the cases involving black defendants and white victims, but it was imposed in only 1 percent of the cases involving black defendants and black victims.[5]

In rejecting the eighth amendment challenge, Justice Powell, writing for a five-justice majority, emphasized that a state legislature was required to remain within constitutionally permissible limits of proportionality in its imposition of the death penalty.[6] As long as the legislature remained within those limits, however, its determination of what acts and aggravating circumstances warranted capital punishment controlled the meaning of the proportionality standard embodied in the eighth amendment. This is because that determination was informed by the legislature's appreciation of contemporary community standards. The language of Justice Powell's opinion is revealing. It states:

Thus, our constitutional decisions have been informed by "contemporary values concerning the infliction of a challenged sanction," . . . In assessing contemporary values, we have eschewed subjective judgment, and instead have sought to ascertain "objective indicia that reflect the public attitude toward a given sanction." . . . First among these indicia are the decisions of state legislatures, "because the . . . legislative judgment weighs heavily in ascertaining" contemporary standards. . . . We also have been guided by the sentencing decisions of juries, because they are "a significant and reliable objective index of contemporary values." [Citations omitted][7]

In addition, Justice Powell emphasized that in order to withstand eighth amendment scrutiny, imposition of the death penalty in particular cases had to result from the jury's exercise of discretion after considering all of the surrounding circumstances, which by hypothesis must include the defendant's race. The language of the opinion is again revealing. It states:

Thus, it is the jury that is a criminal defendant's fundamental "protection of life and liberty against race or color prejudice." . . . Specifically, a capital sentencing jury representative of a criminal defendant's community assures a " 'diffused impartiality,' " . . . in the jury's task of "express[ing] the conscience of the community on the ultimate question of life or death." [Brackets in original; citations and footnote omitted][8]

The opinion incorporates majoritarian preferences into the meaning of the governing constitutional principle in two distinct ways. First, it holds that within the range of acceptable punishments the content of the eighth amendment proportionality requirement mirrors what the majoritarian legislature views as appropriate punishment for a given criminal act. Second, and more striking, the Court holds that the eighth amendment principle proscribing cruel and unusual punishment *requires* the exercise of jury discretion. This holding is striking because the jury is a majoritarian institution. Indeed, it is precisely because the jury is a repository of majoritarian values that the Court elects to make jury discretion the operative act in the state's imposition of capital punishment.

A jury of one's peers could be viewed as a countermajoritarian institution that served to inhibit government oppression. In theory, a government intent on advancing the interests of one interest group at the expense of another would find it more difficult to effectuate its exploitative intent if it had to secure the cooperation of a jury composed of the defendant's peers than of a jury composed of members of the government's own favored interest group. The Supreme Court nominally embraced such a conception of the jury in *Duncan v. Louisiana*.[9] It seems unlikely, however, that the Court takes this countermajoritarian conception of the jury very seriously. It has declined to hold that criminal defendants are entitled to petit juries whose membership actually includes members of their own race, reasoning that a prohibition on state-sanctioned discrimination in the selection of the jury venire from which the petit jury is drawn is sufficient to guard against the dangers of government oppression.[10]

Conceiving of the jury as a majoritarian institution seems much more plausible. As pointed out by Justice Stevens in *McCleskey*,[11] and elaborated upon by Professor Kennedy,[12] if McCleskey's allegations are true, the jury—like the population at large—values the lives of blacks less than it values the lives of whites. In fact, the jury undervalues the lives of blacks to such an extent that it makes the deterrent and retributive protections of the criminal law four times more available to white citizens than it does to black citizens.[13]

Such judicial deference to a majoritarian body in defining the operative content of a constitutional safeguard is, of course, inconsistent with judicial protection of minority interests from majority control. But under the facts of *McCleskey*, such deference is affirmatively alarming. The case not only tolerates, but actually *constitutionalizes*, the level of racial discrimination that exists in the community from which the jury is drawn. Because of the nature of McCleskey's claim—that the Georgia statute permitted juries to discriminate on the basis of race in the imposition of capital punishment—the Court's own insistence on jury discretion appears to be an affirmative endorsement of such discrimination. McCleskey's evidence demonstrates that when juries in Georgia exercise the discretion to impose capital punishment, in a statistically significant number of cases they will do so *because* of the victim's race. As a result, when the Court insists on giving dispositive discretion to this institution in making capital punishment determinations, the Court reads the Constitution to require the level of discriminatory bias that the majoritarian jury reflects. Knowing that juries are inclined to discriminate on the basis of race, the Court remarkably insists, as a matter of constitutional law, that this discriminatory inclination be present in death penalty deliberations. In this way, the Court not only incorporates majoritarian preferences into the meaning of the constitutional standard, but it does so even though those preferences are assumed to be discriminatory.

In addition to the occasions on which the Court explicitly incorporates majoritarian preferences into the meaning of governing principles, there are occasions on which the Court incorporates such preferences implicitly. The primary way that the Court effects implicit incorporation is through deferential standards of review. When the range of permissible represent- ative branch discretion is broad, majoritarian preferences will in most cases control the disposition of minority interests because the Court will not intervene. The operative meaning of the governing legal principle, there- fore, is the meaning that the representative branch has assigned to it.

Incorporation through Deference

Many minority challenges to majoritarian actions are framed as equal protection claims. The standard of review applied in typical equal pro- tection cases is the rational basis standard. To withstand scrutiny under this standard of review, a legislative or executive classification need only bear a rational relationship to a legitimate governmental objective.[14] The standard is extremely deferential, and governmental actions almost always survive constitutional challenge when this standard is invoked.[15] When a majoritarian enactment *is* invalidated under the rational basis standard, some other factor is typically the actual cause of judicial invalidation.[16] Where suspect classifications are involved, however, the Court—at least nominally—applies a heightened standard of review, which requires the government to show both that its classification is necessary to achieve a compelling governmental objective, and that there is a tight fit between that objective and the means that the government has chosen to pursue it.[17] The tightness of the fit is often measured by the presence or absence of less restrictive alternative means of achieving the desired result.[18] Con- stitutional challenges are much more likely to be successful if this strict level of scrutiny is applied. Race is considered to be one of the suspect bases for classification, sufficient to trigger heightened scrutiny, because the relative political powerlessness of racial minorities demands close Su- preme Court monitoring of majoritarian classifications that adversely affect racial minority interests.[19] In *United States v. Carolene Products*,[20] which laid the groundwork for the heightened judicial scrutiny now accorded majoritarian enactments that differentiate on the basis of race, Justice Stone, writing for the majority, suggested that the Court should decide

whether prejudice against discrete and insular minorities may be a special condition, which tends seriously to curtail the operation of those political processes ordinarily to be relied upon to protect minorities, and which may call for a correspondingly more searching judicial inquiry.[21]

This suggestion has now developed into a full-fledged theory of constitutional jurisprudence, known as the representation-reinforcement theory, which has been popularized by Professor Ely.[22]

Despite the nominal availability of strict scrutiny for racial classifications, there are three reasons why the Court may nevertheless decline to upset majoritarian dispositions of minority interests. First, the Court may simply decline to apply heightened scrutiny to a case even when that case intuitively appears to be a race case. The Court did this in *Washington v. Davis* when it applied rational basis scrutiny to adjudicate a claim alleging that the qualifying examination used to select District of Columbia police officers was racially discriminatory.[23] The Court held that because the allegation of racial discrimination related to the discriminatory impact of the qualifying exam and not to any discriminatory intent on the part of the officials who administered it, the constitutional standard of strict scrutiny did not apply.[24] The distinction between discriminatory intent and discriminatory effects is discussed more fully in Chapter 4.

Second, the Court may determine that the representative branches have in fact made the demanding showing that is required under the heightened standard of review. Such determinations are not common, but they do occur. Moreover, they tend to occur in contexts that highlight the ultimate inability of the Supreme Court to protect minority interests from majoritarian abrogation. One of the most famous examples of such a determination is the Supreme Court decision in *Korematsu v. United States*.[25] The case arose out of a military program under which American citizens of Japanese descent were interned in concentration camps after the outbreak of World War II. It upheld that portion of the program that excluded Japanese-Americans from certain areas along the West Coast of the United States, finding that the exclusion did not violate the equal protection clause despite the Court's concession that the actions of Congress and the President in authorizing the internment of a specified racial minority were subject to strict scrutiny.[26] The decision was a product of wartime hysteria and racial resentment, and it has been widely criticized.[27] Nevertheless, the decision does illustrate that when majoritarian insistence on the exploitation of minority interests is most intense, Supreme Court protection of racial minorities is likely to be least effective. A peacetime example of a governmental classification that has effectively survived strict scrutiny is provided by the Supreme Court's now-infamous decision in *Naim v. Naim*,[28] issued one year after *Brown v. Board of Education*,[29] where the Supreme Court failed to invalidate a Virginia miscegenation statute even though the statute seems to have fallen squarely within the prohibition of *Brown*.[30]

The third reason that the Court may decline to protect racial minorities from a classification that adversely affects their interests is that the Court may never reach the merits of the equal protection claim. Justiciability doctrines such as standing, ripeness, mootness, and the political question doctrine often result in tacit affirmance of the majoritarian action being challenged. For example, in *Warth v. Seldin*[31] the Supreme Court declined to reach the merits of an equal protection challenge to a municipal zoning ordinance that restricted the construction of low- and moderate-income housing. The black plaintiffs claimed that the ordinance had the unconstitutional purpose and effect of preventing blacks from living in the area. The Court held that the plaintiffs lacked standing because they failed to establish that the housing they desired would be constructed in the absence of the ordinance. As a result, the plaintiffs had not demonstrated the type of redressable injury that was required under the law of standing.[32] The Court's standing disposition seems to have been result-oriented. The standing issue could easily have been resolved the opposite way, as it was two years later in *Village of Arlington Heights v. Metropolitan Housing Development Corp.*,[33] where the Court granted standing to virtually identical plaintiffs under virtually identical facts, and then ruled against the plaintiffs on the merits. Indeed, some commentators have argued that the Court will elect to reject a claim on justiciability grounds rather than deny it on the merits where the political costs to the Court of doing so are lower.[34] But even assuming that the decision was not result-oriented, it still illustrates a failure of the Court to protect minority interests. The end result was that the Court again had factored majoritarian preferences into the operative equal protection standard. The Court effectively held that the equal protection clause permitted majoritarian discrimination against the class of racial minorities who would not be able to establish standing to the Court's satisfaction.

This formulation of the Court's holding is a realistic one because there are instances in which the Court has used various combinations of standing, mootness, and ripeness requirements in a way that seems to preclude some challenges from ever being cognizable on the merits. In a series of cases alleging a pattern and practice of racially discriminatory police harassment and prosecutorial misconduct in major metropolitan areas, the Court repeatedly declined on justiciability grounds to reach the merits of the plaintiffs' claims for injunctive relief. For the plaintiffs who had already been injured by the challenged misconduct, the claims were moot. The other plaintiffs either lacked standing, or the threatened injuries that they alleged were not ripe.[35] The effect was to make the type of pattern and practice misconduct about which the plaintiffs complained effectively unreviewable—as if the claim itself amounted to a nonjusticiable political question, for which majoritarian preferences are conceded to be dispositive. The pattern-and-practice claim asserted by the plaintiffs, alleged the type of racially discriminatory conduct that was later documented in the now-famous home video that captured a brutal instance of police brutality committed by several members of the Los Angeles Police Department.[36]

Theoretically, damage actions by individuals who had already been injured could serve as a basis for reaching the merits of the constitutional claims, although as a practical matter, the success of such actions would likely be frustrated by the doctrines of official and sovereign immunity. *Will v. Michigan Department of State Police*[37] holds that such suits can now be maintained only against municipalities,[38] with all of the difficulties that are attendant to successful maintenance of such suits, or against a government official seeking funds from only the official's personal assets,[39] which may well preclude such litigation from being cost-justified. Regardless of the ultimate viability of damage actions, however, the decided cases do create the impression of a distinct reluctance on the part of the Court to reach the merits of the constitutional challenges.

In *Allen v. Wright*,[40] the Court hinted at a possible reason for its frequent incorporation of majoritarian preferences into the meaning of constitutional standards in racial discrimination cases. There, the Court held that the parents of black school children, who had filed a nationwide class action suit challenging the IRS practice of allowing private schools to retain their tax exemptions despite their racially discriminatory policies, lacked standing to maintain the suit. As in *Warth* and the police brutality cases, the Court held that the various injuries alleged by the plaintiffs were not sufficiently redressable to provide a basis for standing, because the revocation of tax exemptions might not cause the discriminatory schools to change their policies.[41] However, in discussing its reluctance to adjudicate cases involving claims of broad-based racial discrimination, the Court revealed a preference for the resolution of such claims by the political branches of government. Justice O'Connor's majority opinion stated:

"When a plaintiff seeks to enjoin the activity of a government agency, even within a unitary court system, his case must contend with 'the well-established rule that the Government has traditionally been granted the widest latitude in the "dispatch of its own internal affairs." . . .' . . ." The Constitution, after all, assigns to the Executive Branch, and not to the Judicial Branch, the duty to "take Care that the Laws be faithfully executed." . . . We could not recognize respondents' standing in this case without running afoul of that structural principle.[42]

Although the Court's reluctance to engage in structural social reform may be understandable, it does disable the Court from serving as an effective buffer between the majority and the minority in areas where such reform is what is at stake.

One might argue that the problem of majoritarianism by incorporation is not a systemic problem but merely reflects remediable Supreme Court insensitivity to the need to develop substantive legal doctrines in a way that does not permit majoritarian desires to control. After all, the doctrines into which majoritarian preferences have been incorporated, either explicitly or incidentally, are not written in stone. The Court is free to modify those doctrines so that they permit more effective judicial protection of minority interests. But that is precisely why the problem *is* systemic. The doctrines can be modified only because they are imprecise and subject to evolution. Their content at any particular point in time is therefore a function of Supreme Court discretion, which in turn is a function of the personal attitudes of the justices. As a result, the suggestion that the problem of majoritarian incorporation could be overcome by having the majority-socialized justices reformulate the offending principles simply begins a regress that recreates the original problem. The only way that the socialized preferences of the justices could be excluded from the judicial decisionmaking process would be through a more determinate process of principled adjudication. Greater doctrinal determinacy, however, appears to be hopelessly elusive, both because of difficulties encountered in identifying the governing principles and because of difficulties encountered in ascertaining what outcomes the principles produce.

CHAPTER 4

Selection of Principles

The process of principled adjudication begins with specification of the legal principles that govern proper resolution of a disputed issue. A variety of legal principles will arguably be relevant, but the Court must somehow decide which of the candidates actually apply. Selecting applicable principles is an act of loosely constrained discretion that once again creates opportunities for a judge's personal attitudes to enter into the decision-making process. Where obviously controlling rules or precedents exist, the problem may appear to be insignificant, but in fact, serious difficulties often lurk beneath the surface of such apparent certainty. Moreover, in cases of first impression, or cases in which it is unclear which lines of developed precedent a court should apply, the problem of identifying the proper legal principles can be especially troublesome. It is difficult to see how such a selection could be made other than through a judge's submission to his or her own values, which in turn will reflect majoritarian preferences.[1]

The problem can be illustrated by examining three sets of legal principles that are of frequent concern in race discrimination cases. First, intent and effects principles have traditionally competed for control of race discrimination law. Although the Court purports to have resolved the competition in a context-dependent manner, it is difficult to identify any meaningful constraints that can be said to have insulated the Court's resolution from the dangers of majoritarian influence. The Court seems simply to have preferred one principle to the other for unspecified reasons. Second, the Court's treatment of the state action principle indicates that even in areas where superficial analysis might suggest a clear answer to the question of what principle should control, deeper analysis can reveal the continued existence of a problem. Although the language of the fourteenth amendment explicitly requires the presence of state action in order to establish a legally cognizable act of discrimination, the Court does not always acquiesce in explicit constitutional commands. It is unclear, therefore, how the Court decides to honor or ignore the state action requirement in the particular race discrimination cases that it decides. Third, even a principle as basic as the principle prohibiting discrimination itself may at times be inapplicable to something that at first blush appears to be a discrimination case. The Court has developed parallel lines of precedent, one of which condemns discrimination and the other of which favors majoritarian discretion. Selection of the proper line of precedent turns on how the case is characterized, but it is unclear how the Court knows in a given case which of the competing characterizations is appropriate. Because legal principles are not self-actuating, judicial resolution of the problems that are entailed in the identification of governing principles raises the danger of majoritarian domination over minority interests, thus further exacerbating doubts about the countermajoritarian capacity of the Court.

Intent v. Effects

In order to advance its antidiscrimination objectives, a legal system could rationally choose to prohibit actions that were motivated by an intent to discriminate against minority interests, or it could extend the prohibition to encompass even neutrally motivated action that had a disproportionately adverse effect on minority interest. Strong arguments can be made to support either approach, but each approach poses serious problems as well. Not surprisingly, the academic literature is replete with articles advocating one approach or the other, as well as articles suggesting the desirability of recognizing additional alternatives.[2]

The basic argument in favor of focusing on intent is that a prohibition on innocently motivated, neutral actions that simply happen to have a racially disparate impact would unduly restrict the ability of governmental decisionmakers to use precise and efficient classifications that are directly responsive to the merits of the regulatory problems with which they are confronted. It is sometimes argued that an intent test is preferable to an effects test because the Constitution guarantees procedural regularity but not particular outcomes. That argument, however, merely states a preference for intent over effects. It does not offer a justification for why the Constitution should be viewed as simply a procedural document. In order to justify such a view of the Constitution, one would have to fall back on the types of arguments that are made below. The major drawback of focusing on intent is that evidence of intentional discrimination is often difficult or impossible to secure, thereby permitting acts of intentional discrimination to escape invalidation by masquerading as acts of neutral policymaking. The basic argument in favor of focusing on effects is that harmful effects are harmful regardless of the intent with which they are produced. The major drawback of focusing on effects is that such a focus would require governmental decisionmakers to consider explicitly race as a factor in formulating social policy, thereby contravening the very principle of racial neutrality that is embodied in our antidiscrimination laws.[3]

In *Washington v. Davis*,[4] the Supreme Court held that the applicable principle for equal protection clause purposes is the intent principle. Although the Constitution affirmatively prohibits governmental actions taken with the purpose of discriminating against racial minorities, it does not prohibit unintentional acts of discrimination that have a racially disparate impact.[5] Discussion of the policy reasons for the Court's selection of the intent rather than the effects principle was noticeably absent from the decision. The Court stated only that a wide range of actions might potentially be invalidated by an effects principle.[6] The Court also asserted that application of the antidiscrimination principle to effects rather than intent was a legislative rather than a judicial function, but it offered not even a hint as to why this should be the case.[7] Presumably, the Court was making an inchoate effort to reconcile *Washington v. Davis* with *Griggs v. Duke Power*,[8] a case that is discussed below. The Court's failure to offer any policy justification for its holding was surprising in light of the Court's recognition that many of its own prior decisions had suggested that effects rather than intent should be dispositive.[9] In addition, the Court recognized that many federal courts of appeals had held that disparate impact alone was enough to establish an equal protection violation.[10]

The Court's lack of policy discussion becomes even more peculiar when one realizes that the Supreme Court itself had earlier construed the antidiscrimination provisions of Title VII to prohibit disparate impact as well as intentional discrimination. Title VII of the 1964 Civil Rights Act prohibits discrimination in employment based upon race, color, religion, sex, or national origin.[11] In *Griggs v. Duke Power*,[12] the Court expressly rejected the view that Title VII was limited to intentional discrimination, finding that the intent of Congress to reach discriminatory effects as well as intent was "plain from the language of the statute."[13] The Court went on to hold that such an "effects" reading of the statute was necessary to prevent facially neutral practices from prospectively freezing a status quo that had been created through historical acts of discrimination.[14]

The question that naturally arises is how the Court knew that the intent principle governed discrimination claims that were asserted under the equal protection clause, while the effects principle governed claims asserted under Title VII. Although one might initially suspect that the drafters of the two provisions must have had different intents, there is absolutely no evidence to support such a suspicion. The drafters of the fourteenth amendment appear to have left no evidence of their views concerning which principle should apply to equal protection claims—at least the *Washington v. Davis* Court cited no such evidence in support of its "intent" decision. And contrary to the Court's assurance in *Griggs*,[15] there is nothing in the language or legislative history of Title VII that compels the adoption of an "effects" test for statutory claims of discrimination. The language of Title VII provides in pertinent part:

Sec 703(a). It shall be an unlawful employment practice for an employer—

*   *   *

(2) to limit, segregate, or classify his employees in any way which would deprive or tend to deprive any individual of employment opportunities or otherwise adversely affect his status as an employee, *because of* such individual's race, color, religion, sex, or national origin.[16]

It is difficult to see how this language favors effects any more than it favors intent. In fact, use of the phrase "because of" might well evidence congressional contemplation of an intent test. Although the statutory language is not dispositive, the Court failed to offer any legislative history in support of its effects construction. Moreover, in arriving at its effects construction, the Supreme Court was required to reverse the district court and the court of appeals, both of whom had read the statute to require intent.[17]

If the two decisions are to be reconciled, it will have to be on policy grounds. But the policy advantages and disadvantages associated with each principle seem to be equally present in both cases.[18] There is no obvious reason to suppose that the presence or absence or relative weight of these policy considerations should vary with the constitutional or statutory nature of the underlying cause of action, and the Court has offered no nonobvious reason why this should be the case. One might be tempted to argue that Title VII's more expansive effects test could properly be imposed by a politically accountable Congress, whereas the politically unaccountable Supreme Court could not properly read such an expansive test into the meaning of the Constitution where it would be immunized from congressional revision. This argument, however, posits the majoritarian Congress, rather than the countermajoritarian Supreme Court, as the more effective guardian of minority rights. Moreover, because antidiscrimination remedies can adversely affect the interests of certain classes of white workers, who themselves might not be adequately represented in Congress, countermajoritarian Supreme Court intervention might be required to prevent Congress from utilizing an effects test for Title VII purposes. This, of course, is the subject of the contemporary affirmative action debate, which is discussed more fully in Chapter 8.

More recent Supreme Court decisions have made matters even more confused. When called upon to decide whether the intent or the effects principle governed challenges to subjective employment and promotion standards alleged to have been applied in a discriminatory manner, the Court nominally adopted one standard, but appears effectively to have adopted the other. In *Watson v. Fort Worth Bank & Trust*,[19] the Court held that Title VII challenges to subjective employment standards had to be adjudicated under the *Griggs* effects test, even though prior subjective-standard cases had been resolved under an intent test.[20] The Court reasoned that use of an effects test was necessary to prevent employers from evading *Griggs*. If subjective-standard cases were to be judged under an intent test, employers could neutralize the *Griggs* effects test simply by combining their objective employment standards with a subjective standard, such as a personal interview.[21] Justice O'Connor's plurality opinion in *Watson* also contained dicta reallocating the burden of proof in subjective standard cases.[22]

The *Watson* dicta was turned into holding the following Term in *Wards Cove Packing Co. v. Atonio*.[23] Justice White's majority opinion in *Wards Cove* reaffirmed *Watson*'s use of the effects test in subjective-standard cases,[24] but added that statistical disparities in racial representation between various segments of an employer's work force could not alone establish the plaintiff's prima facie case.[25] The Court then went on to hold that the plaintiff in a disparate-impact subjective-standard case also had the burden of proving that particular employment practices, rather than the aggregate effect of the employer's hiring and promotion policies, were the legal cause of the disparate-impact of which the plaintiff complained.[26] Finally, the Court held that the plaintiff had the burden of proving that the challenged practices were not justified by business necessity,[27] even though business necessity had traditionally been treated as an affirmative defense that employers were required to prove in order to defeat a showing of disparate impact.[28]

Both *Watson* and *Wards Cove* nominally extend the effects test to Title VII subjective-standard cases. However, the stringency of the new proof requirements that those cases impose upon Title VII plaintiffs is so high that the evidence needed to satisfy those standards is likely to be sufficient to sustain an inference of discriminatory intent. For example, the facts giving rise to the disparate-impact claim in *Wards Cove*, which included segregated housing and dining facilities, were sufficiently egregious that the dissenters found them to "bear an unsettling resemblance to aspects of a plantation economy."[29] If facts egregious enough to warrant this characterization are not sufficient to satisfy the Court's new effects test, it is difficult to divine a meaningful difference between this new test and the traditional intent test.

An innocent interpretation of these two recent decisions indicates that the intent and effects standards are quite confused. A less sanguine interpretation would depict the decisions as intentional efforts by the Court to cut back on the scope of Title VII protections in order to bring Title VII into line with prevailing political opinion. Although this is arguably permissible in the statutory context of Title VII, it poses obvious problems for a countermajoritarian model of the Supreme Court to the extent that it suggests an inclination on the part of the Court to defer to political opinion in a constitutional context.[30] For present purposes, however, it does not matter which interpretation is correct. It is sufficient that none of the Court's opinions adequately explain why the Court selected the principle that it selected in each of the pertinent contexts. The Court could easily have resolved the intent v. effects issue either way in each of the cases that it considered. Indeed, the nature of judicial accountability is such that the Court believed itself free to issue opinions that essentially announced rather than explained the results that the Court chose to reach. However, even if the Court had tried to offer serious policy justifications for its holdings, the policy arguments seem to have roughly equal force in each of the contexts that the Court has considered. Again, the Court would easily have been able to come out either way. In many cases at least, the act of identifying the governing principle of law will be an act of unconstrained judicial discretion. And where unconstrained judicial discretion is invoked, the danger of majoritarian influence is necessarily present.

State Action v. Private Autonomy

Arguably, the dangerous discretion that exists when the Court is forced to select a principle under first-impression conditions dissipates as the constraints governing principle selection become more explicit. If precedents or external texts, such as statutes and constitutional provisions, explicitly provide for the application of particular principles, the amount of judicial discretion entailed in deciding when to apply those principles might seem to be acceptably low. In actuality, however, vast amounts of discretion are present even in such superficially clear cases. There are three reasons for this. First, the Court has reserved for itself the discretion to forego compliance with certain provisions of law despite their textually explicit applicability. Second, not even sincere efforts by the Court to bind itself under the doctrine of stare decisis can eliminate judicial discretion, because the Court always possesses the power to overrule itself if it wishes to avoid the application of a prior principle in a subsequent case. Third, the existence of legal fictions makes it possible for the Court to feign application of one principle while in fact applying another. The Court's state action decisions illustrate all three of these reasons.

One might think that the amount of Supreme Court discretion present in the selection of governing principles would be minimized by the existence of an explicitly applicable principle of law. The problem, however, is that the Court does not always acquiesce in explicit constitutional commands. In fact, there are many constitutional provisions that the Court either blatantly ignores or drastically rewrites. As noted above,[31] since the New Deal the Court has essentially ignored the safeguards of federalism and separation of powers, despite their integral importance to the system of government envisioned by the framers.[32] Supreme Court attention to other express constitutional provisions waxes and wanes over time, as evidenced by the Court's variable enforcement of the contract clause,[33] and the privileges and immunities clause.[34] Other provisions, such as the ineligibility and incompatibility clauses,[35] appear never to have been taken very seriously by the Court.[36] And there are provisions whose texts the Court appears never to have even read, such as the second amendment,[37] the ninth amendment,[38] and the eleventh amendment.[39] Although one could argue that the Court's actions simply indicate that it deems political rather than judicial enforcement of such provisions to be appropriate, such an account lends little support to the argument that the Supreme Court can be counted on to operate as an effective bulwark against majoritarian racial insensitivities.

The Court's state action decisions involving the Reconstruction civil rights statutes illustrate how the Court sometimes avoids explicit constitutional and statutory requirements in the context of racial discrimination. The Civil War ended in 1865.[40] Later that same year, Congress adopted and the states ratified the thirteenth amendment, which abolished slavery.[41] Many southern states attempted to blunt the impact of the thirteenth amendment by enacting "Black Codes," which severely restricted the ability of freed slaves to exercise the rights of ordinary citizenship. As a result, Congress enacted the Civil Rights Act of 1866,[42] § 1 of which gave blacks the same right as whites to make contracts, participate in judicial proceedings, and own property. However, federalism-based doubts concerning the power of Congress to enact this legislation under its thirteenth amendment authority prompted Congress to adopt the fourteenth amendment, which was ratified in 1868. The fourteenth amendment made blacks citizens of the United States, and prohibited states from abridging the privileges and immunities of that citizenship or from denying to any person due process or the equal protection of the laws. In addition, it explicitly authorized Congress to enforce the antidiscrimination provisions of the amendment through appropriate legislation.[43] Congress then reenacted the 1866 statute as part of the Enforcement Act of 1870,[44] the pertinent provisions of which are now codified in Title 42 of the United States Code.[45] Section 1981 of Title 42 gives blacks equal rights to make contracts and participate in judicial proceedings,[46] and § 1982 gives blacks equal rights to own property.[47]

A recurring question confronting the Supreme Court has been whether the antidiscrimination provisions of §§ 1981 and 1982 prohibit acts of private discrimination or whether a state action requirement limits the prohibitions of those sections to acts of discrimination mandated or specifically authorized by state law. The state action limitation is significant for two reasons. First, as a practical matter, adherence to a state action requirement has the effect of limiting the range of discriminatory acts for which the Court will offer a remedy, because it precludes judicial interference with private acts of discrimination. Second, as a federalism matter, a state action restriction has the effect of making the states, rather than the federal government, the primary guardians of individual civil rights. In order to establish state authorization, one would first have to establish that state law did not itself prohibit and provide a remedy for the deprivation of civil rights being alleged. The exhaustion of state legal remedies necessary to make this showing gives the states the initial opportunity to protect the rights in question. One would only impose such a state action/exhaustion requirement if one trusted the states to detect and correct the majority of civil rights violations.[48]

The Reconstruction statutes, which are plainly intended to prohibit racial discrimination, are plainly authorized by the fourteenth amendment, which plainly imposes an explicit state action requirement on the scope of their coverage.[49] However, as the foregoing chronology indicates, the Reconstruction statutes may also have been authorized under Congress's thirteenth amendment authority. The thirteenth amendment contains no explicit prohibition on racial discrimination, but neither does it contain an explicit state action requirement. By its terms, the thirteenth amendment simply abolishes slavery, which can exist with or without state authorization.[50] Accordingly, the issue of whether the state action limitation applies to §§ 1981 and 1982 is amenable to several plausible resolutions. Ultimately, resolution of this issue turns on distinct assessments of congressional intent in enacting the Reconstruction statutes and in adopting the Reconstruction amendments. Because the same Congresses contemporaneously drafted both the statutes and the amendments, however, it is likely that the relevant legislative intents coincide. It might be that the Reconstruction statutes do require state action because they are authorized only by the fourteenth amendment, which by its terms contains a state action limitation. Or it might be that the state action limitation does not apply because the thirteenth amendment is alone sufficient to authorize the Reconstruction statutes, and the thirteenth amendment does not require state action. Or it might be that state action is required even though the thirteenth amendment authorizes the statutes, because the thirteenth amendment itself contains a tacit state action limitation. Although it seems clear that the thirteenth amendment's abolition of involuntary servitude applies to private as well as state action, it may be that whatever prohibitions that amendment imposes on the *incidents* of involuntary servitude are subject to a state action requirement. Or it might be that both the thirteenth and fourteenth amendments independently authorize the statutes, but the state action requirement of the fourteenth amendment overrides the absence of such a requirement in the thirteenth amendment, because the fourteenth amendment is more specifically addressed to the types of discrimination barred by the Reconstruction statutes. Accordingly, even though the fourteenth amendment contains an explicit state action limitation on the scope of congressional authority to promulgate antidiscrimination legislation, a discretionary judicial determination is nevertheless required in order to ascertain whether that limitation is ultimately operative in §§ 1981 and 1982 antidiscrimination suits.

The manner in which the Supreme Court has exercised its discretion in resolving the state action issues has been inconsistent. Initially, the Court held that the state action limitation applied to what are now §§ 1981 and 1982 claims. In the *Civil Rights Cases*,[51] which were decided roughly contemporaneously with the enactment of the Reconstruction statutes and amendments, the Court held that fourteenth amendment authorization for the antidiscrimination legislation was limited by the state action principle.[52] The Court also held that, although the thirteenth amendment authorized Congress to reach private conduct in order to eliminate the "badges and incidents of slavery," ordinary racial discrimination did not constitute such a badge or incident that could be regulated in the absence of state action.[53] Other contemporaneous Supreme Court interpretations were in accord.[54]

Contemporary Supreme Court decisions have now abandoned this limited interpretation of the Reconstruction statutes. In 1968, the Court held in *Jones v. Alfred H. Mayer*[55] that § 1982 prohibited private discrimination in the sale or rental of real property, and that so construed the statute was authorized by Congress's thirteenth amendment power to eliminate the "badges and incidents of slavery" that had been referred to in *The Civil Rights Cases*.[56] In 1976, the Court adopted a similar reading of the § 1981 prohibition on discrimination in the making of contracts. In *Runyon v. McCrary*,[57] the Court held that the prohibition applied to private refusals to contract on account of race, and that so construed § 1981 too was a valid exercise of congressional power under the thirteenth amendment.[58] In 1989 the Court reconsidered its *Runyon* decision. The Court first ordered reargument in *Patterson v. McLean Credit Union*,[59] expressly requesting the parties to address the issue of whether *Runyon* should be overruled. After reargument, however, the Court reaffirmed the *Runyon* holding that § 1981 applied to private action, although it did adopt a narrow interpretation of the substantive scope of § 1981.[60]

The difficulty that the Court has had in adopting a stable resolution of the state action issue with respect to the scope of §§ 1981 and 1982 attests to the difficulty that can be encountered in determining the ultimate impact of even explicitly applicable principles of law. Although the text of a legal provision may make the provision applicable by its terms, other considerations such as competing provisions of law, contrary legislative intent, or contemporary political exigencies may militate against a literal interpretation. Once again, the arguments for applying or avoiding a literal reading can be so equally balanced that a court's application determination will necessarily amount to an act of very loosely constrained discretion. The contemporaneous §§ 1981 and 1982 cases may have correctly ascertained congressional intent. The plaintiffs in *Runyon* were the parents of black children who had been excluded from Virginia private schools and summer day camps solely because they were black.[61] It seems unlikely that the 1866 Congress that drafted § 1981 would have desired the desegregation of private schools that was ultimately required by *Runyon*, a point that Justice Stevens makes in his concurring opinion.[62] However, the contemporary cases may have correctly responded to modern aspects of education and race relations that make the 1866 legislators' intent as inapposite as their views about airplanes and cable television. In order to decide which of the Court's application determinations was correct, one would have to do something no less discretionary than derive an entire theory of statutory and constitutional interpretation.

Like §§ 1981 and 1982, most federal civil rights legislation has been based upon the congressional authority granted by the Reconstruction amendments. Some statutes, however, such as the Civil Rights Acts of 1964[63] and 1968,[64] which include prohibitions on various types of discrimination in public accommodations, education, employment, and housing, also invoke other powers of Congress, such as the commerce power,[65] and the spending power.[66] In determining whether those other sources of congressional power were sufficient to preclude the state action requirements of the fourteenth amendment, the Court had to make assessments similar to those required in connection with §§ 1981 and 1982. In general, congressional reliance on these additional sources of constitutional authority have been upheld without judicial insistence on state action.[67] Because the scope of the commerce power has been extremely broad since the New Deal,[68] it seems that the commerce power will always be available whenever the Court wishes to avoid the fourteenth amendment state action restriction.

The state action decisions also illustrate a second problem entailed in any effort to exclude discretion from a court's application determinations. As *Runyon* and *Patterson* reveal, the Supreme Court is always free to change its mind and to overrule itself in a subsequent case. This means that the Court cannot even bind itself under the doctrine of stare decisis in a way that limits its own future discretion. By the Court's own terms, it does not have the unlimited authority to reverse its statutory precedents. Various factors must be considered before the Court can properly overrule itself. These factors, however, are quite nebulous and are unlikely to impose any significant constraint on the Court's discretion. In *Patterson* the Court held that it could properly overrule statutory precedents only: where intervening changes in governing law "removed or weakened the conceptual underpinnings from prior decisions" or rendered prior decisions "irreconcilable with competing legal doctrines or policies"; where "inherent confusion created by an unworkable decision" or tension with "important objectives embodied in other laws" made the precedent "a positive detriment to coherence and consistency in the law;" or where a precedent "becomes outdated[,] and after being ' "tested by experience, has been found to be inconsistent with the sense of justice or with the social welfare" ' ".[69] This is not to say that there are no constraints imposed under the doctrine of stare decisis. The Court cannot reverse itself too frequently or overrule cases that have attracted substantial popular support without risking a loss of legitimacy. These operative constraints, however, are political in nature. As such, they contribute little to the Court's counter-majoritarian capabilities.

A third way in which the Court preserves the opportunity to exercise discretion in determining whether to apply an explicitly applicable principle of law is through the use of legal fictions. Again, the Court's Civil Rights Act cases provide an illustration. In addition to the provisions of § 1 of the 1866 Civil Rights Act, which prohibited discrimination in contract and real property transactions,[70] § 2 of that Act further prohibited any person acting "under color of" state law from interfering with the rights guaranteed by the statute.[71] That provision, which is now codified as § 1983 of Title 42 of the United States Code,[72] was intended to prevent state officials from using their authority to harass, intimidate or otherwise discriminate against blacks, as they had shown a propensity to do under the Black Codes. In addition, Congress wished to ensure that the federal courts would be available to redress claims of discrimination because the state courts had often been unwilling to redress those claims.[73]

The Court has construed the "under color of" language in § 1983 to be identical to the fourteenth amendment state action requirement, holding that only those vested with indicia of official authority are subject to the prohibitions of § 1983.[74]

This interpretation of § 1983—as well as a state action interpretation of §§ 1981 and 1982—poses a serious eleventh amendment problem. The eleventh amendment bars the federal courts from entertaining most suits filed against state governments.[75] However, a primary purpose of the Civil Rights Act of 1866 was to permit civil rights claims to be adjudicated in federal court, precisely because the southern state courts had exhibited hostility toward those claims. An eleventh amendment bar to such suits, therefore, would seriously undermine this fundamental Reconstruction objective. On its face, the problem is logically insoluble. The very state action that is required to establish a substantive § 1983 cause of action deprives the federal courts of jurisdiction under the eleventh amendment. Either the state action requirement applies or it does not, but it cannot both apply and not apply at the same time.

The Supreme Court resolved this dilemma by inventing the *Ex Parte Young* fiction. In *Ex Parte Young*,[76] the Court held that a suit filed against a state official alleging a fourteenth amendment violation was not barred by the eleventh amendment, because if the challenged action was indeed unconstitutional, it could not under the supremacy clause be validly authorized by state law, and was not therefore state action barred by the eleventh amendment.[77] The fiction that *ultra vires* actions of a state official are not actions of the state is as strained as it is ingenious. The fiction not only makes it impossible for a state qua state ever to act unconstitutionally—something that seems counterintuitive—but it also defeats the symbolic purpose of the eleventh amendment by forbidding the state from invoking its sovereign immunity until it has first established that it will prevail on the merits of the constitutional challenge that has been asserted against it. However, the fiction does permit the constitutionality of a state's actions to be tested before the eleventh amendment bar can ever be triggered. To the extent that the Reconstruction statutes and amendments evidence a shift in the allocation of responsibility for the protection of constitutional rights from the state to the federal courts, this would appear to be the desired result.

The Court obviously had broad discretion in deciding whether or not to invent a fiction that would permit it to circumvent the explicitly applicable eleventh amendment. That discretion was almost certainly guided by the Court's assessment of how judicial power was to be properly distributed in the aftermath of the Civil War. However, that judicial assessment in turn appears to have rested upon majoritarian enactments—the Reconstruction statutes and constitutional amendments. It is unlikely that the Court would have thought itself free to initiate such a radical departure from the then-accepted tenets of federalism in the absence of those enactments, or some other evidence of a popular mandate to do so.

The Court not only possessed considerable discretion in deciding whether to invent the *Ex Parte Young* fiction, but its subsequent decisions reveal that it possesses considerable discretion in deciding how to implement the fiction as well. In order to be subject to suit under § 1983, the defendant must be a "person" within the meaning of that section.[78] Although the fiction was created precisely to permit the constitutionality of state action to be tested, the Court has ironically held that a state is not a "person" for § 1983 purposes.[79] The Court reasoned that because it had previously held in *Monroe v. Pape*[80] that a municipality was not a § 1983 "person," a state could not be a "person" for § 1983 purposes either.[81] These holdings, which purport to be based upon the intent of Congress in enacting § 1983,[82] are difficult to square with the *Ex Parte Young* fiction. Why should the shift in federal-state judicial responsibility embodied in the intent of the Reconstruction Congress be potent enough to prompt the *Ex Parte Young* fiction but insufficient to create § 1983 "personhood?" The Court then began to reverse itself. In *Monell v. New York Department of Social Services*,[83] it reconsidered the legislative history of § 1983 and overruled *Monroe v. Pape*, holding that municipalities were, after all, "persons" within the meaning of § 1983.[84] Although some subsequent Supreme Court cases seemed tacitly to assume that after *Monell*, states too were § 1983 "persons,"[85] in *Will v. Michigan Department of State Police*,[86] the Court held that this was not the case.[87] In passing, the final paragraph of the opinion noted that state officials sued in their official capacities were not § 1983 "persons" either, because a state could act only through the actions of its officials.[88] Then, apparently realizing that this holding was potentially fatal to the entire *Ex Parte Young* fiction, the Court added in a final footnote that its official-capacity holding did not apply in cases seeking injunctive relief.[89]

The § 1983 law that emerges from this collection of cases is unstable and contorted. What the Court appears to be grappling for is a doctrinal regime under which the constitutionality of state action can be tested in federal court without putting at risk the money contained in the state treasury.[90] The Court's distinction between injunctive and monetary relief may or may not have practical significance, but it is difficult to see how it could have theoretical or symbolic significance with respect to the fundamental federalism issues that underlay the eleventh amendment and § 1983. Nevertheless, accepting for the sake of argument the desirability of this objective, it is worth noting that such a regime could easily have been achieved in a doctrinally more elegant manner. The *Will* Court could simply have held that states, municipalities, and state officials acting in their official capacities were all "persons" within the meaning of § 1983, but that the eleventh amendment ultimately barred the assessment of monetary awards that would have to be paid from state treasuries.[91] By preserving high levels of doctrinal complexity, however, the Court has wittingly or unwittingly advanced another objective. It has preserved the wrinkles and creases in which high levels of doctrinal discretion can be stored—discretion that can produce unconstrained patterns of decisions such as the § 1983 decisions discussed above. As a result, increased doctrinal complexity ultimately increases the opportunities for majoritarian domination of the judicial process.

In deciding whether to apply an explicitly applicable provision of law, a court must make a variety of nonobvious discretionary determinations.

It must decide whether the provision is one that should be taken seriously, or one that should be ignored. In addition, it must decide whether its own prior precedents should be followed or overruled. Finally, it must decide whether its actions should be fictitiously portrayed or candidly disclosed. In making each of these decisions the Court exposes its deliberations to the risk of majoritarian infiltration. And that risk persists with respect to even the most fundamental decision that the Court must make—the decision about how the case is to be characterized.

Discrimination v. Discretion

As the intent v. effects and the state action v. private conduct debates suggest, legal principles tend to travel in competing pairs. One way to conceptualize the manner in which the Court chooses between these competing legal principles is that the Court first identifies the relevant nature of the case before it, and then applies the principle that properly governs cases of that type. Accordingly, if the case is a statutory rather than a constitutional case, the Court will apply the effects test rather than the intent test in deciding whether the case involves impermissible discrimination. Similarly, if the case is an ordinary discrimination case rather than a "badges of slavery" case, the Court will apply the fourteenth amendment state action requirement and decline to remedy purely private misconduct. It would seem, therefore, that one could predict with confidence that the Court would at least believe itself bound to apply antidiscrimination principles to race discrimination cases. However, even that prediction is problematic. This is because identification of a case as a true discrimination case turns out to be less a matter of passive recognition than a matter of active characterization. As a result, in order to determine when to apply the antidiscrimination principles that govern discrimination cases, the Court is once again called upon to draw subtle legal distinctions with little nondiscretionary guidance.

The legal principle that prohibits illegitimate discrimination has as its benign complement a competing principle that favors desirable forms of differentiation. In race cases, this benign complement tends to be articulated as a need for discretion in the exercise of governmental functions. Although invidious discrimination is socially undesirable and legally indefensible, the presence of humanizing discretion prevents the legal system from becoming artificial, insensitive, and mechanistic. Accordingly, before the Court can properly apply antidiscrimination principles to a case that the plaintiff alleges to involve racial discrimination, the Court must determine whether it is really a discrimination case or whether it is actually a case that involves the desirable exercise of discretion. This is the precise problem with which the *McCleskey* Court was confronted when it insisted on the need for jury discretion, even though it knew that such discretion was likely to be exercised in a racially discriminatory manner.[92] The Court's jury selection decisions further illustrate the complications that can be encountered in judicial efforts to arrive at the proper characterization of a putative race discrimination case.

The paradigm jury selection case is one in which a prosecutor intentionally exercises peremptory challenges to exclude blacks from the jury that will hear a case involving a black criminal defendant, believing that a conviction is more likely to be obtained from an all-white jury than from an integrated or all-black jury. Thus described, the case certainly seems amenable to characterization as a race discrimination case. The prosecutor is intentionally according differential treatment to potential jurors solely on the basis of their race, in order to secure a litigation advantage over the defendant that will materialize solely because of the defendant's race. Viewed from another perspective, however, the case can easily be characterized as a pure discretion case. The prosecutor is making jury selection decisions based upon his or her best assessment of what combination of jurors is most likely to result in a conviction. The fact that race is merely incidental to this motive is demonstrated by the fact that racial considerations will never outweigh likelihood-of-conviction considerations in the prosecutor's deliberations. If tomorrow it is revealed that blacks are actually *more* likely than whites to convict black defendants, the prosecutor will then seek to exclude all whites from a black defendant's jury. It is, of course, possible that a prosecutor could be motivated by a species of racial animus that would cause him or her to exclude blacks even when such an exclusion would decrease the likelihood of a conviction, simply because the prosecutor disliked blacks very intensely. That, however, is not the case that I have in mind, and it does not seem to be the paradigm case that the Supreme Court has considered. As is apparent, the problem of proper characterization can be a difficult one.

In theory, difficult characterization problems can be resolved by adopting that characterization that appears likely to produce the most desirable consequences. However, even such a consequentialist analysis can be ambivalent, because consequences themselves are subject to characterization. From the prosecutor's perspective, the justification for peremptory challenges is that it permits attorneys to respond to the inarticulable misgivings that they may have about individual jurors. Realizing that the elaborate array of procedural formalities with which we have saturated the criminal justice system cannot completely secure the objectives of fairness and justice that we desire, we have carved out peremptory challenges as the one area in which attorneys can exercise unconstrained compensatory discretion. Moreover, it would be imprudent to disqualify the prosecutor's discretion solely because of its association with race. In a culture that is as race-conscious as ours, the human instincts that are indispensable to the effective operation of the system are almost certain to be tinged by the factor of race.

From the defendant's perspective, the consequentialist analysis looks quite different. The whole point of judicially scrutinizing race-sensitive classifications is to neutralize race-conscious governmental decisionmaking of the precise type in which the prosecutor has engaged under the facts of the paradigm case. By acquiescing in racially offensive tactics of prosecutorial expediency, a court will inevitably end up perpetuating the counterproductive preoccupation with race on which that expediency is based. Moreover, ingenious suggestions that the prosecutor may technically have been discriminating on the basis of some factor other than race simply camouflage the fact that a potential juror's race will *always* be the dispositive factor guiding the prosecutor's selection decisions, no matter which correlation between race and likelihood of conviction the prosecutor ultimately comes to adopt. Judicial acceptance of such clever modes of argumentation can only serve to increase the artificiality of the legal system and make it incomprehensible to the ordinary citizens on whom it depends for its continued legitimacy.

The latitude available to a court attempting proper characterization of the paradigm case is broad, and the Supreme Court has utilized a considerable amount of that latitude in resolving the two incarnations of the paradigm case that it has encountered. The first time that the Court considered the jury selection issue was in *Swain v. Alabama*.[93] The defendant in *Swain* was a black man who had been convicted of raping a seventeen-year-old white woman and sentenced to death.[94] Prior to *Swain*, the Court had held that the fourteenth amendment prohibited the exclusion of blacks from the jury venire, because such discrimination denied both the excluded jurors and the criminal defendant the equal protection of the laws.[95] In *Swain* the Court went on to hold that although the Constitution prohibited systematic use of a prosecutor's peremptory challenges to exclude blacks from the juries of black defendants over the range of cases, it did not prohibit the prosecutor from systematically excluding blacks from a particular jury in a particular case.[96] In other words, a case alleging systematic exclusion in multiple cases was a discrimination case to which the anti-discrimination principles of the fourteenth amendment applied, but a case alleging systematic exclusion in that one case alone was a discretion case to which fourteenth amendment antidiscrimination principles did not apply.

Lest one think that it is I rather than the Court who is taking liberties with proper characterization, I should emphasize that the Court held the prosecutor's conduct in a single case to be wholly beyond judicial examination precisely because judicial scrutiny would undermine the well-established need for discretion upon which the long tradition of peremptory challenges was based. The Court stated:

> With these [historical] considerations in mind, we cannot hold that the striking of Negroes in a particular case is a denial of equal protection of the laws. . . . To subject the prosecutor's challenge in any particular case to the demands and traditional standards of the Equal Protection Clause would entail a radical change in the nature and operation of the challenge. . . .
>
> In the light of the purpose of the peremptory system and the function it serves in a pluralistic society in connection with the institution of jury trial, we cannot hold that the Constitution requires an examination of the prosecutor's reasons for the exercise of his challenges in any given case. The presumption in any particular case must be that the prosecutor is using the State's challenges to obtain a fair and impartial jury to try the case before the court. The presumption is not overcome and the prosecutor therefore subjected to examination by allegations that in the case at hand all Negroes were removed from the jury or that they were removed because they were Negroes. Any other result, we think would establish a rule wholly at odds with the peremptory challenge system as we know it.[97]

It is apparent that the Court was not simply applying some fourteenth amendment balancing test. Rather, it was holding that because of the importance of discretion, antidiscrimination principles were rendered wholly inapplicable.

It is also interesting to note that the Court justified its decision not to apply the fourteenth amendment by relying on a legal fiction—the irrebuttable presumption that the prosecutor properly exercised the State's peremptory challenges in an effort to obtain an impartial jury.[98] The Court's reliance on this fiction in *Swain* is particularly fascinating because the facts of the case suggest that the prosecutor may well have been motivated by a desire to capitalize on particular prejudices of white jurors precisely because those prejudices might not have been shared by black jurors.

The basis for the *Swain* distinction between systematic exclusion in multiple cases and systematic exclusion in a single case is less than self-evident. It may be possible to justify a distinction between discrimination in the selection of the jury venire and discrimination in the selection of the petit jury. The exclusion of blacks from the jury venire implies that blacks are not capable of sitting on *any* jury—an implication that is constitutionally unacceptable—while the exclusion of blacks from particular juries simply implies that blacks are not capable of being impartial in those particular cases because of their likely racial identification with the defendant—an implication that may not be constitutionally impermissible.[99] However, assuming that such an argument is susceptible to a noninvidious interpretation, it nevertheless fails to explain why one should distinguish between the systematic exclusion of blacks from one petit jury and the systematic exclusion of blacks from many petit juries.

What is more puzzling for advocates of a countermajoritarian judiciary is the fact that the *Swain* distinction seems to be backwards. Under the *Marbury* model of judicial review, it is the isolated cases of discrimination, rather than the range of discriminatory cases, that present the most compelling need for judicial intervention. In the range of cases, it is at least possible for the class of discrimination victims to pool their political resources and to pressure the prosecutor into ceasing his or her discriminatory conduct. But in the individual case, where the single victim is politically most powerless, only countermajoritarian judicial review offers any hope of vindicating the right to be free from invidious prosecutorial discrimination. Note also that the Court's actions in the jury selection cases seem to be inconsistent with its decision in *McCleskey v. Kemp*,[100] which was discussed in Chapter 3, where the Court refused to remedy allegations of racial discrimination practiced by petit juries precisely because the alleged discrimination was systemic rather than isolated.[101]

The *Swain* Court also held that, although the systematic exclusion of blacks in multiple cases would amount to a fourteenth amendment violation, the defendant had not established a prima facie case of such discrimination.[102] This holding was striking because the defendant's proof established not only that systematic exclusion had been practiced in his own case, but that in the entire history of Talladega County—the Alabama county in which the case had arisen—there had never been a black on a civil or a criminal jury.[103] The Court, however, viewed the existence of other nondiscriminatory explanations for this statistic to be so probable that it did not see the need even to require the prosecutor to come forward with such evidence.[104]

Perhaps in response to the fragility of its *Swain* decision, the Supreme Court reexamined the paradigm case in *Batson v. Kentucky*,[105] and—once again—overruled itself. Although Justice Powell's majority opinion stated that it was overruling only the evidentiary portion of *Swain*,[106] the opinion actually seems to have a broader reach. Justice Rehnquist's dissent asserts that, despite its disclaimer, the majority opinion actually recognizes a substantive right on the part of individual defendants to a jury from which blacks have not been systematically excluded, thereby overruling one of the fundamental holdings of *Swain* and imprudently undermining the utility of peremptory challenges.[107] Moreover, Justice White's concurrence asserts that the decision reverses the principle holding of *Swain* by authorizing judicial scrutiny of a prosecutor's exercise of peremptory challenges.[108] In *Batson*, therefore, the Court appears to have held that individual exclusion cases should be characterized as discrimination cases rather than discretion cases.

The problem with the *Batson* characterization is that it too seems quite fragile. By suggesting that the paradigm case is a discrimination rather than a discretion case, the *Batson* Court minimizes the importance of discretion as a mechanism for responding to perceptions and suspicions that are too subtle to be articulated. The danger of such minimization can be appreciated by imagining that it is the defendant rather than the prosecutor who wishes to exercise peremptory challenges in order to exclude jurors of a particular race. Although the *Batson* majority purported not to address this issue,[109] it is necessarily implicated in any principled resolution of the case. Indeed, a perceived inability to distinguish meaningfully between the racially motivated exercise of peremptory challenges by prosecutors and defense counsel caused Justice Marshall to advocate the elimination of peremptory challenges entirely.[110] Moreover, imagine that the defendant wishes to exclude those jurors out of fear that they will exercise racial prejudice against the defendant. Because a defendant would typically be unable to disqualify a juror for cause solely on the basis of heartfelt misgivings about the juror's racial tolerance, we might well wish to elevate discretion over discrimination considerations in order to permit defensive use of peremptory challenges. Indeed, if we were not willing to do so, the whole point of characterizing the paradigm case in *Batson* as a discrimination rather than a discretion case would be defeated. By declining to elevate the defendant's discretion needs over our competing antidiscrimination objectives, we would be permitting an increased level of subtle discrimination to occur, thereby directly thwarting the very antidiscrimination objectives that we wished to advance.

If you are tempted to argue that a state action requirement could be used to prohibit racially motivated use of peremptory challenges by prosecutors while permitting their use by defendants, you would first have to confront the difficulties inherent in ascertaining whether the state action requirement applied. This difficulty was discussed earlier in the present chapter.[111] Then, you would have to confront the difficulties inherent in ascertaining when state action is present. Those difficulties are discussed below in Chapter 5.[112] Ultimately, such differential treatment could not be justified on any principled basis.

The Court's most recent forays into the interstices of the jury selection issue came in 1991. In *Powers v. Ohio*,[113] the Court held that the right to challenge the constitutionality of criminal juries for racial exclusion also extended to white criminal defendants who wished to complain about the exclusion of blacks from their juries. Later that same Term in *Edmonson v. Leesville Concrete Co.*,[114] the Court held that the *Batson* prohibition on racially motivated use of peremptory challenges by prosecutors in criminal cases also extended to the racially motivated use of peremptory challenges by private litigants in civil litigation. The pervasiveness of state involvement in the litigation process was viewed as sufficient to render a private litigant's use of peremptory challenges a delegated exercise of the government's power to empanel a jury, whether the litigation was criminal or civil.[115] Although the majority opinion did not so hold, the dissenters asserted with some plausibility that the *Edmonson* decision would necessarily bar criminal defendants from using racially motivated peremptory challenges because they, like criminal prosecutors and civil litigants, would be state actors.[116] Both of these decisions seem to be permissible interpretations of the fourteenth amendment, but neither seems to be compelled by the fourteenth amendment. One could easily have concluded, for example, that on balance the reduced danger of racial discrimination to which white defendants were exposed from the exclusion of black jurors in *Powers* did not warrant interference with the prosecutor's use of peremptory challenges. In addition, one could easily conclude that the dangers of state-sanctioned discrimination in the context of private civil litigation, to which the government is not a party, did not warrant interference with the use of peremptory challenges by private litigants in *Edmonson*.

Although *Powers* and *Edmonson* appeared to expand the protections of *Batson*, a third jury selection case that was decided that Term appeared to contract those protections. In *Hernandez v. New York*,[117] the Court indicated that relatively weak explanations by prosecutors for their exclusion of minority jurors would suffice to defeat a charge of racial motivation in the use of peremptory challenges. In *Hernandez*, the Court upheld as nondiscriminatory a prosecutor's explanation that Latino jurors who had been excluded through the use of peremptory challenges were permissibly excluded because of the prosecutor's fear that they would rely on their own understandings of Spanish language testimony rather than relying on the court's English language translation of that testimony.[118] In addition, the Court held that trial judges should be permitted to exercise considerable discretion in ruling on the adequacy of a prosecutor's justification for suspect peremptory exclusions.[119]

It is difficult to imagine how a judge could decide whether a jury exclusion case was a discrimination case or a discretion case without relying heavily on his or her own discretion. Not only is proper characterization less than self-evident, but the arguments for each of the competing characterizations seem to be equally compelling. Moreover, as the string of inconsistent Supreme Court decisions in this area reveal, principled analysis cannot be relied upon to guide the way to proper judicial characterization. When subjected to sufficiently intense analysis, the competing principles simply merge. A judge's views concerning proper characterization, therefore, would seem by default to be a function of the judge's own societally influenced priorities and values.

The process of principled adjudication on which we rely to insulate our judges from their own majoritarian inclinations begins with identification of the governing principle. This first step, however, is so ripe with discretion that it is difficult to imagine a judge selecting an applicable principle of law free from the influence of majoritarian preferences. This is true even when identification of the governing principle initially seems obvious because of precedent, textual specificity, or fundamental appropriateness of one of the alternatives. Accordingly, the process of principled adjudication will be colored by majoritarian preferences before it begins. And once the process begins, matters are likely to get even worse.

CHAPTER 5

Application of Principles

In theory, once a governing legal principle is identified, it eliminates the danger of majoritarian exploitation of minority interests because the governing principle rather than majoritarian-influenced judicial discretion will generate case outcomes. A legal principle can emanate from a constitutional provision, a statute, a regulation, or from common law precedents. But regardless of its source, proper application of a principle to the facts of a case, in accordance with the accepted tenets of logical analysis, will control the outcome of the case. Even if the principle does leave room for the exercise of some discretion, the sphere within which that discretion can properly be exercised will be narrow enough to minimize the risk of majoritarian domination of the adjudicatory process. Notwithstanding this theoretical construct, however, there are two reasons why the safeguard of principle cannot work. First, principles will be acceptable only if they are so general that the level of judicial discretion they demand is also high enough to reintroduce the dangers of majoritarianism. Second, the process by which principled adjudication proceeds makes it unrealistic to expect even a precise principle to generate only one result to the exclusion of contradictory results.

The nature of pluralist politics requires legal principles to be articulated at a relatively high level of abstraction in order to secure general approval. If principles are stated with such precision that they leave little uncertainty concerning the results that they will produce in controversial cases, interest groups who oppose those results will form coalitions to prevent the principles from being incorporated into statutes, regulations or constitutional provisions. In addition, those interest groups will also use the threat of "remedial" legislation to prevent such principles from being incorporated into judge-made common law. As a result, the only legal principles that will typically acquire operative status are principles that interest groups on each side of the relevant issues can reasonably believe will give them a chance of winning particular disputes. Arguably, there are exceptions. In *Roe v. Wade*,[1] the Court articulated fairly specific rules in order to implement an extremely *non*specific right of constitutional privacy. However, the court nevertheless preserved a fair degree of ambiguity in defining the scope of the right on which those specific rules rested.[2] Moreover, uncertainty concerning peripheral issues such as abortion funding made it unclear precisely how far the *operative* right to an abortion would extend.[3] *Roe* has been subjected to considerable "majoritarian" political pressure,[4] and although the case itself has not been overruled, its ostensible specificity does appear to have been.[5] Similarly, the highly specific rule of law announced in *Miranda v. Arizona*[6] was designed to implement an extremely nonspecific principle of voluntariness, and subsequent decisions have left the actual parameters of the *Miranda* right quite fuzzy.[7] In addition, despite its apparent specificity, *Miranda* leaves fundamental issues unclear, such as which interests are ultimately advanced and which are frustrated by the Court's decision.[8] Accordingly, even when the Court appears to adopt specific rules, the essential uncertainty that pluralist political theory predicts will be present in a governing principle can typically be uncovered. It should be noted that several commentators have distinguished between "principles" or "standards" on the one hand, which operate at a high level of abstraction and tend to be phrased in terms of functional policy objectives, and "rules" on the other hand, which operate at a high level of specificity and are designed to implement the "principles" from which they emanate.[9] However, this distinction is unimportant for present purposes, because I am prepared to argue that even highly specific rules cannot eliminate majoritarian discretion.

If it were politically possible for a precise principle to achieve controlling status, the principle would still demand recourse to dangerous judicial discretion in order to effect its implementation. Since the emergence of legal realism in the 1920s and 1930s, which demonstrated the futility of relying on linguistic conceptual analysis to arrive at correct case outcomes, the process of principled adjudication has subsisted on functional policy analysis.[10] Contemporary legal analysis tends to concede the linguistic indeterminacy of legal principles, as well as the profound ambiguity inherent in the quest for legislative intent. It justifies outcomes by arguing that one result is preferable to another because it will advance rather than frustrate the policy objectives on which a legal principle is based. However, reliance on policy analysis to reduce the indeterminacy of even seemingly precise legal principles ultimately proves to be misplaced. Postmodern legal scholarship has demonstrated the inevitable indeterminacy of legal principles by subjecting them to the process of deconstruction. A principle is deconstructed by undermining its connection to a particular policy objective and demonstrating that the principle actually advances a conflicting policy. This process is sometimes referred to as the inversion of hierarchy because the outcome associated with the policy objective that is favored by the relevant principle is severed from that objective and reattached to an outcome that is disfavored by the principle.[11] The principle's connection to the conflicting policy can then be reinverted, or undermined again, and the principle reattached to its original policy objective. This makes it unclear which policy objective the principle actually serves. As a result of this indeterminacy, legal principles can acquire operative meaning only through recourse to the same type of judicial discretion that proved to be always present when the principle was selected. And this once again raises all of the majoritarian dangers that are attendant to the presence of such discretion. The problem of indeterminacy can be illustrated by deconstructing the intent, state action, and discrimination principles identified in Chapter 4, demonstrating that each is capable of generating contradictory outcomes under a given set of facts. As a result, the Supreme Court always has the analytical option of applying a legal principle in a manner that will generate any outcome that the Court desires. Once again, the only way in which the Court can select among the available applications is through recourse to majoritarian-influenced judicial discretion.

Intent

If the Court identifies the principle of intent as controlling the discrimination issue in a particular case, as it has done with respect to race discrimination cases that allege a violation of the fourteenth amendment,[12] it must next apply that principle to the facts of the case. Consistent with the foregoing hypothesis,[13] the terms in which the principle is stated are too abstract to generate a result directly. The mere injunction to apply a requirement of intentional discrimination does not indicate who must intend to discriminate against whom with what degree of conscious deliberation. Proper resolution of these ambiguities requires consideration of which outcomes will best serve the policy objectives of the intent principle. Such functional policy analysis, however, is typically indeterminate because the relationship between principles and the outcomes that they produce is fluid.

Assume that the legislature enacts a statute designed to ameliorate the problem of drug abuse by authorizing random police searches of private residences in neighborhoods having more than a specified incidence of drug-related crime. Assume further that 90 percent of the individuals whose homes would be searched under the program are black. If challenged on equal protection grounds, the Court would then have to determine whether enactment of the drug search statute did or did not constitute an act of racial discrimination within the meaning of the intent principle. Any fourth amendment invasion of privacy problems that the legislation might pose are irrelevant for present purposes. Only the potential equal protection problems are of concern.

As noted above,[14] the policy reason for adopting an intent principle is that a prohibition on legislative classifications having a mere disparate impact on racial minorities would unduly interfere with the legislature's ability to tailor its remedial actions narrowly so that they were precisely responsive to the problem that the legislature was confronting. An effects principle might require random searches of the population at large in order to avoid an equal protection violation even though the drug problem was highly concentrated in particular neighborhoods. An intent principle, however, would permit the legislature to focus remedial efforts on neighborhoods in which they would do the most good. Moreover, an effects principle would force governmental decisionmakers to engage in race-conscious rather than race-neutral decisionmaking by forcing them actively to consider the racial impact of the legislative strategies that they were considering. An intent principle, however, would permit the legislature to focus solely on the effectiveness of a remedy without ever having to think about race. It appears, therefore, that the intent principle would require the Court to uphold the drug search legislation as long as the available direct evidence of legislative intent indicated that the statute was genuinely enacted for the purpose of reducing the drug problem and not for the purpose of imposing the burdens of drug enforcement on blacks rather than whites.[15] However, closer analysis reveals that the policy objectives lying beneath the intent principle are actually better served through application of an effects principle.

The degree to which the objectives of legislative precision and race-neutral deliberations will be advanced is likely to be a direct function of the incentives imposed upon the legislature by the threat of judicial invalidation. Under the equal protection clause, suspect classifications are not automatically invalidated but rather are subjected to strict judicial scrutiny. Therefore, if the legislature was in fact operating with a high degree of precision in directing the drug searches to the neighborhoods from which drug problems emanate, the statute will be upheld. If, however, there are other legislative classifications that would generate a tighter fit between the problem and the remedy—perhaps legalization for certain categories of drugs or mandatory sentencing for certain categories of sellers—judicial review should provide an incentive for the legislature to use those more precise classifications. As long as the legislature is genuinely concerned with reducing drug abuse, an intent test provides little incentive for the legislature to use the most precise classification available. An effects test, however, will ensure that the legislature has an incentive to legislate with the highest possible precision in disparate impact cases, because an effects test will trigger strict scrutiny even when the legislative purpose is pure.

Similarly, an effects test is more likely than an intent test to advance the objective of race-neutral deliberation. This is true both because an intent test entails more consideration of race than is commonly thought to be the case, and because an effects test entails less. Contrary to superficial appearances, an intent test does not relieve the legislature of the need to consider the racial effects of proposed legislation, but rather promotes race-conscious deliberation. A properly administered intent principle would require strict scrutiny of all legislation having a racially disparate impact because mere legislative toleration of disparate impact can amount to an act of intentional discrimination. Even under an intent principle, therefore, a legislature wishing to ensure the validity of its legislation will have to engage in a race-conscious evaluation of effects, just as it would have to do under the effects test itself. For example, when a legislature decides to focus drug searches on neighborhoods having a 90 percent black population rather than imposing those searches on the population at large, it is making an intentional decision to impose upon blacks rather than whites a high percentage of the social costs entailed in reducing the drug problem. As a result, a reviewing court will have to invalidate that legislation even under an intent test unless the legislature makes the showing required to justify an act of intentional discrimination. The legislature, therefore, will have to consider the racial impact of such legislation just as it would have to do under an effects test.[16]

Even if the legislature is initially unaware of the racially disparate impact of its legislation, the legislation will still be subject to invalidation under an intentional discrimination standard in a way that preserves the need for race-conscious legislative deliberations. A legislative decision to proceed in the absence of any given item of information entails a legislative cost-benefit determination to risk whatever adverse consequences would have been revealed by such information in order to save the administrative costs required to obtain it. In contemporary society, where racial minorities are disproportionately represented among those who lack social, economic, and political power, a decision to forego the acquisition of additional information cannot be viewed as race-neutral. Because the adverse consequences of proceeding in the face of uncertainty are more likely to be borne by racial minorities than by the majority, a legislative action having a racially disparate impact can be invalid under the intent test even when the legislature is unaware of the disparate impact that its legislation will have. A legislature wishing to avoid this result will again be forced to engage in race-conscious deliberations in order to maximize the likelihood that its legislation will be upheld.

Our failure to appreciate the strong correspondence that exists between intent and effects causes us to understate the degree to which the intent principle requires race-conscious legislative deliberations. That same failure also causes us to overstate the relative amount of race-conscious deliberation that is necessitated by the effects principle. As indicated above, a diligent reviewing court will draw inferences concerning discriminatory intent from the circumstantial evidence of disparate impact. However, a reviewing court will also rely upon any direct evidence of legislative intent that is provided by the statutory language and legislative history.

Because a legislature is a multimember body whose intent is difficult to ascertain, aberrant evidence of discriminatory intent can pose serious problems. Suppose, for example, that a majority of the legislature favored the drug-search legislation discussed above free of any discriminatory animus that would cause a reviewing court to invalidate the legislation under an intentional discrimination standard. Suppose further, however, that a small but vocal group of additional legislators favored the legislation for invidious reasons, and that they disclosed those reasons in floor statements and portions of the relevant committee reports. Although the votes of the invidious discriminators were not needed to enact the statute, the statute nevertheless now carries with it direct evidence of discriminatory intent that might result in its invalidation.

Under an intent test, the danger of invalidation can be quite real. Under an effects test, however, there is no danger of invalidation at all because direct evidence of discriminatory intent is simply irrelevant. By focusing on both direct and circumstantial evidence of discriminatory intent, the intent test requires the legislature to think about race a lot. Not only does it have to be concerned with the avoidance of disparate impact, but it also has to avoid anything that might be construed as direct evidence of improper legislative motivation. Although the effects principle also requires race-conscious consideration of legislative effects, it relieves the legislature of the need to concern itself with direct evidence of discriminatory intent. As a result, the intent test actually requires the legislature to think about race *more* than the effects test does. Despite initial appearances, both the policy favoring legislative precision and the policy favoring race-neutral legislative deliberation are better served by the effects principle than by the intent principle.

The intent principle has now been deconstructed. The policy justifications initially thought to be promoted by that principle have been shown to be fostered more effectively by a principle that focuses on disparate impact. Before becoming too comfortable with this inversion of principles and policy objectives, however, it is necessary to realize that the effects principle can also be deconstructed, thereby permitting the relationship between each principle and its associated policy to be inverted yet again.

Although the effects principle seems to enhance the incentive for legislatures to draft statutory categories with precision, it ignores the fact that judicial deference is needed in order to secure optimal legislative precision. If the Court were strictly to scrutinize every legislative classification having a racially disparate impact, permitting only what it considered to be the tightest fitting classifications to stand, the Court would itself be exercising the policymaking discretion that the Constitution reserves to the legislature. Because courts are institutionally ill-suited to balancing the benefits and burdens of particular legislative classifications in order to find out which one is best, a measure of judicial deference to legislative discretion is necessary to prevent judicial usurpation of legislative policymaking functions. Indeed, that is the very reason for which courts adhere to particular standards of review when ruling upon the constitutionality of legislative enactments. The effects principle discounts this need for judicial deference whenever a legislative classification happens to have a racially disparate impact. As a practical matter, an effects test applied at any given level of judicial scrutiny will be more intrusive than an intent test applied at that same level of scrutiny, because evidence of disparate impact will be more readily available than evidence of invidious intent. As a result, an effects test increases the risk of judicial usurpation over what it would be under an intent test, regardless of the particular standard of review that is employed. The intent principle, therefore, better serves the standard-of-review function that is called for. By risking the danger of judicial usurpation only when purposeful discrimination has been established, the intent principle accords the legislature the deference needed for optimal precision in the formulation of legislative categories.

Similarly, although the effects principle seems to reduce the degree to which legislators will ultimately have to engage in race-conscious deliberations, any reduction is actually shortsighted. If our long-term policy objective is to establish social conditions under which race neutrality will flourish, the most effective means of pursuing that objective is to engage in short-term race-conscious deliberations designed to compensate for present societal imperfections that make governmental race neutrality not yet viable. That means that thorough legislative consideration should be encouraged with respect to all aspects of racially relevant classifications. Both the intent and effects associated with such legislation should be fully ventilated and explored. The effects principle truncates such plenary consideration by making legislative consideration of racial impact the only thing that is constitutionally relevant. The intent principle, however, not only fosters legislative consideration of both intent and effects, but such contemplation inevitably conveys the important insight that the two are inextricably intertwined.

The process of deconstruction can go on and on indefinitely—or at least until the analyst reaches the limits of his or her energy or imagination. The reason for this is that the concepts upon which most legal principles rest lack stable content. The concept of intent can mean purpose, or it can mean toleration of known effects, or it can mean knowing toleration of ignorance about likely effects. This lack of stable content deprives legal principles of the capacity to have any dispositive meaning. The recent intent v. effects cases of the Supreme Court, which have already been discussed,[17] illustrate how the Court has capitalized on this instability. Although the Court nominally applied the effects principle to those cases, the proof requirements on which it insisted seem actually to implement a principle of intent. The court generated this confusion by silently shifting between nominal principles and their evidentiary attributes in the same way that the process of deconstruction shifts between principles and their policy objectives.

The content given to a principle in any particular context seems to depend heavily upon the purposes and preferences of the person supplying that content. As a result, the only way that a judge who somehow manages to identify a particular principle as controlling can actually apply that principle in a particular case is through an act of judicial discretion. And once judicial discretion is given controlling importance, the dangers of majoritarian influence become unavoidably high.

State Action

The state action principle can be similarly deconstructed. Once a court selects the state action rather than the private conduct principle as controlling in a particular case, it must then decide how that principle applies to the facts of the case. Again, ambiguities are present. It is not clear precisely who constitutes the "state," and precisely what constitutes "action." Accordingly, the court must resolve those ambiguities in the manner that best serves the objectives of the state action principle. As with the principle of intent, however, the fit between the state action principle and its objectives is loose enough to permit the principle to be deconstructed. This can be illustrated by analyzing another paradigm case whose variants the Court has considered on multiple occasions.

A white seller agrees to convey to a black purchaser a parcel of real property that is subject to a racially restrictive covenant prohibiting sale of the property to blacks. The Court is then called upon to determine the validity of the covenant in a suit filed by other whites living in the seller's neighborhood to enforce the racial restriction. The restrictive covenant has typically been inserted into the seller's deed by a prior owner of the property, or by the real estate developer of the property, who has an economic rather than an associational interest in maintaining the racially segregated nature of the development.[18] The Court decides that the state action rather than the private conduct principle applies to the case and, therefore, must determine whether enforcement of the covenant would constitute state action in order to determine its validity.

The purpose of the state action requirement is to isolate a sphere of personal autonomy in which private parties are able to exercise their associational freedoms.[19] It is premised on the belief that, as distasteful as invidious discrimination may be, unlimited governmental intrusion into private affairs can be even more undesirable. When state action is present, a prohibition on discriminatory conduct advances our societal interest in promoting racial equality without undermining our desire to protect autonomy and associational freedom. This is because it is the state, rather than private parties, that must conform its conduct to specified norms. In the absence of state action, however, a requirement to conform behavior to government specified norms *would* interfere with individual autonomy and associational freedom. Accordingly, the state action principle requires government neutrality. The state must make its legal enforcement ma-chinery available to blacks and whites on an equal basis so that the state itself is not guilty of discrimination, and it must do so without regard to the associational preferences of private parties so that it does not interfere with their personal autonomy. The state action principle, therefore, pro-motes individual autonomy and associational freedom while ensuring that the state does not selectively elevate the associational preferences of one race over those of another. The private conduct principle, on the other hand, would undermine both autonomy and associational freedom, and require the state itself to discriminate among those to whom it extended its enforcement services.

In light of these objectives, the court should determine that the state action requirement is not satisfied in the paradigm case. The restrictive covenant was placed in the white seller's deed as the result of a private contractual agreement between the white seller and the previous owner of the property. As long as that agreement was knowingly entered into as part of a freely bargained-for exchange, judicial invalidation would subvert the autonomy of the parties by denying them the ability to protect their associational preferences. Moreover, judicial invalidation would under-mine the objective of government neutrality, because it would result in state enforcement of the associational preferences of the black buyer who wanted to live with the white seller's neighbors, while denying enforcement to the preferences of the white neighbors who did not wish to associate with the black buyer. The state itself would then be guilty of discriminatory enforcement, in direct violation of the state action principle.

This is the result that the Supreme Court reached the first time that it considered the paradigm case. In its little-known *Corrigan v. Buckley* decision,[20] the Court held that the absence of state action was so clear that the issue did not even raise a constitutional question substantial enough to trigger the Court's appellate jurisdiction.[21] Then, in *Shelley v. Kraemer*,[22] the Supreme Court deconstructed its own prior decision, hold-ing that the paradigm case did, after all, involve state action. The *Shelley* Court distinguished the two cases by arguing that *Corrigan* concerned only the validity of the restrictive covenant rather than its enforceability.[23] The distinction may at first seem artificial. However, as the discussion below will demonstrate, it is manipulation of this precise distinction that ultimately permits the state action principle to generate whatever outcome is desired. Although the restrictive covenant was a wholly private agree-ment that did not entail state action, judicial enforcement of that agree-ment *would* amount to state action prohibited by the fourteenth amendment. Ultimately, the presence or absence of state intervention, backed by the full panoply of the government's coercive powers, is what would determine whether the willing buyer and seller were able to effectuate their exchange.[24]

In functional terms, the *Shelley* Court can be viewed as having inverted the connection that *Corrigan* had initially established between each of the competing principles and the policy objectives that they served. Protection of individual autonomy and associational preferences was not, as *Corrigan* had suggested, advanced by characterizing the paradigm case as a state action case. In reality, this characterization nullified the autonomy of a willing buyer and seller by denying them their preference for voluntary mutual association. In so doing, the state also abandoned its role as a neutral arbiter by agreeing to enforce the real property exchanges of those who wish to sell to whites but not of those who wish to sell to blacks. These are the disfavored policy consequences associated with the private conduct principle, not the desired policy objectives associated with the state action principle. The desired policy objectives are best advanced by characterizing the paradigm case as a state action case, so that the fourteenth amendment can be invoked to prevent the state from frustrating the preference of the buyer and seller to associate with each other, and from selectively enforcing its real property laws in a way that denies individuals with certain associational preferences the ability to make legally enforceable agreements. The Court reaffirmed this deconstructive inversion of policies and principles in *Barrows v. Jackson*,[25] when it refused to require the white seller to pay damages for breach of the restrictive covenant to the seller's white neighbors. The Court held that, like the equitable relief sought in *Shelley*, a judicial award of money damages at law would also constitute coercive state action.[26]

After *Shelley* and *Barrows* the law appears to be that restrictive covenants are valid agreements, effective to the extent that they can command voluntary compliance. However, they are not legally enforceable, because legal enforcement would constitute discriminatory state action. Of course, the state action principle can be further deconstructed in a way that calls the soundness of even this formulation of current law into question. Assume that the white seller refuses to sell to the black buyer, for the express reason that the seller wishes voluntarily to comply with the restrictive covenant. The black buyer then sues to have the covenant declared invalid.

Should the Court decline to intervene because the covenant is now being "enforced" through voluntary private action rather than state action? After all, in this case, unlike *Shelley*, the Court does not have the final say as to whether the deal will go through; the private seller's associational preference will ultimately be dispositive. This is the view of state action that the Court seems to have adopted in *Evans v. Newton*.[27] There, the Court held that the Georgia Supreme Court's transfer of title from the City of Macon, Georgia, to a board of private trustees, in order to permit the park to remain racially segregated as required by the terms of the will that initially bequeathed the park to the City, constituted state action. *Even though* the state Court was attempting to remain neutral with respect to private associational preferences by terminating the City's involvement with the park, the state Court's actions impermissibly facilitated the private testator's discriminatory intent.[28]

Or, should the Court choose to intervene because judicial abstention would constitute state action that facilitated the private seller in his or her efforts to exclude blacks? After all, in this case as in *Shelley*, the Court has the final say as to whether the deal will go through; effectuation of the private seller's associational preference is completely dependent upon how the Court rules on the state action issue. This is the view of state action that the Court seems to have adopted in *Evans v. Abney*.[29] There, in a subsequent case involving the same Macon park, the Court held that the Georgia Supreme Court's reversion of title to the testator's estate, in order to permit the park to remain racially segregated as required by the terms of the will that initially bequeathed the park to the City, did *not* constitute state action. This time, *because* the state court was attempting to remain neutral with respect to private associational preferences by applying the Georgia law of *cy pres* to terminate the City's involvement with the park, the state Court's actions did not impermissibly facilitate the private testator's discriminatory intent.[30]

The problem is insoluble. In a liberal legal system, the objective of protecting a sphere of private autonomy is generally viewed as normatively desirable. Indeed, from a Hobbesian perspective, such facilitation constitutes the only justification for the state's existence.[31] However, judicial efforts to advance that objective simply generate a paradox. Once a court declines to remedy an act of private discrimination, the act can no longer retain its character as a private act, precisely because the court has chosen to protect the discriminator's private autonomy. Because the court is a state actor, judicial facilitation of what begins as an act of private discrimination transforms the act into conduct that constitutes state action. As a result, the state action principle requires that whenever the private character of a discriminatory act compels a court to refrain from intervening, the court's own act of restraint will automatically make judicial intervention compulsory.

Because of the paradoxical nature of the state action conundrum, there can be no hope of principled judicial resolution of state action issues. Not even recourse to the Court's fundamental countermajoritarian function can assist the Court in applying the state action principle, because the principle of countermajoritarianism can be deconstructed as well. The Court can never know with confidence whether its job is to protect potential black buyers from majoritarian white sellers who wish to discriminate against them, or to protect individual white sellers from the majoritarian government that would deny them their unpopular associational preferences.[32] Dangerous judicial discretion again appears to hold the only hope of ever giving operational content to the state action principle.[33]

Discrimination

Like the intent and state action principles, the discrimination principle can also be deconstructed by manipulating its connection to particular policy objectives. As the following discussion demonstrates, the concept of discrimination is inherently ambiguous. Once the Court decides to apply the principle in a particular case, it will have to resolve that ambiguity by determining whether the policy reason for which the principle was selected would be advanced or frustrated by a finding of discrimination in that case. The policy objective of the discrimination principle is perhaps the most fundamental in all of Anglo-American jurisprudence. It stems from the *a priori* belief that like cases should be treated alike. However, because cases are both alike and different in a vast number of ways, some basis must be found for distinguishing between the similarities and differences that are legally relevant and those that are not. The discrimination principle is designed to implement this distinction.

When the representative branches of government accord differential treatment to cases based upon legitimate differences that exist between those cases, the representative branches are behaving in an appropriate manner that warrants judicial deference. The discretion principle cautions the Court not to intervene in such cases because the selection of relevant similarities and differences has properly been made by a politically accountable majoritarian branch of government. I am here using the discretion principle as shorthand for the entire range of permissible bases of majoritarian differentiation. When a majoritarian branch of government draws legislative or executive classifications based upon permissible factors, it is using its discretion in determining that those factors are important enough to merit differential treatment. If, however, the governmental differentiation is based upon similarities or differences that the government cannot properly make the basis of disparate treatment, the countermajoritarian Court is obligated to invalidate that differentiation under the discrimination principle. Although a wide variety of factors may properly serve to justify governmental differentiation, for purposes of the discrimination principle we refuse to recognize race as such a factor. The Supreme Court established in *Brown v. Board of Education*,[34] when it outlawed the separate-but-equal doctrine of *Plessy v. Ferguson*,[35] that racial discrimination constitutes inherently unequal treatment that operates to the disadvantage of the minority race.[36] The discretion principle, therefore, encourages differential treatment based upon neutral factors because such differentiation promotes politically accountable policymaking by the majoritarian branches of government. The discrimination principle, however, prohibits differential treatment based upon the immutable characteristic of race because it constitutes a form of invidiousness that we believe to be unfair, inequitable, and immoral, all in contravention of a fundamental tenet of Anglo-American jurisprudence.

I have offered a formulation of the discrimination principle that is somewhat stronger than the principle actually applied by the Supreme Court. The Court does not invalidate all racial classifications. Rather, it deems such classifications to be suspect and subjects them to strict judicial scrutiny. As a result, some racial classifications are, in fact, upheld by the Court—specifically, those that the majoritarian branches can establish are narrowly tailored to advance a compelling state interest.[37] However, the compelling state-interest formulation of the discrimination principle causes the principle to inject majoritarian preferences into its own meaning.[38] These preferences will enter the analysis either through judicial deference to the representative branches under the applicable standard of review or through the Court's own socialized discretion in ascertaining what does and does not constitute a compelling state interest or a tight-enough fit. The advantage of the stronger formulation that I have offered is that it does not openly call for the exercise of majoritarian discretion—although ultimately, recourse to such discretion will still be required.

Deconstruction of the discrimination principle can be illustrated by considering the facts of *Lee v. Washington*,[39] a brief per curiam decision of the Supreme Court that has come to be known more for its plurality dicta than for its holding. There, black and white prison inmates challenged the constitutionality of certain Alabama statutes, and official practices taken in accordance with those statutes, that required the racial segregation of prisoners in state and local prisons. The State argued that such racial segregation was necessary in order to ensure prison safety and discipline, and that the Court should defer to the expert discretion of the prison administrators in determining the need for segregation.[40] Nevertheless, in a one paragraph opinion, the Supreme Court affirmed the invalidation by a three-judge district court of the Alabama statutes. Although the statutes were invalidated on equal protection grounds, the constitutional permissibility of limited-duration segregation in order to deal with emergency situations appears to have been conceded both by the Supreme Court and the district court, albeit in advisory dicta.[41] When the case is cited, it tends to be cited for the proposition that, in extreme cases, race-based classifications will be tolerated in order to advance sufficiently important state interests.[42] However, it is very difficult to determine whether the Court's resolution of the case was or was not correct.

Assuming the truth of the state's assertion that racial segregation in Alabama prisons is necessary to ensure prisoner safety, the discrimination principle nevertheless requires invalidation of the segregation statutes because they constitute impermissible race-based classifications. Since race is not a legitimate basis for differential treatment, state statutes that are expressly drawn in racial terms cannot constitute valid forms of governmental differentiation. This is the very form of majoritarian illegitimacy that the discrimination principle requires a countermajoritarian court to detect and neutralize. Moreover, the judicial deference that the discretion principle typically accords majoritarian policymaking determinations in order to promote political accountability would be inappropriate here, where it is precisely that accountability that has spawned the mandatory segregation statutes. Functional application of the discrimination principle, therefore, requires invalidation of the Alabama statutes.[43]

The discrimination principle can be deconstructed by inverting the policies associated with the competing principles. Despite their explicit reliance on racial classifications, the Alabama statutes are actually based upon the legitimate factors of prisoner safety and discipline. That grouping of prisoners resulting in greater degrees of prisoner safety and discipline is simply preferred to other groupings that are likely to result in prison riots. Although the State relies upon an explicit racial classification to advance this objective, race is merely a correlative rather than an actuating basis for the differential treatment. Invalidation of the State's prisoner segregation statutes, therefore, would actually frustrate rather than advance the goals of the discrimination principle by setting aside a majoritarian policy determination that was based upon permissible safety factors rather than upon the impermissible factor of race. Moreover, upholding the segregation statutes would advance the deference to politically accountable policymaking that the discretion principle is intended to serve. Accordingly, it is by upholding rather than invalidating the Alabama segregation statute that the discrimination principle is properly applied.[44]

Or, the discrimination principle can be further deconstructed so that it once again requires invalidation of the Alabama statutes. Semantic niceties concerning danger-based differentiation notwithstanding, the operative basis for discrimination in the prison riot situation must realistically be viewed as race. Race is the factor that created the danger of prison riots, and by hypothesis, racial separation is the only remedy that will be adequate to eliminate the danger. Beginning the analysis at the level of prison safety and discipline, while ignoring the fact that the problems of safety and discipline themselves derive from the underlying problem of racial friction, makes the analysis unacceptably artificial. It overlooks the fact that our current race-relations problems stem from a history of official majoritarian discrimination. The discrimination principle should, therefore, be applied to invalidate the racial segregation statutes rather than to permit continued deference to majoritarian desires concerning interracial association.

The reason that the discrimination principle can be repeatedly deconstructed is that there is a fundamental ambiguity inherent in the concept of discrimination that is subject to both intentional and inadvertent exploitation during a particular analysis. The principle assumes that there is an "actual" basis of discrimination in cases involving differential treatment, which can be identified and then classified as legitimate or illegitimate. However, as the problems encountered in analyzing *Lee v. Washington* suggest, there is no particular reason to believe that acts of governmental differentiation are the result of only one cause or motive. Moreover, even if a single or primary basis for differential treatment could be identified, an additional problem would remain. It is not clear how a court could reliably distinguish between legitimate and illegitimate uses of a particular basis for differentiation. The Supreme Court's school desegregation cases reveal the complexity of this problem, as well as the elusiveness of any principled resolution.

The Supreme Court's decision in *Brown v. Board of Education*[45] held that racially segregated public school systems were unconstitutional, and that segregated "dual" systems had to be dismantled and replaced by desegregated "unitary" systems.[46] Although *Brown* was decided in 1954, and the injunction to desegregate the public schools "with all deliberate speed" was issued in 1955,[47] the Supreme Court did not become actively involved in the implementation of *Brown* until the mid- or late-1960s.[48]

The major doctrinal difficulty in implementing *Brown* came in attempting to ascertain the difference between a dual system and a unitary one. Because the *Brown* requirements apply only to dual systems, and not to unitary systems, the distinction between the two is constitutionally significant.[49] However, one cannot distinguish a dual system from a unitary system simply by looking at it. The existence of racial imbalance among students or teachers does not alone establish that a system is dual. Rather the distinction between a dual and a unitary system depends upon the factors to which that racial imbalance is traceable. Racial imbalance that is traceable to impermissible discrimination on the part of school officials causes a school system to be characterized as an unconstitutional dual system. However, racial imbalance that is traceable to the exercise of permissible discretion by school officials in making decisions of educational policy permits the system to be characterized as a unitary system despite its racial imbalance. Accordingly, the difference between an unconstitutional school system and a constitutional system turns on the elusive distinction between discrimination and discretion.

The test on which the Supreme Court has settled for determining whether a racially imbalanced school system is the product of discrimination or discretion is whether the racial imbalance in the system is *de jure* or *de facto* in nature.[50] *De jure* racial imbalance, which results from an intentional policy of racial segregation that is expressed in state laws or intentionally discriminatory practices, is deemed to be the product of impermissible discrimination. *De facto* racial imbalance, which results primarily from segregated residential patterns, is deemed to be the product of permissible discretion in the formulation of school district lines, attendance zones, school busing programs, and the like.[51] Accordingly, the four segregated school systems that were held to be unconstitutional in *Brown* itself were dual systems because they resulted from official and explicit policies of public school segregation.[52] However, the school systems in suburban Detroit, which the Supreme Court in *Milliken v. Bradley*[53] permitted school officials to exclude from a constitutionally compelled plan for the desegregation of Detroit's inner-city schools, were unitary systems because their overwhelmingly white character had resulted from residential patterns rather than from an official policy of school segregation.[54]

When a state or local school system admits that it is engaged in *de jure* racial discrimination, as the school systems did in *Brown*,[55] it is a relatively simple matter to conclude that the system is an unconstitutional dual system. However, when a school system asserts that its racial imbalance is merely the *de facto* result of racially neutral policies that were designed to advance educational objectives unrelated to racial segregation, proper characterization of the system as dual or unitary becomes extremely problematic. On one level, proper characterization is problematic because it poses the same insoluble dilemma that is encountered whenever one seeks to apply the intent principle in the context of racially disparate treatment.[56] Just as the prison segregation in *Lee v. Washington* could be viewed as the product of either impermissible discrimination based upon race or permissible discretion based upon safety, the racial imbalance of a school system can be viewed as the product of either impermissible *de jure* discrimination or permissible *de facto* imbalance that is attributable to the formulation of educational policy. An additional problem is encountered, however, even when the factor of intent is held constant.

Perhaps the most striking feature of the school desegregation issue is the depth of the white opposition that it arouses.[57] Whether one focuses on the need to send federal troops to desegregate the schools in Little Rock, Arkansas,[58] Governor George Wallace blocking the schoolhouse doors to prevent the desegregation of public schools in Alabama,[59] or the intense racial violence that accompanied efforts to desegregate the school system of South Boston,[60] it is plain that public school desegregation is an issue that many whites regard with vehement hostility. Although the liberal white majority that supports *Brown v. Board of Education* favors school desegregation in theory,[61] no one seems to want his or her own children to attend a desegregated school. In the context of "white flight" to suburban and private schools that is designed to escape the desegregation of inner-city school systems,[62] it is difficult to accept the assurance of school officials that factors such as the optional attendance zones, school closings, new school site selections, and opposition to busing that have had the effect of increasing rather than decreasing public school racial imbalance is really the exercise of discretion concerning matters of educational policy that have nothing to do with race. Nevertheless, by declining to recognize *de facto* segregation as evidence that is sufficient to establish the existence of a dual school system, the Supreme has imposed upon itself the burden of distinguishing between permissible and impermissible forms of racial imbalance. The Court's decisions have been predictably inconsistent, because the discrimination principle lacks sufficient content to control them.

In 1973, the Court held in *Keyes v. School District No. 1, Denver, Colorado*,[63] that the predominantly white schools surrounding the predominantly black and Latino inner-city schools in Denver were dual. A year later, in *Milliken v. Bradley*,[64] the Court held that the predominantly white schools surrounding the predominantly black inner-city schools in Detroit were unitary. More specifically, when the school officials in Denver continued to honor existing attendance zone lines rather than redraw those lines in a way that would permit desegregation of the inner-city schools, the Court held that this decision was an impermissible act of discrimination. The fact that officials had engaged in past *de jure* discrimination with respect to some schools was evidence that every school in the district was tainted by *de jure* discrimination, thus requiring a constitutionally acceptable desegregation plan to include all of the schools.[65] However, when the school officials in Detroit continued to honor existing school district lines rather than redraw those lines in a way that would permit desegregation of the inner-city schools, the Supreme Court held that this decision was a permissible exercise of discretion. Although the officials had engaged in past *de jure* discrimination with respect to the inner-city schools, the record did not reveal any *de jure* discrimination with respect to the surrounding schools whose predominantly white character was the result of residential patterns.[66]

The two cases are indistinguishable. Both entail efforts by white school officials to preserve the *de facto* racial imbalance that resulted from residential patterns by refusing to include surrounding white schools in a desegregation plan that was constitutionally required for inner-city schools. Moreover, both cases involved heavily minority, inner-city schools that simply could not be desegregated without the inclusions of white students who lived outside of the inner city in the applicable desegregation plan. The distinction that the Supreme Court offered between the two cases is untenable. It held that the school district lines in *Milliken* were distinguishable from the attendance zone lines in *Keyes* because the school district lines in *Milliken* reflected the need for local control over the operation of schools but the attendance zone lines in *Keyes* did not. Accordingly, the Court rejected the trial court's conclusion that "[s]chool district lines are simply matters of political convenience and may not be used to deny constitutional rights."[67] The distinction, however, is both non responsive and artificial.

The distinction is non responsive because the bare assertion that local control is important says nothing about *how* important local control is relative to the independent goal of attaining a meaningful level of school desegregation. If the objective of local control is not important enough to preclude an effective remedy for the southern *de jure* segregation that was found to exist in *Brown*, why does it become important enough to preclude an effective remedy for the northern *de jure* segregation that was found to exist in *Milliken*? Indeed, the whole point of *Brown* was that the national interest in school desegregation was sufficiently strong to override regional preferences for segregated schools. The distinction is artificial because there is no necessary correlation between school district lines and local control. One can view schools as being controlled by single unelected principals, by unelected regional directors, by elected school boards, by elected state officials who enact education legislation, or by elected federal officials who make conditional grants of educational funds available to the states. The point along this continuum at which control changes from local to nonlocal is not self-evident. Moreover, there is nothing inherent in a school district's size or population that makes a school district line the natural line of demarcation between local and nonlocal control. In some states, school districts are small enough to include only a few schools serving a small number of students.[68] In other states, urban school districts are large enough to encompass literally hundreds of the small school districts that exist in more rural jurisdictions.[69]

Even if the distinction between school district lines and attendance zone lines were meaningful, it would be easy to deconstruct that distinction so that it produced the opposite results in *Keyes* and *Milliken*. Assuming that local control over the formulation and implementation of educational policy is important, local control is more closely related to the attendance zone lines that the Court disregarded in *Keyes* than to the school district lines that it honored in *Milliken*. Because attendance zones are by hypothesis smaller than school districts within a given jurisdiction, respect for attendance zone lines will result in more local control than respect for school district lines. The officials who set policy for an attendance zone are more likely to be familiar with the educational policy preferences of the residents of that attendance zone than school board officials who live in distant parts of a large school district. Moreover, because attendance-zone policymakers will tend to be unelected professional educators rather than politically vulnerable elected school board members, the attendance-zone officials will be free to focus on the needs of their own attendance zones without engaging in the process of political compromise that necessarily colors the policies of elected school board officials, who must balance the divergent interests represented in their larger and less-homogeneous school districts. In addition, the day-to-day operational decisions that are made by attendance-zone officials, relating to matters such as discipline, teaching methods, and extra-curricular activities, are more likely to be the sorts of decisions for which local control is desirable—more likely than district-wide decisions that can implicate matters of national importance, such as the nature and scope of school desegregation in the district. Accordingly, if the Supreme Court were genuinely interested in fostering local control, it would have made more sense for the Court to have honored the attendance-zone lines in *Keyes*, which relate to matters of permissible discretion in the formulation of educational policy, than to honor the school district lines in *Milliken*, which relate to matters that tend merely to camouflage impermissible discrimination.

The suggestion that the distinction between impermissible discrimination and permissible discretion is what really accounts for the divergent results in *Keyes* and *Milliken* simply lacks plausibility. A much more credible account is that the Supreme Court, responding to its innate majoritarianism, simply changed its mind during the interval between *Keyes* and *Milliken* about the advisability of intermingling white suburban students and black inner-city students. Moreover, this change of heart seems to have coincided with a decline in popular support for school desegregation. When school desegregation was an issue that affected only southern schools, southern regional opposition to desegregation was strong, but national support for desegregation was even stronger—strong enough to override southern opposition. However, as school desegregation moved north in the 1970s, national support for desegregation began to subside, and the Supreme Court began to invalidate school desegregation plans.[70]

In the 1970s, political opposition to desegregation began to be more vocal. President Nixon, who had been elected in 1968 on a political platform that included opposition to busing, was reelected in 1972. That same year, Congress also enacted the Education Amendments of 1972, which prohibited the appropriation of federal funds for busing that was intended to achieve racial balance. In 1974, Congress amended this statute so that it prohibited federal courts from requiring the busing of students beyond the nearest neighboring schools in an effort to remedy *de facto* segregation. This political opposition continued to grow during the Republican administrations of the 1970s and 1980s, as Congress proposed constitutional amendments to ban busing, and as the Reagan administration ultimately pledged not to seek busing remedies and to construe narrowly the Court's earlier desegregation precedents.[71]

The Supreme Court's desegregation decisions tracked this increasing political opposition to school desegregation. The early desegregation cases that arose in the south strongly favored desegregation plans that promised to work. For example, *Green v. County School Board*[72] invalidated freedom of choice plans because they were empirically unlikely to result in meaningful levels of school desegregation. Similarly, *Swann v. Charlotte-Mecklenburg Board of Education*[73] authorized the use of race-based pupil assignment and busing to achieve meaningful levels of desegregation. *Keyes* suggested that the Court would continue to insist on meaningful desegregation even in northern urban school districts.[74] In fact, for twenty years after its 1954 decision in *Brown*, the Court had never invalidated a desegregation plan. The first Supreme Court decision to do so was its 1974 decision in *Milliken*, which refused to order the inclusion of suburban schools in a desegregation plan for inner-city Detroit.[75]

From 1974 until 1979, the Court's response to desegregation plans fluctuated. In the 1976 case of *Hills v. Gautreaux*,[76] the Court authorized metropolitan-area remedies for public housing discrimination even though it had rejected such remedies for public school desegregation in *Milliken*, thereby suggesting that the *Milliken* holding would not be fatal to desegregation efforts. However, in 1976 the Court also held in *Pasadena Board of Education v. Spangler*[77] that annual readjustment of attendance zones was not required to ensure that desegregated schools did not revert to predominantly minority schools as a result of population shifts. In 1977, the Court once again considered *Milliken v. Bradley*,[78] this time holding that remedial education in lieu of the race-based pupil assignment authorized in *Swann* could be used to remedy past *de jure* segregation in heavily black inner-city school systems. Also in 1977, the Court rejected the need for a system-wide desegregation plan for the city of Dayton, Ohio, in *Dayton Board of Education v. Brinkman*, only to change its mind two years later in 1979 when it affirmed a system-wide plan for that same city.[79] In a second 1979 case, the Court also affirmed a system-wide desegregation plan for the city of Columbus, Ohio, in *Columbus Board of Education v. Penick*.[80]

Since 1979, the Supreme Court's decisions have been more uniform in their tolerance of majoritarian efforts to dilute the desegregation obligations imposed on public school systems—efforts that were increasingly shared by black parents who had become disillusioned with the potential of desegregation to improve the education of black children.[81] In 1982 the Court issued two companion decisions that had the effect of permitting school systems to terminate their efforts to remedy *de facto* segregation through busing. In *Washington v. Seattle School District No. 1*,[82] the Court invalidated a state-wide initiative that prohibited school districts from ordering busing beyond the confines of a student's neighborhood. In *Crawford v. Board of Education of the City of Los Angeles*,[83] the Court upheld a similar initiative that prohibited state courts from ordering busing to eliminate *de facto* segregation. The Court offered esoteric justifications for its differential treatment of the two cases, but even the *Seattle* case left local school districts free to reject busing remedies if they wished.[84] In the 1986 case of *Bazemore v. Friday*,[85] the Court upheld a freedom-of-choice remedy for *de jure* segregation practiced by 4-H Clubs that were organized through the segregated North Carolina public schools, even though the plan was seemingly identical to the freedom of choice plans that the Court had invalidated eighteen years earlier in *Green v. County School Board*.[86]

In 1990, the Court decided *Missouri v. Jenkins*,[87] which invalidated on federalism grounds a trial court order increasing Kansas City, Missouri, property taxes in order to pay for a sweeping desegregation order. The majority held that, although the Court did not have the power to increase taxes itself, it did have the power to order local government officials to increase taxes to pay for a valid desegregation order. The Court did not, however, reach the question of whether the district court's order was a valid order.[88] In the 1991 case of *Board of Education of Oklahoma City Public Schools v. Dowell*,[89] the court held that desegregation orders were intended to be temporary in nature and that they could be dissolved after good faith compliance for a reasonable period of time that eliminated the vestiges of past discrimination to the extent practicable, despite the continued existence of avoidable one-race schools. The Supreme Court has also heard argument in two desegregation cases that will give it a further opportunity to determine whether previously dual systems become unitary after a period of compliance with a desegregation plan that has been frustrated by resegregation or by school board policies that fail to minimize racial imbalance.[90]

Because the discrimination principle is imprecise, it is able to capture simultaneously both faces of our cultural ambivalence about school desegregation in a way that permits the principle to be deconstructed at will. This, in turn, enables the Supreme Court to approve or disapprove desegregation plans as it deems appropriate in its discretion. Once again, because that discretion will reflect majoritarian preferences, the discrimination principle cannot be expected to insulate racial minorities from popular political pressures. The increasingly unreceptive trend of the school desegregation cases, which corresponds to an increasingly unreceptive popular response to the prospect of continued efforts at meaningful school desegregation, illustrates that the Supreme Court is much more likely to respond to shifts in majoritarian attitudes about topical issues than to resist those shifts.

The difficulties inherent in properly interpreting the discrimination principle are endemic to all efforts at principled interpretation. Because legal principles can be deconstructed, they provide little assistance to a Court seeking to limit the implication of its own discretion in the application of the principles on which it relies. This is because the result produced by a legal principle reflects little more than the point at which the Court chooses to end the analytical process—a process that can in theory continue indefinitely, producing first one result and then another. Rather than serving a constraining function, legal principles ironically end up increasing the Court's dependence on majoritarian-influenced discretion, minimizing only the degree to which the impact of such majoritarian influence is likely to be detected.

The phenomenon of deconstruction illustrates but one of the many difficulties that inhere in the traditional model of judicial review. Ultimately, the traditional model cannot work because the countermajoritarian assumptions on which it is based are untenable. The traditional model posits the existence of a Supreme Court that is capable of protecting the interests of racial minorities by superseding the majoritarian preferences that are socialized into the justices who sit on the Court. However, the mechanisms relied upon to ensure this countermajoritarian capability are ineffective. Neither the formal safeguards of life tenure and salary protection nor the operational safeguard of principled adjudication can successfully insulate the adjudicatory process from majoritarian domination. The formal safeguards do not even address the problem of unconscious majoritarianism, which can significantly influence the actions of a socialized judiciary. Although the operational safeguard of principled adjudication nominally *is* addressed to that problem, it cannot effectively guard against unconscious majoritarianism because the adjudicatory process is unable to insulate judicial decisionmaking from the vast amounts of judicial discretion that are required to make the process work. Even when legal principles do not directly incorporate majoritarian preferences into their meanings, the loosely constrained discretion that is entailed in the selection and application of governing principles provides ample opportunity for majoritarian concerns to determine judicial outcomes. Ultimately, the Supreme Court operates as yet another majoritarian branch of government, whose primary commitment is to the advancement of majoritarian desires. For self-interested reasons, the contemporary majority in the United States favors the continued subordination of racial minorities. However, it is also in the interest of the majority to have this subordination accomplished in subtle rather than conspicuous ways. Part II of this book describes how the Supreme Court serves the majority by perpetuating such subtle subordination.

PART TWO

Perpetuating Subordination

CHAPTER 6

The Political Alternative

Contemporary minority attraction to judicial review has been premised on the belief that the framers' political safeguards against factionalism could not adequately protect the interests of racial minorities who would effectively be under-enfranchised by their discrete and insular character.[1] Moreover, any effectiveness that the structural safeguards might initially have had was further called into question by the substantial dilution of those safeguards that occurred during the New Deal.[2] However, reexamination of these assumptions in light of the majoritarianism inherent in judicial review suggests that whatever their defects, the political safeguards hold more promise for contemporary racial minorities than continued reliance on judicial review. Part I of this book has suggested that Supreme Court dispositions of legal claims will ultimately be governed by the majoritarian-influenced personal preferences of the justices who consider those claims. This means that the judicial process is ultimately a political process—preferences rather than principles will determine outcomes. Accordingly, the appropriate minority response to such judicial majoritarianism should be a political response.

In light of the failure of countermajoritarianism, minorities could rationally choose to forego reliance on judicial review altogether and concentrate their efforts to advance minority interests on the overtly political branches of government. The framers had faith in the ability of pluralist politics to protect the minority interests with which they were concerned. Moreover, the political branches have historically done more than the Supreme Court to advance minority interests. In addition, the predominant role of the Court, consistent with its veiled majoritarian design, has been to retard the rate at which minority claims of entitlement could prevail at the expense of majority interests. As is discussed in Chapter 7 below, it turns out that even *Brown v. Board of Education*,[3] the case most often cited as establishing the viability of countermajoritarian review, can be better understood as a product of veiled majoritarianism than as a triumph of the traditional model. Therefore, to the extent that it is possible for minorities to forego Supreme Court guardianship over their interests in favor of the protections available through the pure political process, the political option has considerable appeal. However, it is not possible to exclude the Supreme Court from the political process. Moreover, when the Court does intervene, its intervention will be inherently conservative.

Pure Politics

In a contest between competing societal interests that is ultimately to be judged by political considerations, minorities might well prefer to compete in an arena that is openly political, rather than one from which political concerns have nominally been excluded. In an overtly political process, minority interests will receive whatever degree of deference their innate strength can command, subject only to limitations in the bargaining and organizational skills of minority politicians. In a positive sense, therefore, the overt political process is pure. Outcomes are determined by counting votes, with no need to consider the reasons for which those votes were cast. Moreover, the process purports to be nothing more than what it is— a pluralistic mechanism for the generation of binding results. Although rhetorical principles may accompany the solicitation of political support, the principles themselves are inconsequential. No one cares much about their content, and their meaning is measured only by the extent to which their rhetorical invocation proves to be effective.

For racial minorities, the overt political process has two attractions. The first is that it is definitionally immune from distortion because it essentially has no rules that can be violated. In the film *Butch Cassidy and the Sundance Kid*,[4] Butch Cassidy was able to prevail in a knife fight over one of his adversaries by exploiting the absence of formal rules. Butch first suggested that he and his adversary needed to clarify the rules of the knife fight. As the adversary—put off-guard by Butch's suggestion—protested that there was no such thing as "rules" in a knife fight, Butch kicked the adversary very hard in a very sensitive part of his anatomy. With this one action Butch was able both to establish the truth of the proposition being asserted by his adversary and to capitalize on that proposition in order to win the fight.

As a matter of legal positivism, the pure political process is nothing more than the process of casting and counting votes. Outcomes cannot be right or wrong, nor can they be just or unjust. They are simply the outcomes that the process produces. Although outcomes may be determined by how the issues are framed, how support for those issues is secured, and even by who is permitted to vote, minorities should not be distracted by considerations relating to whether the process is operating fairly. The process simply works the way it works. What minorities should focus on is how best to maximize their influence in that process. Minority participation in pluralist politics can, of course, take the form of voting, running for office, or making campaign contributions, but it is not limited to those forms of involvement. Minority participation can also take the form of demonstrations, boycotts, and riots. Although such activities may be independently illegal, for purposes of positive politics their significance is limited to their potential for increasing or decreasing political strength. This is not to say that there are no rules at all governing the positive political process. There are operative rules that determine which strategies will increase and which will decrease political power. However, the operative rules are not only too complex and contingent to permit them to be articulated accurately, but there is no need to articulate those rules, because the selective responsiveness of the political process itself will promote compliance with those rules without regard to the accuracy of their formal expression. The process of positive politics—like a knife fight— cannot be distorted because it has no formal rules. And the operative rules that do govern the process tend to be self-enforcing. In this sense, the pure political process is not only positivist, but realist as well.

There are, of course, competing conceptions of the political process under which the process is more principled than it is under my conception. Because those conceptions postulate adherence to principle, however, they share the same weaknesses that are inherent in a principled model of judicial review. The value of politics as I have conceptualized it here is that it escapes the need to depend upon principle for its proper operation. Nevertheless, I do not wish to overstate the degree to which pure politics need be a self-regulating endeavor. Bribery, ballot box stuffing, and vote miscounting could be considered forms of misconduct that require external regulation—although strong realist arguments could be made that even these abuses are subject to correction by the political process itself. Nor do I wish to obscure the fact that differential access to the political process can drastically affect political outcomes. Rather, the present argument is that despite these potential abuses, the political process may still be preferable to policymaking processes involving the Supreme Court. I also realize that some advocates of political pluralism hold the political process in high regard, according its outcomes the imprimatur of democratic legitimacy.[5] The advantages of positive politics on which I am focusing, however, do not rest upon normative claims of external validity.

The second attraction of the overt political process is that it permits minorities to assume ultimate responsibility for their own interests. There are, of course, inherent limits on the political strength of any interest group. Within those limits, however, positive politics gives minorities themselves control over the degree to which minority interests are advanced. It is minorities who determine how important it is for minorities to engage in political activity; it is minorities who determine how much political activity is appropriate; and it is minorities who decide what minority priorities should be in selecting among competing political objectives. Positive politics gives minorities both the credit for minority advances and the blame for minority failures. By thus promoting minority self-determination, positive politics elevates minority dignity and self-esteem in a way that is likely to be of more long-term significance than minority success in advancing any particular interest.

The politics inherent in the process of judicial review is of a different order. Where the overt political process is transparent and unassuming, the Supreme Court political process is opaque and pretentious. The Court requires its political bargaining to be conducted in the vernacular of legal principle, and its referenda to be cloaked in the mantle of reasoned deliberation. Moreover, because judicial convention requires the justices to camouflage the political preferences that ultimately govern their applications of principle, political negotiation with the Court is haphazard and imprecise. Judicial opinions must be deciphered for the clues that they contain regarding the concessions for which a justice will commit his or her vote. And once a commitment is made, members of the Court are largely impervious to any leverage through which future fidelity to that commitment could be enforced. Unlike the positive political process that is effectively immune from distortion, the Supreme Court process is itself a distortion that renders the outcomes of ordinary politics uncertain. Moreover, because it is the Court rather than the pluralist process that has the final say over which of the competing political interests will prevail, it is the Court, rather than the affected minority group, that retains ultimate control over the fate of the minority group's interests.

The positive reasoning that permits one to conceive of the overt political process as immune from the possibility of distortion also makes it possible to characterize the Supreme Court political process in such terms. However, this does not undermine the reasonableness of a preference that minorities might have for a simple process that does not involve the Supreme Court over a complex process that does. It is easier for less experienced players to master the skills required for effective participation in a simple process than to acquire the skills demanded of a complex process. Moreover, a preference for simplicity is particularly sensible if complexities are differentially beneficial to participants depending on whether they wish to maintain or to change the status quo. There is reason to believe that Supreme Court political complexity creates just such a differential benefit, working to the disadvantage of minorities who typically wish to alter rather than preserve the socioeconomic status quo.

The Supreme Court adjudicatory process is political, but its political dimensions are complex and obscure. Even though all of the interest groups competing for Supreme Court endorsement will be burdened similarly by the complexities of the Supreme Court process, a rational minority response to those complexities would nevertheless be to prefer the candor and elegance of representative politics. Pluralist politics is, of course, no panacea. Its historical loss of favor reflects genuine grounds for concern.[6] Nevertheless, pluralist negotiation offers more to minorities than continued reliance on judicial review. As is discussed below, political theory suggests that minority interests can successfully influence majoritarian politics. Moreover, minority interests have historically been better served by the representative branches than by the Supreme Court, notwithstanding New Deal evisceration of the structural minority safeguards.

Minority Influence in Pluralist Politics

There are at least three reasons for which majoritarian institutions can be expected to respond to minority political preferences. First, the logrolling process through which pluralist political theory predicts that majoritarian public policy will be developed gives minorities a degree of influence over policy formulation that is commensurate with minority political strength. Second, it will often be in the long term best interest of the majority itself to protect minority interests. Third, minorities can negotiate political concessions from the majority by invoking the apparent need of majoritarian institutions to conceive of themselves as capable of countermajoritarian acts. Although innate political strength imposes a theoretical limit on the concessions that minorities are ultimately able to secure from the majority, minority political skills are likely to have the most immediate impact on the scope of such concessions.

Pluralist political theory predicts that in a representative democracy, majoritarian public policy will be formulated through a process of negotiations between interest groups. Some theorists, often referred to as civic republican theorists, view the negotiation process as an opportunity for collective deliberation through which virtuous civic policies can be developed that transcend the selfish desires of the negotiating interest groups.[7] For these theorists, the interests of racial minorities will be protected by the prevailing moral theory to which the deliberants collectively adhere.[8] Others, often referred to as public choice theorists, view the political process as an inherently self-interested one in which the most powerful special interests will combine forces to impose their will on less powerful interest groups, often to the detriment of the overall public welfare.[9] For these theorists, the interests of racial minorities will be protected only to the extent that racial minorities have the political power to protect themselves.[10] Even assuming that the less flattering public choice depiction is correct—that public policy results simply from a process of logrolling during which interest groups selfishly pursue their own interests by trading votes on one issue for support on another with no regard for the overriding public good—contemporary racial minorities possess sufficient political influence to participate effectively in that process. Indeed, the less flattering characterization may be the one that is preferable to minorities, because it minimizes the need for external regulation of the political process, which could reintroduce the dangers of veiled majoritarianism. Any theory which requires the majority to adhere to a substantive moral theory, or even to a theory of elaborate procedural regularity, requires some mechanism to enforce that adherence. To the extent that the mechanism resembles judicial review, all of the problems associated with veiled majoritarianism are posed once again.

One could debate whether racial minorities have always possessed the power to protect their own interests through participation in the pluralist political process. Obviously, the history of *de jure* racial disenfranchisement in this country makes such an argument difficult to maintain. The argument is not an impossible one, however. Sometimes, surrogate representation can compensate for the lack of power to vote directly. For example, white women almost certainly had a higher standard of living than black men between enactment of the thirteenth and the nineteenth amendments, even though black men could vote and white women could not.[11] Moreover, white children presently have a higher standard of living than black adults, even though black adults can vote and white children cannot.[12] In addition, despite their disenfranchisement, blacks and women were somehow able to secure the right to vote through operation of the political process, even after the Supreme Court had failed them.[13] For present purposes, however, it is not necessary to determine whether racial minorities have always possessed the power to protect their own interests through pluralist politics.

Today, it is plain that minorities do possess significant political power. This is demonstrated by evidence as varied as the success of black political candidates among white voters in recent regional elections,[14] the strength of Jesse Jackson's showings in the 1984 and 1988 presidential campaigns,[15] the adoption of minority set-aside programs such as the one that the Supreme Court invalidated in *City of Richmond v. J.A. Croson Co.*,[16] and the notable presence of minority actors in television shows and commercials.[17]

Pluralist political strength stems in part from numerical voting strength as a percentage of the total electorate. Today, minority groups comprise a large percentage of the total electorate. Blacks currently comprise approximately 10 percent of the electorate.[18] Latinos comprise another 8.2 percent, and the Latino population is growing five times faster than the population at large.[19] By the middle of the next century, whites will constitute a minority.[20] Accordingly, in sheer numerical terms, racial minorities can form voting coalitions of either a temporary or a lasting nature that have sufficient political strength to demand concessions from the majority.[21] Of course, pluralist political power does not result solely from innate voting strength. Minority voting strength can be supplemented by the support of majority voters who perceive a correspondence between their own interests and minority interests on particular issues, as well as by majority voters who are simply sympathetic to minority preferences. Such majority-minority coalitions will not be formed if the discrete and insular nature of a minority group causes majority members to refuse to bargain with that group. However, that does not seem presently to be the case. The available evidence indicates that the majority *is* currently bargaining with racial minorities.

Not only does the varied evidence discussed above belie the suspicion that whites will refuse to bargain with racial minorities, but the remarkable popularity enjoyed by the Bill Cosby television show attests to the erosion of feelings of alienation that might preclude such bargaining. The fact that *The Cosby Show*, which weekly—even daily in some markets—depicted blacks, whites, and Latinos interacting in a relaxed and uneventful manner, was able to achieve considerable popularity among white viewers suggests the beginnings of cultural assimilation that will increase the likelihood of future majority-minority coalitions. As the degree of assimilation grows, race will ultimately come to lose its status as a characteristic around which interest group identities will be formed. The prospective barriers to pluralist bargaining are likely to be more economic than racial—the *Cosby* characters are firmly upper-middle class. Although there may be many sound reasons for which one would object to the loss of distinctive cultural identity attendant to assimilation into the dominant culture, in terms of the single goal of advancing pluralist political power, assimilation seems likely to be beneficial.

The welfare of minority interests is not limited solely to gains that can be attributed to minority political power in the logrolling process. Minority interests can also benefit incidentally from selfish actions that the majority takes in order to advance its own interests. Slavery offers a crass example. Assuming that slave owners have no concern for the welfare of minority human beings, productivity concerns will nevertheless cause slave owners to make food, clothing, and shelter concessions to their minority slaves. Although one could argue that these productivity concerns in fact give slaves the political power to demand concessions, that characterization seems unrealistic. The cost to slaves of exercising whatever bargaining leverage they may theoretically be said to possess is simply prohibitive. It is more meaningful to conceive of such concessions as incidents of majority efforts to advance their own interests, which occur independent of the exercise of minority political power. This suggests that minorities can maximize their welfare by allocating the political capital that they do possess to interests that are not subject to such derivative advancement.

To the extent that minority politicians are skillful in framing the presentation of political issues, they can define issues relevant to minority interests in ways that make them appear to be issues that advance majority preferences. The current abortion controversy may provide a contemporary example. If one assumes that liberal access to abortion services will advance minority interests—something that is, of course, open to debate—it might make sense for minority politicians to allocate their political resources to different issues, believing that politically powerful white middle-class women will ensure such liberal access for themselves and incidentally for minority women. This is a useful example, because it also illustrates the potential danger of pursuing such an allocation strategy. It may well be that the political preferences of white middle-class women will ultimately prevail on the abortion issue, but that their victory will be obtained by deflecting anti-abortion opposition away from themselves and toward minority abortions. Arguably, that is precisely what happened after *Roe v. Wade*,[22] when liberal access to abortion services was available but abortion funding was not.[23] Accordingly, although minority political strength can be enhanced by freeriding on majority preferences, the strategy can be a risky one.

In addition to its inherent voting strength, supplemented by participation in voting coalitions, effective minority political power can also be enhanced by playing upon the majority's own need to believe itself capable of countermajoritarian sensitivities. The countermajoritarian model of judicial review was not preordained. Rather, it was a liberal political invention designed to counteract majoritarian threats to individual liberty that the majority itself perceived to be quite real.[24] Paradoxically, continued faith in the viability of this invention is essential to continued majority acquiescence in majoritarian authority. This means that the Supreme Court must exhibit sufficient deference to minority interests during the process of judicial review to reassure the majority of the Court's countermajoritarian capabilities. In addition to the victories that minorities are able to secure through the overt political process, therefore, minorities can also win some political victories before the Supreme Court, which by hypothesis they could not win through the political branches. As is discussed below,[25] effective use of the Supreme Court as a political institution can be both difficult and risky enough that, if given the option, minorities would choose simply to avoid the Court. To the extent that the option of avoidance is unavailable, however, skillful use of the Court can provide yet another method for increasing the amount of operative political power that minorities possess.

In theory, the magnitude of minority political influence is subject to innate limits that correspond to inherent minority political strength. Those limits, however, are of more theoretical than practical interest because they will never be reached. Variations in operative minority political power are so likely to result from the manner in which minorities make their political judgments and exercise their political skills that the innate limitations become relatively insignificant. Questions concerning when to form coalitions, when to freeride on majoritarian preferences, how to frame political issues, and when to involve the Supreme Court are so complex that there will always be opportunities for minorities to increase their political strength by increasing their political skills.

Minority Frustrations in the Supreme Court

The influence that pluralist theory predicts minorities will have in the majoritarian political process has been borne out empirically. Minorities have not only secured significant concessions from the representative branches, but the representative branches have typically done *more* than the Supreme Court to advance minority interests. In fact, the Supreme Court's civil rights performance has historically been so disappointing that it lends little, if any, support to the traditional model of judicial review. Rather, the Court's decisions serve more as a refutation than a validation of countermajoritarian judicial capacity.

The advancement of minority interests in the United States has typically been secured through the political process. The most obvious example is the manumission of black slaves. Slavery itself was a political creation that the majoritarian framers chose to accord some degree of constitutional protection. The Constitution contains three provisions that are explicitly addressed to slavery.[26] Article I, section 9, clause 1 prohibits Congress from terminating the importation of new slaves until 1808, and authorizes the imposition of a federal tax on imported slaves.[27] Article I, section 2, clause 3 apportions legislative representation in the House of Representatives on the basis of state population, counting each slave as three-fifths of a person for apportionment purposes.[28] Article IV, section 2, clause 3 prohibits one state from according free status to a slave who has escaped to that state from another state.[29] At the time that the Constitution was ratified, slavery was a very contentious issue that the framers anticipated would continue to be the focus of future political attention.[30] That attention gradually resulted in total emancipation. First, some northern states enacted legislation that abolished slavery within their jurisdictions.[31] Then, Congress enacted federal legislation prohibiting slavery in the new territory acquired through the Louisiana Purchase.[32] Next, in 1861 after the outbreak of the Civil War, President Lincoln issued the Emancipation Proclamation, which abolished slavery in the southern states.[33] Finally, in 1865 after the end of the Civil War, Congress adopted and the states ratified the thirteenth amendment, abolishing slavery throughout the United States.[34] Manumission illustrates that even the interests of completely disenfranchised minorities will be advanced through the political process when they correspond to the perceived interests of the majority.[35]

Manumission also illustrates that the political process can prove to be much more advantageous to racial minorities than the judicial process. When the Supreme Court was given the opportunity to limit slavery six years before the Emancipation Proclamation in the infamous *Dred Scott* case,[36] it declined to do so, issuing an opinion so demeaning to blacks that it reads like a parody of Supreme Court insensitivity to minority interests. In rejecting the claim of free status asserted by a slave who had been taken by his owner to a free state, then to the Louisiana Territory where slavery had been prohibited, and then brought back to the owner's original slave state, Chief Justice Taney's opinion made two assertions that are remarkable coming from a purportedly countermajoritarian institution.

First, the opinion asserted that the court lacked jurisdiction over the suit because the subhuman character of the black plaintiff deprived him of the capacity for citizenship required to invoke the Court's diversity jurisdiction. The opinion states:

> The words "people of the United States" and "citizens" are synonymous terms, and mean the same thing. . . . The question before us is, whether [blacks are] a portion of this people. . . . We think they are not and that they are not included, and were not intended to be included, under the word "citizens" in the Constitution, and can therefore claim none of the rights and privileges which that instrument provides for and secures to citizens of the United States. On the contrary, they were at that time considered as a subordinate and inferior class of beings, who had been subjugated by the dominant race, and, whether emancipated or not, yet remained subject to their authority, and had no rights or privileges but such as those who held the power and the Government might choose to grant them.

> *   *   *

> It is difficult at this day to realize the state of public opinion in relation to that unfortunate race, which prevailed in the civilized and enlightened portions of the world at the time of the Declaration of Independence, and when the Constitution of the United States was framed and adopted. But the public history of every European nation displays it in a manner too plain to be mistaken.

> They had for more than a century before been regarded as beings of an inferior order, and altogether unfit to associate with the white race, either in social or political relations; and so far inferior, that they had no rights which the white man was bound to respect; and that the negro might justly and lawfully be reduced to slavery for his benefit.[37]

Second, even though the Court lacked jurisdiction, the opinion went on to declare that the provision of the Missouri Compromise statute that prohibited slavery in the Louisiana Territory was unconstitutional because it deprived slave owners of a property interest in their slaves. The opinion states:

> [The] right of property in a slave is distinctly and expressly affirmed in the Constitution. The right to traffic in it, like an ordinary article of merchandise and

property, was guarantied to the citizens of the United States, in every State that might desire it, for twenty years. And the Government in express terms is pledged to protect it in all future time, if the slave escapes from his owner. This is done in plain words—too plain to be misunderstood. And no word can be found in the Constitution which gives Congress a greater power over slave property, or which entitles property of that kind to less protection than property of any other description. The only power conferred is the power coupled with the duty of guarding and protecting the owner in his rights.[38]

The first assertion is remarkable because it evidences an unmistakably strong attitudinal predisposition that would seem to be disqualifying for an institution charged with safeguarding minority interests. Considering the range of political positions concerning slavery that existed at the time, the subhuman position adopted by the Court seems to have been the *most* disadvantageous to blacks. Although Chief Justice Taney purported to be reporting the views of the framers rather than his own views concerning the status of blacks,[39] the tone of Taney's opinion belies any suggestion that Taney himself did not share those views. Although slavery has existed in numerous societies and cultures, the brand of slavery that existed in the American south developed to the highest degree a slaveholder ideology under which the honor of the slaveholder was directly dependent upon the degradation of the slave.[40]

The second assertion is remarkable because it reveals that this sub-human-property predisposition of the Court was so strong that the Court felt itself obligated to invalidate a *majoritarian* enactment limiting the spread of slavery. And it did so after having relied upon the need to defer to majoritarian policymakers as a justification for its jurisdictional holding. In justifying its conclusion that the subhuman character of blacks made them incapable in the eyes of the framers of acquiring the citizenship necessary to give the Court jurisdiction, the opinion states:

> It is not the province of the court to decide upon the justice or injustice, the policy or impolicy, of these laws. The decision of that question belonged to the political or law-making power . . . [41]

It is more than a little ironic that the Court found itself to lack jurisdiction to entertain suits filed by those whose interests it was required to protect under the traditional model.

Although it is possible to argue that Chief Justice Taney was deferring to the majoritarian framers rather than to the majoritarian Congress that enacted the Missouri Compromise, arguments of this type pose insoluble analytical difficulties. Where the framers did not specifically provide otherwise,[42] it is reasonable to conclude that they desired congressional preferences to govern resolution of future issues that would arise concerning slavery.[43] However, the framers may have specifically "provided otherwise" by including in the Constitution the protections for private property on which Chief Justice Taney relied to invalidate the Missouri Compromise prohibition on slavery.[44] It is precisely this sort of analytical difficulty that Part I of this book argues can be resolved only through recourse to the personal preferences of individual judges. It is also possible to argue that the *Dred Scott* Court was engaged in an act of countermajoritarianism precisely because it *did* invalidate the majoritarian Missouri Compromise, in order to prevent the majoritarian abrogation of individual property rights. This argument, however, is suspect because the Missouri Compromise appears to have been politically dead at the time of its judicial invalidation, thereby making the Court's decision more majoritarian than countermajoritarian.[45]

Most of the judicial encounters with slavery that occurred prior to the Civil War resulted in judicial invalidation of majoritarian efforts to limit slavery.[46] *Dred Scott* was the second Supreme Court decision to invalidate a congressional enactment on constitutional grounds; *Marbury* itself was the first. *Dred Scott*, therefore, can be seen as continuing the Supreme Court tradition established in *Marbury* of sacrificing the interests of those that the Court is charged with protecting in order to advance ulterior political objectives.[47]

The major advances that racial minorities have made since manumission have also come from the representative branches. The fourteenth amendment overruled *Dred Scott* by granting citizenship to blacks, and it provided constitutional validation for the Reconstruction civil rights statutes now codified in §§ 1981, 1982, and 1983 of Title 42 of the United States Code.[48] After a post-Reconstruction lapse in congressional responsiveness to minority interests, there was a mid-twentieth century revival of congressional civil rights activity. The Civil Rights Acts of 1957[49] and 1960[50] created federal remedies for voting discrimination. The omnibus Civil Rights Act of 1964 prohibited various types of public and private discrimination. Among its most significant provisions are Title II, which prohibits discrimination in public accommodations,[51] Title IV, which authorizes the Attorney General to maintain school desegregation suits,[52] Title VI, which prohibits segregation in schools receiving federal funds,[53] and Title VII, which prohibits discrimination in employment.[54] The Voting Rights Acts of 1965,[55] 1970,[56] and 1975[57] substantially enhanced the federal safeguards against voting discrimination contained in the 1957 and

1960 Acts by suspending literacy tests for voter registration and by re-quiring Attorney General preclearance of apportionment changes that might be used to dilute minority voting strength.[58] The Fair Housing Act of 1968[59] contains provisions that prohibit discrimination in the sale or rental of housing, and it imposes increased federal criminal sanctions for the violation of individual civil rights.[60] The Public Works Employment Act of 1977 contained minority set-aside provisions requiring that ten percent of the funds given to state and local governments for construction purposes had to be used to secure goods or services supplied by minority-owned enterprises.[61]

In addition to congressional enactments, the executive branch has also made concessions to minority interests. For example, the President by executive order has imposed affirmative action obligations on federal con-tractors.[62] Moreover, the school desegregation guidelines used to imple-ment the Title VI fund cut-off provisions under the 1964 Civil Rights Act were developed by the Department of Health, Education, and Welfare.[63] In addition, the Equal Employment Opportunity Commission has devel-oped guidelines to implement the Title VII employment discrimination provisions of the 1964 Civil Rights Act,[64] and the Department of Housing and Urban Development has developed guidelines to implement the fair housing provisions of the 1968 Civil Rights Act.[65] Obviously, the repre-sentative branches have not been uniformly or consistently deferential to minority interests. Rather, they have made concessions to minority interests when the overall political climate has been conducive to such concessions.

The Supreme Court has greeted majoritarian efforts to advance minority interests with a mixed response. On occasion those efforts have been validated, as when the Court upheld the federal minority set-aside program established by the 1977 Public Works Employment Act in *Fullilove v. Klutznick*.[66] Sometimes the Court has shown even more sensitivity to minority interests than the representative branch taking the action that the Court was validating. For example, in holding that the Reconstruction statutes reached private as well as official government conduct, the Court may well have gone beyond the actual intent of the Reconstruction Con-gress in its solicitude for minority interests.[67] On other occasions, major-itarian efforts to advance minority interests have met with marked judicial hostility, as they did in *Dred Scott*.[68] For example, although the Court upheld the federal minority set-aside program in *Fullilove*, it recently in-validated a similar municipal program in *City of Richmond v. J.A. Croson Co.*[69] And although it recently reaffirmed the applicability of the Recon-struction statutes to private action, it simultaneously redefined the substantive scope of prohibited discrimination in a way that excluded much discrimination that did not constitute state action. In *Patterson v. McLean Credit Union*,[70] the Court held that although the 42 U.S.C. § 1981 prohibition on discrimination in the formation and enforcement of contracts applied to private acts of discrimination, discriminatory *performance* of a contract through racial harassment of an employee did not come within the scope of the § 1981 prohibition. Discriminatory enforcement occurred only if the state made enforcement remedies for breach of contract selectively available on the basis of race.[71] The net effect of this holding was to reimpose a state action requirement in § 1981 suits with respect to discriminatory contract performance. Like the representative branches, the Supreme Court has not been uniform or consistent in its deference to minority interests. Rather, the Court too has made concessions to minority interests when the overall political climate has been conducive to such concessions.

I have argued that a rational minority response to the veiled majoritarian nature of the Supreme Court would be to abandon efforts to influence the Court and to concentrate minority political activities on the representative branches, because minorities are more likely to secure concessions from an overtly political branch of government than from a branch whose political dimensions are covert. I have also argued that comparison of the historical performances of the representative branches and the Supreme Court provides empirical support for this theory, because the representative branches have done more than the Court to advance minority interests. One might object to this asserted preference for the representative branches by arguing that if the actions of each branch are ultimately determined by majoritarian political preferences, it should not matter which branch minorities choose as the focus of their political efforts. The response to this objection is that, although the Supreme Court is a majoritarian branch of government, the Court responds to different types of political preferences than the preferences to which the representative branches respond.

A Political Model of the Supreme Court

Although representative politics is more promising than Supreme Court politics for minority interests, minorities do not have the luxury of concentrating their efforts exclusively on the representative branches. When minorities secure political concessions from the majoritarian branches, nonminority interest groups disadvantaged by those concessions can force minorities to defend their political victories before the Supreme Court. Many of the affirmative action gains that minorities have made through the political process have been subject to just such nonminority challenges.[72] In addition, minorities will often be compelled to seek judicial enforcement of the political gains that they make before the representative branches. The assistance of the Court will be required both to resolve ambiguities in majoritarian enactments and to prompt compliance by recalcitrant nonminority interests.[73] Supreme Court intervention in the political process affecting minority interests is, therefore, inevitable. Moreover, structural features of the Supreme Court ensure that when this inevitable intervention occurs it will also be politically conservative.

Part I of this book suggested that life tenure and salary protection are unable to provide any meaningful safeguard against the influence that a judge's own socialized majoritarian preferences will have on the adjudicatory process.[74] That does not mean, however, that life tenure and salary protection are irrelevant to judicial outcomes. They are designed to permit Supreme Court justices to remain on the bench for extended periods of time. The average age of a Supreme Court justice when appointed during this century has been 55. The average length of a justice's stay on the Court has been 16 years.[75] That means that the contemporary Supreme Court has been staffed by justices who serve from ages 55 to 71. Institutionally, a Supreme Court staffed by such individuals is likely to be receptive to two types of political arguments.

Professor Tushnet has identified the first type of argument.[76] The Court will respond to arguments advancing political preferences that are durable rather than transitory in nature. The amount of political power that a pluralist voting coalition possesses is a direct function of its longevity. A coalition that can secure majoritarian support for its position on a single issue will be able to prevail upon that issue, but it will not be able to implement a political agenda that encompasses multiple issues or even repeated tests of a single issue. In order to advance a political agenda, a coalition must command sustained political support.

A coalition that can sustain majority support for a two-year period can control the House of Representatives, all of whose members are elected every two years. More specifically, in order to control the vote of a representative, a coalition must have the popular votes needed to secure the initial election of that representative and, in addition, must for two years be able to maintain a credible threat that failure to comply with the wishes of the coalition will result in the failure of the representative to secure reelection. Such a coalition, therefore, will be able to prevail in those contests where the position of the House of Representatives is dispositive. The position of the House alone will be dispositive with respect to issues such as impeachment, which the Constitution assigns exclusively to the House of Representatives.[77] However, the position of the House can also be dispositive with respect to issues over which the distribution of political power and the prevailing political climate give practical control to the House. Such issues will arise frequently when the House is controlled by a different political party than the party controlling the Senate and the White House. In such circumstance, the House of Representatives will have a meaningful veto power over legislative initiatives.

A coalition that can sustain majority support for a period of four years is in a much stronger position to advance its political agenda. It can control not only the House of Representatives for two terms, but it can also control the President, who is elected to a four-year term. In addition, because one-third of the Senate is elected every two years, a four-year coalition can also control the Senate, by controlling the votes of two-thirds of its members. A coalition durable enough to last four years, therefore, can control the entire federal government. Except for the judiciary. Because of their longer "terms of office" Supreme Court justices can only be controlled by political coalitions having a political durability that is substantially longer. Professor Tushnet postulates that a coalition must command majority support for approximately a decade before it can control the judiciary.[78]

Tushnet does not offer a prediction for how much time it would take to control the Supreme Court alone, although the ten-year estimate seems reasonable for the Supreme Court as well. As has been noted, the average tenure of a justice on the Supreme Court has historically been approximately sixteen years.[79] If each justice serves for sixteen years, on average, one of the nine justices will leave the Court every 1.75 years. This means that it will take approximately nine years for a five-justice majority of the Court to turn over. This corresponds roughly to how long it took the Reagan-Bush conservative coalition to wrest control of the Supreme Court from the prior liberal coalition that supported the decisions of the Warren Court. President Reagan was elected in 1980, and he made his first Supreme Court appointment in 1981.[80] President Bush gained control of the Supreme Court in the period between 1990 and 1991 with the appointment of Justices Souter and Thomas as replacements for Justices Brennan and Marshall.[81] A political coalition with a nine- or ten-year duration, therefore, seems powerful enough to gain control over the Supreme Court— and theoretically, over the entire federal government.[82] This means that, regardless of the particular political preferences that individual justices may have, the Supreme Court as an institution will be receptive to legal arguments advancing political positions that have the support of durable rather than transitory majorities. The ultimate effect of this selective sensitivity is to render the Court a force for preservation of the political status quo. Proponents of political change will be less successful before the Court than will their opponents.[83]

The second type of argument to which the Supreme Court will respond favorably is an argument advancing an issue whose political support, while transitory, is both broad-based and intense. This is due, in part, to the ability that proponents of such issues possess to raise a credible threat of removal. Because Supreme Court justices have life tenure, political control over individual justices must normally be exercised at the selection stage. Under ordinary circumstances, politically motivated threats of retaliatory removal are unlikely to have much credibility in light of the political difficulty of securing impeachment. Tushnet's theory would predict that a political coalition having a four-year durability would be required to impeach and convict a justice. This is because the Constitution requires controlling influence over a simple majority in the House and a two-thirds majority in the Senate for impeachment and conviction.[84] In light of the reluctance of interest groups to use impeachment for ordinary political purposes, such a coalition would normally be quite difficult to amass. In a climate of intense political fervor, however, the threat of impeachment might be more credible. Both individuals and electorates are capable of taking actions in the heat of the moment that they would not take after calmer reflection.[85] More subtly, to the extent that the justices view intense popular resistance as a threat to the perceptions of legitimacy that the Court needs in order to issue decisions that will be able to claim the support of short-term majority coalitions, the justices will be responsive to expressions of popular disapproval intense enough to jeopardize the Court's continued legitimacy, even if that disapproval is not intense enough to pose a credible threat of impeachment.

One might initially suspect that Supreme Court responsiveness to intense bursts of majoritarian political sentiment would make the Court populist rather than conservative in its political outlook. In some contexts that might be true. However, in the context of judicial protection of minority interests, vulnerability to intense expressions of majoritarian desires makes the Court conservative in the sense that it is unable to perform its countermajoritarian function. Cases like *Korematsu v. United States*,[86] in which the Court upheld the World War II geographic exclusion of Japanese-

Americans from certain locations on the West Coast, illustrates the problem of such judicial submission to an intense political preference. It is difficult to understand *Korematsu* as anything other than an instance of judicial deference to popular desires for retribution against the Japanese after the bombing of Pearl Harbor. As such, the decision has been widely criticized as the unfortunate product of wartime hysteria and racial resentment.[87] And as such, the decision demonstrates the danger inherent in believing that the Supreme Court possesses the political capacity to resist majoritarian efforts to exploit racial minority interests.

Although the Supreme Court is a majoritarian institution, it does not merely replicate the actions of the other representative branches of government. The manner in which a representative branch reflects popular preferences is a function of its political sensitivities. The House of Representatives is sensitive to local majorities, the Senate is sensitive to state majorities, and the President is sensitive to the national majority. The Supreme Court can best be understood as a representative branch that is politically sensitive to conservative majorities. Because life tenure gives the justices longer terms of office than elected governmental officials, the Court is most responsive to durable political interest groups that are able to exert sustained pressure for the adoption of their political agendas. This model of the Supreme Court suggests that the Court will lag rather than lead the overtly representative branches in the protection of minority rights, and history has borne this prediction out. In matters ranging from the early controversy over slavery to the contemporary debate about affirmative action, the Court has done more to impede the social and economic progress of racial minorities than it has to advance minority interests.

The Supreme Court has frequently disappointed racial minorities by ruling against them in particular cases. However, the Court's most effective contribution to the cause of conservative racial politics has derived from its ability to structure the law in a way that perpetuates minority subordination. The Court has done this in three ways. First, its decision in *Brown v. Board of Education* has established a dependency relationship between racial minorities and the Supreme Court that permits the Court to regulate the social and economic status of its minority wards. Second, the Court has centralized the law of race relations in a manner that makes it more difficult for racial minorities to utilize their local political power to its maximum advantage in advancing minority interests. Third, the Court has legitimated a set of assumptions about racial minorities and minority demands for equal rights that virtually assures that those demands will not be met. The next three chapters consider each of these three subordinating techniques in turn.

CHAPTER 7

Dependency

Brown v. Board of Education[1] is the case typically offered as evidence of the countermajoritarian capacity of the Supreme Court. In the face of massive popular resistance, the Court not only desegregated the public schools, but also invalidated the constitutional standard adopted by *Plessy v. Ferguson*[2] that tolerated separate-but-equal public facilities. Since *Brown*, racial minorities have concentrated their efforts at achieving equality on the Supreme Court, because the Court has appeared to be more receptive to minority claims of right than the representative branches of government. Despite the countermajoritarian rhetoric that has been cultivated by the *Brown* decision, the case is better understood as a veiled majoritarian effort to perpetuate minority subordination. In terms of motive, *Brown* did not constitute a heroic judicial stance against a racially intolerant majority. Rather, *Brown* was supported by a majority coalition comprised of liberals who were opposed to racial segregation and federal foreign policy interests who viewed segregation as an impediment to the United States in its competition with communism for control over the third world. Although *Brown* may have generated resistance in the south, the national coalition that favored desegregation of *southern* schools chose simply to suppress that local resistance. In terms of effect, *Brown* performed a disservice to racial minorities. *Brown*, of course, did not desegregate the schools; it has been almost four decades since *Brown* was decided and the public schools are experiencing more resegregation than desegregation. In addition, by invalidating the separate-but-equal doctrine of *Plessy*, *Brown* has deprived racial minorities of their only constitutional weapon for securing equal treatment in light of the failure of integration.

Ironically, the racial equality that the Court first championed in *Brown* is the very same racial equality that the Court now invokes to invalidate affirmative action programs that minorities have been able to secure through the political process. The *Brown* experience illustrates the danger of minority dependence on the Supreme Court for the protection of minority interests. Such dependence not only diverts to the Court minority resources that might better be expended on the political branches, but it places minorities in a position that arguably estops them from pursuing race-specific political concessions from the majority. For these very reasons, however, it is in the interest of the majority to promote minority dependence on the Supreme Court.

Brown *and the Political Model*

The desegregation of southern schools mandated by *Brown v. Board of Education*[3] in 1954 was accompanied by predictable massive resistance. According to the traditional understanding, the fact that the Supreme Court was willing to disregard such high levels of majoritarian disapproval in issuing its school desegregation order reveals that the Court must possess countermajoritarian capabilities. This conclusion is further buttressed by the post-*Brown* decisions in which the Court stuck to its convictions and ordered the lower courts to fashion novel equitable remedies such as busing to implement the *Brown* decision, again in the face of massive resistance. Notwithstanding this traditional view, *Brown* is actually better understood as an illustration of the selective political responsiveness of a veiled majoritarian Court.

The *Brown* decision is commonly viewed as having accomplished two things. As a practical matter, it required the desegregation of public schools. *Brown I* declared the maintenance of separate-but-equal public schools to be unconstitutional.[4] *Brown II* issued after reargument addressed to the issue of remedy, ordered segregated public schools to be desegregated "with all deliberate speed."[5] As a doctrinal matter, *Brown* overruled the separate-but-equal principle of *Plessy v. Ferguson*.[6] Although *Plessy* upheld the constitutionality of racially separate public facilities, the case did not by its terms require that those facilities be equal. Nevertheless, subsequent cases did require varying degrees of equality, and *Plessy* is the case that is typically cited for the separate-but-equal requirement.[7] In overruling *Plessy*, *Brown* also established the proposition that race-based classifications are inherently unequal because they inevitably operate to disadvantage the minority race. *Brown I* held that "separate educational facilities are inherently unequal,"[8] because "[t]o separate [school children] from others of similar age and qualifications solely because of their race generates a feeling of inferiority as to their status in the community that may affect their hearts and minds in a way unlikely ever to be undone."[9] As a result, race-based classifications could be sustained only if they satisfied the most exacting scrutiny.[10]

As an actual matter, *Brown* may not have realized these accomplishments at all. Moreover, to the extent that these accomplishments were actually secured by the *Brown* decision, they appear to have corresponded to the political preferences of the durable majority whose interests were represented on the *Brown* Supreme Court. In addition, the Court's advancement of those majoritarian preferences may well have been secured at the expense of long-term minority interests, thereby illustrating the difficulties attendant to minority reliance on the Supreme Court.

The fact that *Brown* is perceived to stand for the two propositions with which it is associated attests to the rhetorical success of the case. When needed, *Brown* is now available for citation in briefs and judicial opinions to support either the limited proposition that the Constitution requires public schools to be desegregated or the broader proposition that race-based classifications in general are unconstitutional. As an actual matter, *Brown* of course did *not* desegregate the schools. A third of the black students attending public school in the United States still attend all-black schools, and 63 percent attend schools that are at least half black. Private schools, gerrymandered district lines, unequal funding, white flight, residential housing patterns, and resegregation are among the many factors that prevented the rhetorical promise of *Brown* from ever becoming a reality.[11] As an actual matter, *Brown* did not terminate governmental use of race-based classifications either. Although subsequent cases issued shortly after *Brown* relied upon the *Brown* decision to invalidate racial segregation in public facilities such as buses, beaches, and golf courses,[12] the Court did not rely upon *Brown* to invalidate all racial classifications. Most notably, the Court declined to invalidate miscegenation statutes, straining to avoid any application of *Brown* that would produce this result.

After issuing its 1954 decision in *Brown I*,[13] invalidating separate-but-equal treatment based upon race, the Court nevertheless declined in *Naim v. Naim*[14] to invalidate a Virginia miscegenation statute, holding that the constitutional issue raised by the statute was not "properly presented."[15] The Court's action not only ignored the holding of *Brown* but it constituted a refusal to exercise mandatory appellate jurisdiction that had been assigned to the Court by statute. Accordingly, *Naim v. Naim* has been the target of considerable criticism.[16] The Court's dismissal is understood to have been a concession to perceived majoritarian pressure in the post-*Brown* era, when it had been asserted that school desegregation would lead to "mongrelization of the race."[17] The Virginia statute was finally invalidated eleven years later in *Loving v. Virginia*.[18] At that time, only sixteen states had miscegenation laws, as opposed to the time of the *Brown* decision, when more than half the states had such statutes.[19]

Realistically, *Brown* had enormous rhetorical success and partial practical success. This combination of substantial rhetorical success and limited practical success appears to have been precisely what the Court's durable majoritarian constituency desired. The massive resistance that accompanied *Brown* does not mean that the decision lacked majoritarian support. Indeed, the resistance was regional rather than national in scope. At the level of national politics—the level of politics at which *Brown* was decided—it is easy to imagine the existence of a national coalition that supported the *Brown* decision. Professor Bell first hypothesized that *Brown* was decided the way that it was because it marked the point of convergence for three national interests.[20] The decision advanced the international objectives of foreign policy interest groups by reducing the embarrassment and competitive disadvantage that domestic racism produced in our competition with communism for influence over third world nations. The decision also advanced the interests of disillusioned post-war blacks who seemed to be missing out on all of the equality that the United States claimed to have been fighting for in World War II. In addition, the decision advanced the interests of whites who saw segregation as an impediment to the economic maturation and development of the south.[21]

Professor Bell also suggested that moral and economic considerations might have played a role in the coalition that he was postulating.[22] Although he did not explicitly claim that the Supreme Court was incapable of countermajoritarian acts, Professor Bell did offer the following Interest-Convergence Theory to account for the *Brown* decision:

The interest of blacks in achieving racial equality will be accommodated only when it converges with the interests of whites; however, the fourteenth amendment, standing alone, will not authorize a judicial remedy providing effective racial equality for blacks where the remedy sought threatens the superior societal status of middle- and upper-class whites.[23]

This caused Bell to conclude that the remedies for *Brown* would be coextensive with white support[24]—something that is consistent with the present thesis.[25]

Professor Dudziak, in an article entitled *Desegregation as a Cold War Imperative*,[26] further developed the idea that *Brown* was a response to national majoritarian interests, emphasizing the particular interest suggested by her arresting title. Professor Dudziak notes that the United States Department of Justice filed an amicus brief stressing the importance of a decision invalidating segregation because "the United States is trying to prove to the people of the world, of every nationality, race and color, that a free democracy is the most civilized and most secure form of government yet devised by man."[27] Just as the victorious northern coalition was able to impose civil rights enactments on the south after the Civil War in order to advance its own political interests, a similar national coalition was able to impose *Brown* on the south in order to advance its political interests.

Not only does the existence of a national coalition provide a plausible account of the *Brown* decision, but the durability of that coalition coincides with the success that minorities have had under *Brown* and its progeny. When the first *Brown* decision was issued, the Court set the case for reargument concerning the issue of remedy.[28] A year later, in *Brown II*, the Court ruled that although school desegregation need not be immediate, it had to be accomplished with "all deliberate speed,"[29] thereby giving both school officials and the Court itself some latitude in implementing the decision. For the next fifteen years, most of the Supreme Court school desegregation decisions issued subsequent to *Brown* were resolved in a manner that was considered favorable to minority interests. All of those decisions involved southern school districts. In the early 1970s, when school desegregation cases involving northern cities began to reach the Court, the Court began to rule against the minority interests.[30] This suggests that after fifteen years, the national coalition supporting *Brown* had broken down, in part because civil rights had ceased to be an important international issue, and in part because northern urban interest groups had withdrawn from the coalition after they were asked to internalize costs of desegregation that had previously been deflected to the south. In a sense, *Brown* was the perfect veiled majoritarian decision. It supplied the majority with rhetorical benefits that were important at the time that the decision was issued and that continue to be important today because of the manner in which they enhance the majority's self-image. However, practical implementation of the decision continued only as long as, and only to the extent that, *Brown* itself continued to command durable majoritarian support.

Brown and the cases implementing it can be understood as the product of a majoritarian coalition that incidentally advanced the immediate interests of racial minorities. It is unclear, however, whether membership in that coalition served to advance long-term minority interests. Professor Seidman has argued that *Brown* in fact advanced white majoritarian interests at the expense of long-term minority interests. By overruling *Plessy* and declaring that separate-but-equal treatment of racial minorities violated the Constitution, *Brown* saved the majority from a *Plessy*-based obligation actually to extend equal treatment to minorities.[31] Today, as a result of property-based tax structures and tax subsidies given to private schools, white students receive a significantly larger share of the governmental resources allocated to education than minority students receive. The Supreme Court upheld this practice of disproportionate funding in *San Antonio Independent School District v. Rodriguez*.[32] Ironically, this practice may well have been unconstitutional under the separate-but-equal doctrine of *Plessy*. *Brown*, however, makes this differential treatment constitutionally permissible. As long as a school district is not engaged in *de jure* segregation and has taken the requisite steps to eliminate the effects of any past *de jure* segregation in which it may have been engaged, its constitutional obligation has been satisfied. Because neither of these obligations entail anything resembling equal treatment, the majority is better off—and racial minorities are worse off—than would have been the case under a faithfully implemented separate-but-equal standard of constitutional law.[33] This is not to suggest that a veiled majoritarian Court could not have contained the damage to majoritarian interests that would have been done by a separate-but-equal standard, just as the Supreme Court was able to contain the damage done by desegregation under *Brown*. However, to the extent that Supreme Court tolerance of the differential treatment presently accorded minority and nonminority children in education would have been more difficult to justify under a separate-but-equal standard, the interests of racial minorities may have been disadvantaged by *Brown*.

To the extent that *Brown* has made it constitutionally difficult for the government to rely upon race-based classifications, *Brown* has also disadvantaged minorities by depriving them of effective affirmative action remedies. As is discussed in Chapter 8, race-conscious remedies, such as minority set-asides, are being invalidated by the Court on constitutional grounds with increasing frequency, and they are being invalidated for the stated reason of preventing unfairness to whites.[34] The Bush administration has even threatened to use *Brown* as a source of legal authority for invalidating minority scholarship programs as a species of unconstitutional affirmative action.[35]

Disillusionment with the results of *Brown* has caused some minority activists to advocate separate minority-controlled schools for minority children.[36] Once again, however, *Brown*'s invalidation of southern school segregation could be used to threaten even the legality of minority colleges and universities that were established to compensate for the historical failure of white institutions to extend meaningful educational opportunities to minority students. Such a challenge could be based upon precisely the same legal theory that the Bush Administration has used to attack the legality of minority scholarships.[37] As is discussed below, if one assumes that a strategy of establishing minority-controlled schools is in the present best interests of racial minorities, *Brown* has again adversely affected minority interests by making that strategy constitutionally impermissible. If one assumes further that the majority itself benefits from the preclusion of minority-controlled minority schools, *Brown* has again advanced majoritarian interests at minority expense. Notably, such a benefit to the majority has ensued by preventing minority children from escaping majoritarian control of the attitude and value formation process to which school children are exposed during the most impressionable years of their lives.[38] It is during these formative years that minority children are inculcated with majoritarian values—especially the value of minority dependence upon the Supreme Court in lieu of minority self-determination.

The Danger of Dependency

The nominal success of *Brown* in establishing the existence of a countermajoritarian Supreme Court has created a relationship between racial minorities and the Court under which minorities have come to depend upon the Court rather than upon their own political strength and judgment in order to advance minority interests. As was discussed in Chapter 6, not only do racial minorities possess the political power to advance their own interests without the intervention of the Supreme Court,[39] but Supreme Court intervention in the political process has more often been a source of frustration than a source of salvation for racial minority interests.[40] Nevertheless, minorities have continued to rely upon the Supreme Court as if it were an ally rather than an adversary in the struggle for racial equality. This is because racial minorities have been taught the countermajoritarian lesson of *Brown* so well that they sometimes seem unable even to imagine their own political self-determination. A more realistic assessment of the lesson to be learned from *Brown* is that measured majoritarian concessions to racial minorities can indefinitely keep racial minority interests dependent upon white majority control. Through this single majoritarian decision, and the tradition of judicial review that it symbolizes, racial minorities have become dependent upon the Supreme Court to control the manner in which minority children are educated, the manner in which minorities conceptualize the nature of their racial difficulties, and even the strategies that minorities select to advance their racial interests.

By now it should be clear that school desegregation simply has not worked—at least not for racial minorities. As good an idea as desegregation may have seemed at the time, it has not resulted in the equalization of educational opportunities for white and minority school children. Nor has it increased the quality of education for minority children in the way that proponents of school desegregation had hoped that it would. Most minority school children still attend schools that are either completely or predominantly minority schools.[41] This is due, of course, to the refusal of the Supreme Court to include white suburban schools in the constitutionally required desegregation plans that it has approved for the heavily minority schools that exist in many of our urban centers.[42] In addition, the Court's approval of drastically disproportionate levels of funding for suburban and inner-city schools has left minority school children with many fewer educational resources than their white counterparts.[43] Moreover, the educational successes that some all-minority schools have had even in the face of their serious underfunding suggests that there is nothing inherent in the concept of integrated education that makes it either a necessary or a sufficient condition for quality education.[44] Continued commitment to desegregation is only likely to make matters worse, as additional white flight increases the racial imbalance in the public schools, with a corresponding increase in the educational difficulties associated with racial imbalance.[45]

School desegregation has not only proven to be less beneficial than its proponents had originally hoped, but in many respects desegregation has proven to be an affirmative burden on the effort to provide quality education for minority school children. Not surprisingly, it is minority students who tend to bear the brunt of the dislocations that are produced by the school desegregation effort. When teachers and administrators must be fired as a result of school consolidations, it tends to be the minority teachers who are fired. When schools have to be closed as a result of redrawn attendance zones, it tends to be the minority schools that are closed. When students have to be bused away from their own neighborhoods in order to improve a school's racial balance, it tends to be the minority students who are bused. Even when schools are formally deseg-regated, informal segregation persists inside the schools, where minority students are disproportionately "segregated" in the slow-track classes, are subjected to disciplinary charges in disproportionate numbers, and must endure the subtle forms of day-to-day racial discrimination that can be inflicted by resentful white students, teachers, and administrators.[46] More-over, because minority parents lack influence in the white communities to which their children are often bused, minority parents tend to be ex-cluded from meaningful input into the educational policymaking process, from active participation in school activities, and from the ability to hold school officials accountable for the education of their children.[47] In sum, desegregation means that racial minorities must cede control over their schools and the education of their children to the white majority.[48]

None of these observations are new. In fact, they are quite old. They were the predicted consequences of school desegregation that were made in the nineteenth and early twentieth centuries by black nationalists and others who predated *Brown*,[49] and they were the assessed consequences of school desegregation that were made by Black Power advocates and others during the 1960s and 1970s after the decision in *Brown* had been rendered.[50] As far back as 1790, blacks in Boston began to seek segregated schools as a means of avoiding the racial mistreatment that had driven all but a handful of black school children out of the then-integrated Boston public schools. However, even two hundred years ago, the now-famous Boston School Committee had developed its instinct for rejecting black requests for quality education. Ironically, the same Boston School Com-mittee that has more recently become known for its resistance to con-temporary school desegregation, then rejected the black community's re-quest for *segregated* schools, on the grounds that the expense entailed in maintaining separate black schools was unwarranted.[51] In 1849, after Bos-ton had itself chosen to adopt a policy of school segregation, black com-munity leader Thomas P. Smith unsuccessfully urged blacks who were then pressing for integration as a means of improving the education of their children not to abandon their black schools because integration would end up actually *reducing* the quality of education that was available for black school children.[52] In the 1930s, when the NAACP was developing the school desegregation strategy that ultimately resulted in the issuance of *Brown*, cofounder W.E.B. Du Bois unsuccessfully urged the organi-zation not to commit itself to a strategy of integration that would sub-ordinate the goal of quality education for blacks to the goal of educating blacks in the same schools as whites.[53]

In the years since *Brown* was decided, fears that desegregation would harm the quality of education for black school children have been reiterated in light of the evidence that has become available concerning the actual effects of the national desegregation effort. In 1963, Malcolm X vigorously advocated minority control of minority schools, explicitly rejecting the suggestion that segregation would lead to inferior education for minority children.[54] Leaders of the politically militant Black Power movement that began in the mid-1960s have not only decried the loss of minority control over minority schools that has resulted from formal desegregation, but have equated integration with white supremacy.[55] Black Power advocates Stokely Carmichael and Charles Hamilton viewed integration as the domination of black culture by white culture through the indoctrination of black children with white middle-class values.[56] Separatist Robert Browne saw integration as a process for transforming black people into white black people.[57] Historian Harold Cruse has emphasized that the assimilation of black culture into white culture was accomplished by enticing the black middle class to force the black working class to abandon black cultural distinctiveness, which had proven embarrassing to the middle class blacks who were seeking to perfect their assimilation into the dominant white culture.[58] Legal scholar Derrick Bell has stressed the harmful effects that school desegregation has had on the black children who were treated as if they were white, and on the black teachers and administrators who were fired for the cause of desegregation.[59] These types of theoretical arguments have even given rise to aggressive efforts by some blacks, during the late 1960s and early 1970s, to seize control of local school districts and to establish autonomous Afro-American Studies departments at major colleges and universities.[60]

There is a long and rich history of minority apprehension about the supposed benefits of school desegregation. This history, however, has been studiously disregarded by mainstream black political leaders. From Thomas P. Smith to W.E.B. Du Bois to Malcolm X, the black political and intellectual leaders who have favored black self-determination have been marginalized by mainstream black leaders so as not to interfere with the promise of black assimilation into white culture. Professor Cruse has stated that "the traditional civil rights leadership will oppose any attempt on the part of an alternative leadership to organize blacks into an independent political bloc."[61] Indeed, this mainstream black opposition to assertions of the need for black autonomy has been surprisingly strong.

In *Calhoun v. Cook*,[62] the Atlanta school desegregation case, the local NAACP branch agreed to a compromise desegregation plan that maintained predominantly black schools but increased both the educational quality of black community schools and the degree of black control that would be exercised over those schools. The national NAACP responded by ousting the President of the local branch and joining in the litigation itself to oppose the compromise plan because the plan did not require the maximum degree of integration that was possible in the school district.[63] The Vice Chairman of the NAACP National Board of Directors stated:

Of one thing we may be sure: the system of racial caste will never be weakened or eradicated by blacks who cooperate with it. Every instance of the acceptance of segregation, whether voluntary or coerced, forges the chains of inequality more firmly. Segregation will not be eradicated by those who abandon integration as a goal, no matter what tortuous logic or euphemistic language may be used to rationalize the expedient compromise.[64]

The national NAACP also sought to intervene in the St. Louis school desegregation litigation to oppose a similar compromise that was favored by local black parents.[65]

When Professor Bell published an article in the *Yale Law Journal* arguing that civil rights lawyers had become more committed to the goal of integration than to the educational interests of minority children,[66] NAACP General Counsel Nathaniel R. Jones published vigorous responses in opposition to Professor Bell's thesis. Mr. Jones argued that segregation was itself the most important educational harm to be remedied because of its connection to institutional racism. Then, as if to prove Bell's point, Jones argued that there was no constitutional right to a quality education but only to an education that was not officially segregated.[67]

A troublesome question is why mainstream racial minorities have chosen so consistently to reject the strategies for minority self-determination that have been espoused by progressive minority leaders. An equally troublesome answer is that mainstream racial minorities have permitted the white majority rather than progressive minority leaders to prescribe minority aspirations. In a sense, this is not surprising. Because the white majority possesses the bulk of the societal resources, the white majority has become the reference group for racial minorities to emulate. Because the white majority controls the media that determine societal tastes and ambitions, the white majority has become the group that gives definition to acceptable forms of social life. Because the white majority controls the schools through which societal values are transmitted, the white majority has become the group that prescribes even the normative preferences of racial minorities. The fact that racial minorities would look to the pervasive white culture for aspirational guidance seems natural. What is surprising, however, is the depth of the minority commitment to white cultural norms. It is as if racial minorities took the Supreme Court seriously in *Brown* when the Court promised minorities that they could be equal participants in the dominant culture.

The danger of minority dependence on the Court's countermajoritarian promise can be detected on multiple levels. On an immediate level, this dependence has permitted the majority to deny educational opportunities to minority children for the nearly forty years since *Brown* was decided. As Professor Seidman has argued, *Brown* conveniently rescued the majority from the potentially burdensome separate-but-equal requirement of *Plessy v. Ferguson* by replacing that requirement with an integration requirement that could be satisfied without really integrating the schools.[68] Moreover, contemporary racial minorities still seem to prefer the demonstrably hollow promise of school desegregation to the more realistic potential of minority-controlled minority schools as a strategy for improving the quality of minority education. A separate-but-equal strategy, which Cruse refers to as "plural but equal" in order to emphasize the inescapable pluralism of contemporary American culture, now seems more promising than a strategy of integration.[69] Nevertheless, school desegregation is still the cornerstone of the NAACP educational policy.[70] Moreover, school desegregation cases are still routinely presented to the Supreme Court despite the hostility of current Court personnel to school desegregation. The Court issued an expansive interpretation of "unitary" schools during its 1990 Term that makes it easier for school districts to escape existing desegregation obligations, and it heard argument in two additional cases during its 1991 Term that give it the opportunity to dilute desegregation obligations even further.[71]

On a deeper level, *Brown* illustrates the danger of minority dependence upon the Supreme Court in defining the manner in which minorities think about the problems of race in contemporary society. A telling example is provided by the arguments that NAACP General Counsel Nathaniel R. Jones offered in defense of the NAACP school desegregation policy. He argued that the elimination of segregation was more important than the elimination of other, more tangible educational harms, and that the Constitution did not guarantee the right to a quality education but only to an education that was not officially segregated.[72] The assertion that segregation is inherently harmful to minority school children comes directly from the Supreme Court's opinion in *Brown*.[73] The assertion that the Constitution prohibits racial segregation but does not protect educational quality is a direct restatement of the Supreme Court's interpretation of the Constitution in *San Antonio Independent School District v. Rodriguez*,[74] which upheld the practice of disproportionate funding for inner-city and suburban schools.[75] In offering these arguments as a defense of the NAACP desegregation policy, Mr. Jones had simply let the Supreme Court define the manner in which he—and mainstream racial minorities—conceptualize the school desegregation issue. Because the Supreme Court favors integration over both local control and educational quality for majoritarian reasons, racial minorities who permit the Supreme Court to dictate the manner in which they think about racial problems are likely to adopt the same conclusions that the Court adopts, despite the majoritarian cast of those conclusions.

There are other ways in which the Court has been able to structure minority thinking about school desegregation. When *Brown* overruled the separate-but-equal doctrine of *Plessy*,[76] it stigmatized separate-but-equal facilities as morally illegitimate. The failed desegregation effort has now made the separate-but-equal strategy seem much more appealing to many progressive minority leaders. However, because of the moral taint that the Supreme Court has placed upon that strategy, mainstream minorities tend reflexively to dismiss the objective of separate-but-equal public facilities as somehow dishonorable or defeatist. Independent minority evaluation of separate-but-equal strategies would reveal the considerable appeal of those strategies to racial minorities, but once again, dependence on the Supreme Court's moral leadership has precluded mainstream minorities from undertaking such independent evaluation.

A closely related corollary is illustrated by mainstream minority acquiescence in the Supreme Court pronouncement that racial segregation itself is per se demeaning to racial minorities, stigmatizing them as inferior.[77] As Malcolm X has pointed out, this notion is simply silly:

I just can't see where if white people can go to a white classroom and there are not Negroes present and it doesn't affect the academic diet they're receiving, then I don't see where an all-black classroom can be affected by the absence of white children . . . . So, what the integrationists, in my opinion, are saying, when they say that whites and blacks must go to school together, is that the whites are so much superior that just their presence in a black classroom balances it out. I can't go along with that.[78]

Unfortunately mainstream minorities *are* able to go along with that. They are able to do so because the Supreme Court has told them to, and because they place more stock in Supreme Court guidance than they place in guidance from their own progressive leaders.

On an even deeper level, minority dependence on the Supreme Court, with respect to both the control of minority schools and the manner in which minorities think about minority schools, generalizes to the entire approach that minorities have taken to the advancement of minority interests. Although racial minorities have the potential to exercise considerable political power to advance their own interests,[79] to date, minorities have been content to rely most heavily on countermajoritarian judicial review to protect minority interests. Because *Brown* is still viewed as an overwhelming success for the countermajoritarian model of adjudication, racial minorities seem more concerned with trying to replicate *Brown* than with escaping the political dependency that has made *Brown* necessary. Contemporary racial minorities have given a low priority to their own self-determination. With only a few episodic exceptions, there have been no race riots; there have been no economic boycotts; there have not even been demands for proportional legislative representation.[80] Moreover, when minorities do engage in political action, it tends to be polite political action that is characterized most strongly by minority participation in coalitions dominated by white political interest groups that debate the proper response to the subtleties of Supreme Court decisions.[81] The enormous political effort that minorities chose to put into the relatively innocuous proposed Civil Rights Acts of 1990 and 1991 is illustrative.[82] Moreover, although minority politicians have recently begun to secure election as mayors of major cities and even as the governor of Virginia, they have done so by structuring their campaigns to appeal to white voters.[83] They have accepted rather than challenged the structure of race relations that has been established by the Supreme Court. In sum, the Supreme Court has been successful in convincing minorities to forego the pursuit of raw political power in favor of continued dependence on the reason, order, and stability of supposedly countermajoritarian adjudication. Because countermajoritarian Supreme Court adjudication is really majoritarianism in disguise, this dependence is intrinsically inimical to racial minorities.

Brown v. Board of Education was not the countermajoritarian gift to racial minorities that it is typically thought to be. Rather, *Brown* was a decision that was motivated by majoritarian political preferences and that was intended to benefit racial minorities only incidentally. Despite this intended incidental benefit, however, *Brown* has actually harmed racial minorities by perpetuating minority dependence on Supreme Court protection in lieu of minority self-determination. Because the Supreme Court is an inherently majoritarian institution, minority dependence upon the

Supreme Court ultimately benefits the white majority by preserving a legal structure in which minority interests can be subordinated to majority interests with minimal minority opposition. The manner in which the Supreme Court has structured the law of affirmative action further illustrates the institutional role that the Court has come to play in this subordinating process.

Centralization

The law of affirmative action is the most significant body of law affecting contemporary race relations in the United States. The Supreme Court, however, has developed the legal doctrines that govern affirmative action in a way that adversely affects the interests of racial minorities. It has done this by insinuating itself into the political policymaking process that governs affirmative action, and by incorporating centralized rather than local standards into the regulatory framework that it has imposed upon that process. In *City of Richmond v. J.A. Croson Co.*,[1] the Court held that state and municipal affirmative action plans were subject to strict judicial scrutiny under the equal protection clause of the Constitution. The practical consequence of this holding is to invalidate virtually all state and local affirmative action plans, because it is extremely rare for an explicit racial classification to survive strict scrutiny. In *Metro Broadcasting v. Federal Communications Commission*,[2] however, the Court held that congressional affirmative action plans were subject to only an intermediate level of judicial scrutiny because of the special powers that Congress possesses as the national legislature. The practical consequence of this holding is to sustain most federal affirmative action plans. Accordingly, the law of affirmative action is centralized rather than local because only the federal government possesses the practical power to implement an affirmative action program.

On a concrete level, this structure places racial minorities at a disadvantage because it increases the amount of political power that they must amass in order to secure the adoption of a valid affirmative action plan. Although racial minorities will often possess the political power to secure enactment of state or local affirmative action plans, those plans will be invalidated as unconstitutional. This is precisely what happened in the *Croson* case, where minorities were able to convince the Richmond City Council to adopt an affirmative action plan, only to have that plan invalidated by the Supreme Court. Although the Court will uphold federal plans, as it did in *Metro Broadcasting*, it is much harder for minorities to secure the adoption of federal plans because minorities will have to possess enough political power to influence a national Congress, not just a local city council. This effectively denies local pockets of minority political strength the power to advance minority interests in the way that they could under a constitutional rule that incorporated local standards.

On a more subtle level, the argument most often relied upon by the Supreme Court to justify its invalidation of affirmative action plans is the need to strive for a colorblind society in which resources will be distributed in a race-neutral manner according to merit, thereby remaining true to the American ideal of treating citizens as individuals rather than as mere members of a racial group. Group identification, however, can be politically very potent. Indeed, it is what has permitted the white majority to amass a disproportionate share of our societal wealth. Just as Americans can be convinced to support a dubious foreign war by the argument that their support is necessary to preserve "traditional American values" or to protect our "vital national interests," racial minorities have the option of making similar "nationalism" appeals in order to secure an increase in minority group solidarity. Moreover, these appeals will be particularly effective if race is viewed as central rather than incidental in American life. However, by denying the centrality of race in American life and insisting upon the importance of race neutrality, the Supreme Court has effectively precluded minorities from responding to appeals for racial solidarity that could facilitate minority realization of racial self-determination.

The Statistical Nature of Affirmative Action

Although laws that prohibit racial discrimination are of obvious social significance, they have less contemporary consequence than the law of affirmative action. In part, this is because the desirability of legal prohibitions on racial discrimination is now generally conceded, while the desirability of affirmative action remains hotly contested. In addition, however, the sophisticated nature of modern discrimination means that the bare prohibitions on racial discrimination that are contained in our antidiscrimination laws can have little effect unless they are accompanied by structural remedies of the type that tend to be associated with affirmative action.

Stated simply, affirmative action is the use of race-conscious classifications for the reallocation of societal resources in a way that benefits minorities. In theory, affirmative action and traditional antidiscrimination laws are analytically distinct. Antidiscrimination laws promote race neutrality by prohibiting the adverse treatment of individuals or groups based upon their race, while affirmative action departs from the immediate goal of race neutrality in order to channel resources to disadvantaged minorities in a way that is designed to advance the long-term objective of racial equality. Despite this theoretical distinction, however, the contemporary relationship that exists between antidiscrimination laws and affirmative action has become so intimate that it rarely makes practical sense to distinguish between the two.

The most significant form of racial discrimination that exists in contemporary American culture is statistical discrimination.[3] Although individualized acts of explicit racism obviously continue to occur, the disproportionate allocation of societal wealth and political power that is presently possessed by the white majority in the United States has resulted from a pattern of racial discrimination that manifests itself most clearly when one consults the statistical data. Consider, for example, the statistical disparities that exist between blacks and whites. Blacks comprise 13 percent of the national population.[4] Nevertheless, in economic terms, whites are considerably better off than blacks. Thirty-one percent of black families live below the federal poverty level while only 11 percent of white families live below the poverty level. In addition, 44 percent of black children live in conditions of poverty while only 16 percent of white children live in poverty conditions.[5] In terms of per capita income, blacks earn only 57 percent of what whites earn, and a black male is twice as likely as a white male to be unemployed. The per capita net worth for whites is $32,667, while the per capita net worth for blacks is only $6,837. Moreover, for every $1 of net wealth possessed by the median white family, the median black family possesses a net wealth of only 9 cents.[6] Health and safety statistics show equally dramatic discrepancies between blacks and whites. Homicide is the leading cause of death for young black males, who constitute 43 percent of the nation's homicide victims, and young black males are six times more likely to be victims of homicide than white males of comparable ages.[7] Infant mortality rates for blacks are twice as high as infant mortality rates for whites.[8] Blacks are also twice as likely as whites to be the victims of serious crimes.[9] In terms of political power, all United

States presidents have been white; all but two United States senators have been white; the overwhelming majority of United States representatives has been white;[10] and all but two United States Supreme Court justices have been white.[11] In terms of its depth, duration, and pervasiveness, statistical discrimination in the United States has been so vast that only the systemic reallocation of resources offers any realistic hope of altering the disproportionate control that the white majority presently possesses over the economic and political resources of the society. Because contemporary antidiscrimination laws and contemporary affirmative action programs both seek to address the problem of systemic discrimination that occurs on a statistical level, the two can easily lose their analytical distinctiveness.

The artificiality of the distinction between antidiscrimination laws and affirmative action can be illustrated by examining President Bush's celebrated political opposition to the proposed Civil Rights Acts of 1990 and 1991.[12] These legislative proposals would have reversed a series of conservative Supreme Court decisions that limited the scope of previously enacted congressional civil rights statutes. Although the legislative proposals were drafted as antidiscrimination amendments intended, *inter alia*, to modify the methods of statistical proof that could be used to establish the existence of racial discrimination, President Bush chose to recast those proposals as affirmative action initiatives in order both to feed and to capitalize on the majoritarian resentment to affirmative action that emerged as the United States economy began to deteriorate during the Reagan and Bush administrations.[13] President Bush was able to do this by arguing that the attention that employers would have to pay under the proposed amendments to the statistical consequences of their hiring and promotion determinations would, in effect, have required employers to use *de facto* racial quotas in making those determinations. Accordingly, President Bush opposed the legislative proposals on the grounds that they called for affirmative action initiatives that were unfair to whites. Note that this argument permits any antidiscrimination law that addresses the problem of statistical discrimination to be opposed as a mere smoke screen for affirmative action. This, in turn, collapses the distinction between race-neutral antidiscrimination laws and race-conscious affirmative action.[14]

Although affirmative action is currently controversial, it is also ubiquitous. Contemporary American culture utilizes an array of affirmative action programs to redistribute resources. Typically, these programs occur in educational and employment contexts, although affirmative action can also occur in other settings, such as the race-conscious establishment of voting districts for legislative apportionment.[15] The most visible affirmative action programs are those that endeavor to increase opportunities for women and racial minorities, both of whom have traditionally been underrepresented in the most lucrative and prestigious societal positions. In addition to these conspicuous programs, many educational institutions utilize less-apparent affirmative action plans, including plans that are designed to increase diversity by attracting geographic minorities, to increase prestige and financial revenues by attracting athletes, and to increase endowment by attracting alumni sons and daughters. Indeed, any selection criterion other than randomness necessarily rests upon a preference that technically constitutes an affirmative action preference. However, the term "affirmative action" has come to connote the use of preferences that are unrelated to merit. Although existing affirmative action programs focus on a number of different groups, the affirmative action programs that are of primary concern in the present context are those that concern racial minorities.

Depending upon the particular justification that is offered for an affirmative action program, the minority benefits that are advanced by the program can be either intentional or incidental. When affirmative action is used as a remedy for the continuing effects of past discrimination, its intended purpose is to provide a direct benefit to those minorities who are viewed as victims of that past discrimination.[16] Legal scholars have been unable to agree upon proper designation of these victims. On some occasions, the victims of past discrimination are defined to be individuals who have suffered identifiable injuries traceable to isolated acts of discriminatory behavior.[17] On other occasions, the victims are defined to be groups that have historically been the objects of invidious societal discrimination.[18] The present Supreme Court tends to be most receptive to an individualized conception of discrimination victims.[19]

When affirmative action is used as a mechanism for providing prospective benefits to a majoritarian institution in the form of enhanced diversity, the direct beneficiary is the majoritarian institution itself.[20] For example, women and minorities are now routinely admitted to law schools under affirmative action programs in recognition of the pedagogical inadequacies inherent in attempting to discuss cases like *Roe v. Wade*[21] or *Dred Scott*[22] in a room that is populated exclusively by white males. Although minorities may stand to benefit from affirmative action that is designed to promote prospective diversity, these minority benefits are incidental rather than primary.

Other justifications for affirmative action are amenable to varying characterizations. For example, role model justifications can be viewed as benefitting either minorities or the white majority.[23] When an affirmative action program places minority individuals in positions of high social or economic prestige, other minorities derive aspirational benefits and enhanced esteem from observing those minorities. For example, men who would not otherwise consider careers in nursing, or women who might not otherwise pursue vocational opportunities in construction work, might choose to do so after having been exposed to role models in those professions with whom they were able to identify. In addition, countless blacks undoubtedly regard military careers as more viable and more rewarding simply because they were exposed to General Colin Powell in the television press briefings that accompanied the war against Iraq.[24] However, the larger majoritarian society also benefits from having minorities in high prestige positions, because the presence of minorities serving in important social roles negates counterproductive cultural stereotypes that distort majority perceptions of minority abilities. For example, it has taken actual confrontation with minority achievement to negate the majority view that minorities could not become successful doctors,[25] lawyers,[26] or even basketball players.[27] Many whites have also undoubtedly altered their perceptions of black military competence as a result of the favorable publicity surrounding General Powell.[28]

Although many justifications have been offered for affirmative action, none has achieved consensus recognition as the most appropriate. Legal scholars have been unable to agree upon the proper basis for assessing the legitimacy of affirmative action,[29] and the Supreme Court has fluctuated between various justifications.[30] Regardless of what justification is offered, however, affirmative action seems destined to remain controversial.

The Centralization of Affirmative Action

One reason for the continuing controversy that surrounds affirmative action flows from its precarious legal status. As has been noted, race-conscious affirmative action is in tension with the race neutrality objectives of our antidiscrimination laws, precisely because affirmative action is race-conscious rather than race-neutral.[31] This makes affirmative action doctrinally problematic, because the Constitution and an array of federal statutes generally prohibit race-based classifications. Although the Constitution that the framers adopted actually protected the race-conscious practice of slavery,[32] adoption of the Reconstruction amendments after the Civil War modified the original Constitution in ways that are relevant to affirmative action.[33] The equal protection clause of the fourteenth amendment states that "[n]o state shall . . . deny to any person within its jurisdiction the equal protection of the laws."[34] Although this constitutional provision only applies to governmental action, Section 5 of the fourteenth amendment authorizes Congress to enforce the provisions of the amendment through appropriate legislation.[35] Pursuant to this authority, Congress has enacted a number of statutes that also prohibit racial discrimination in various nongovernmental contexts, including discrimination in housing, employment, and education.[36] The ironic result of these constitutional and statutory provisions has been to call into question the validity of the race-based classifications upon which some public and private affirmative action programs rest. The role of statutory restrictions on racial discrimination is significant, and Supreme Court majoritarian predispositions can affect these restrictions by making their presence felt during the process of statutory interpretation. However, the majoritarianism of the Supreme Court is most influential in the context of constitutional affirmative action, because Supreme Court constitutional pronouncements cannot easily be overcome by racial minorities through recourse to the political process.[37]

The nation's first affirmative action laws were enacted by Congress during the post-Civil War Reconstruction period, under the authority of the Reconstruction amendments.[38] The civil rights legislation that Congress adopted during that period was intended to benefit the newly freed black slaves by guaranteeing them equal rights of citizenship and a measure of protection from white southern harassment. Although the provisions of those statutes tended to be facially neutral, their unambiguous intent was to benefit blacks. The Supreme Court's initial response to the Reconstruction amendments and statutes was to enforce them after imposing a narrow construction on their scope.[39] Then, however, the Court actually began to invalidate various provisions of the Reconstruction legislation, primarily on federalism grounds.[40] Those narrow constructions and invalidations retained their force until the demise of federalism that occurred during the New Deal, and the second wave of civil rights legislation that was enacted in the post-*Brown* era.[41]

In modern times, the Supreme Court authorized the first extensive constitutional use of affirmative action in the context of school desegregation. *Brown v. Board of Education* invalidated governmental use of racial classifications in holding that *de jure* school segregation was unconstitutional, but the case ironically went on to hold that race-conscious pupil assignment was required to remedy the constitutional violation that it had just recognized.[42] Accordingly, *Brown* has come to stand for both the need to avoid the evil inherent in racial discrimination and the need to engage in racial discrimination in order to counteract that evil. The confusion that has since characterized the law of affirmative action simply reflects the affirmative action dilemma inherent in *Brown*.[43]

The affirmative action dilemma remained dormant as the Supreme Court issued a series of majority opinions through the 1960s and early 1970s that authorized the race-conscious remedies deemed necessary to dismantle the previously segregated southern school systems. As has been noted, however, when the school desegregation effort moved north in the early 1970s, the national political consensus favoring school desegregation had begun to break down, and the Court began to restrict the availability of race-conscious remedies.[44] Moreover, in contexts outside the area of school desegregation, a majority of the Court was unable to agree on a mode of analysis for affirmative action. This resulted in a steady stream of affirmative action cases that were resolved by plurality rather than majority opinions.

After using the doctrine of mootness to avoid ruling on the constitutionality of affirmative action in the 1974 case of *DeFunis v. Odegaard*,[45] the Court upheld the constitutionality of a race-conscious legislative apportionment scheme in *United Jewish Organizations v. Carey*.[46] However, no majority of the Court was able to agree on a rationale for the Court's outcome. Then in the 1978 case of *Regents of the University of California v. Bakke*,[47] the Court invalidated a medical school affirmative action plan that allocated 16 percent of the seats in the school's incoming class to disadvantaged minority students.[48] But once again, the Court was unable to issue a majority opinion. Although a five-justice majority voted to invalidate the particular affirmative action plan that was before the Court in *Bakke*,[49] a different five-justice majority stated that race-conscious affirmative action would be constitutionally permissible in appropriate circumstances.[50] A major source of contention in *Bakke* was whether affirmative action should be subject to the strict judicial scrutiny that is generally accorded racial classifications under the equal protection clause of the fourteenth amendment,[51] or whether the benign nature of affirmative action made a more deferential standard of relaxed scrutiny constitutionally appropriate.[52]

In 1980, the Court upheld a federal set-aside program for minority construction contractors in *Fullilove v. Klutznick*.[53] Once again, however, the Court was forced to resolve the case through the issuance of a plurality opinion. Although the justices were still unable to agree on the proper standard of scrutiny, seven members of the Court did endorse the use of race-conscious remedies for past discrimination,[54] even when those remedies entailed the use of racial quotas.[55] Then, in the 1986 case of *Wygant v. Jackson Board of Education*,[56] the Court issued another plurality decision, this time invalidating a consent decree that protected lower-seniority minority teachers from layoffs at the expense of higher-seniority white teachers in order to maintain the percentage of minority teachers in the school system.[57] The justices who voted to invalidate the program did so primarily because they found the program to be overly burdensome to white teachers.[58] The justices were still unable to agree on the standard of review.[59] In the 1986 case of *Local 28, Sheet Metal Workers International Association v. Equal Employment Opportunity Commission*,[60] and the 1987 case of *United States v. Paradise*,[61] the Court upheld judicially imposed affirmative action orders, but in both cases the Court was yet again forced to issue plurality opinions.

It was not until 1989, after President Reagan's appointment of conservative Justices O'Connor, Scalia, and Kennedy to the Supreme Court, that the Court was finally able to issue a majority opinion in a constitutional affirmative action case. In *City of Richmond v. J.A. Croson Co.*,[62] the Court invalidated, by a vote of 6–3, a minority set-aside program that had been adopted by the City Council of Richmond, Virginia. The Court invalidated the Richmond set-aside plan, even though it had been closely modeled on the federal set-aside program that the Court had previously upheld in *Fullilove*.[63] A year later, in 1990, the Court again issued a majority opinion in an affirmative action case, this time in *Metro Broadcasting v. Federal Communications Commission*.[64] There, the Court upheld, by a vote of 5–4, two broadcast license programs that had been adopted by the F.C.C. in order to give certain preferences to racial minorities in obtaining radio and television broadcast licenses.[65] The current law of affirmative action has been established by these two majority opinions.

The current law, in essence, upholds the constitutionality of centralized affirmative action plans that are adopted by the federal government, but prohibits decentralized plans that are adopted by state and local governments. It does this by applying a deferential standard of intermediate scrutiny to federal plans,[66] while applying a nondeferential standard of strict scrutiny to local plans.[67] This distinction effectively precludes the constitutionality of local plans because strict judicial scrutiny is extremely difficult to overcome, as the outcome in *Croson* illustrates.[68] Under strict scrutiny, a racial classification can be upheld only if it advances a compelling governmental interest and is narrowly tailored to achieving that interest.[69] Intermediate scrutiny, however, is easier to survive, as the Court's decision upholding the F.C.C. racial preferences in *Metro Broadcasting* reveals.[70] Under intermediate scrutiny, a racial classification will be upheld as long as it is substantially related to an important governmental objective.[71]

When the Court invalidated the minority set-aside program in *Croson*, it distinguished the *Fullilove* set-aside plan, which it had previously upheld. It did so by emphasizing that the *Fullilove* plan had been adopted by Congress, whereas the *Croson* plan had been adopted by the Richmond City Council. Justice O'Connor's majority opinion reasoned that Congress was entitled to greater judicial deference than a local city council because of the special powers that Congress possessed as the national legislature.[72] This distinction between federal and local plans was carried forward by Justice Brennan in his *Metro Broadcasting* majority opinion as a basis for distinguishing *Croson*.[73]

At the time that *Croson* was decided, it appeared that Justice O'Connor had simply seized upon the distinction between federal and local affirmative action programs as a convenient method for avoiding the troublesome *Fullilove* precedent in the course of invalidating the Richmond plan. However, when the opportunity to overrule *Fullilove* squarely presented itself the following Term in *Metro Broadcasting*, only four justices were willing to abandon the distinction. Although Justice Brennan had never voted to invalidate any affirmative action program, whether federal or local in origin, his majority opinion in *Metro Broadcasting* nevertheless endorsed the *Croson* distinction between federal and local plans—this time as a convenient method for avoiding the troublesome *Croson* precedent.

Realistically, the operative distinction between *Croson* and *Metro Broadcasting* is that Justices Stevens and White were swing voters who changed their positions in the two cases. A four-justice conservative core consisting of Chief Justice Rehnquist and Justices O'Connor, Scalia, and Kennedy has voted consistently to invalidate the affirmative action programs that the Court has resolved on constitutional grounds. Of these justices, only then-Justice Rehnquist has ever voted to uphold the constitutionality of an affirmative action program, which he did by voting to uphold the voter apportionment scheme that the Court sustained in *Carey*.[74] A three-justice liberal core consisting of Justices Brennan, Marshall, and Blackmun has never voted to invalidate an affirmative action plan that has been presented to the Court. Each of these blocks voted predictably in both *Croson* and *Metro Broadcasting*, but the swing votes determined the outcome in each of those cases.

In *Croson*, the conservative block was joined by Justices White and Stevens. The reason that Justice White appears to have joined the conservative block is that he was converted from a proponent to an opponent of affirmative action as the overall political climate in the nation became more conservative. Justice White voted in favor of affirmative action in the first four constitutional cases that he considered while on the Supreme Court,[75] but he voted against affirmative action in the next four cases that he considered.[76] Justice Stevens appears to have joined the conservative block in *Croson* because he is simply opposed to numerical set-asides. This view is supported by the fact that Justice Stevens had also voted to invalidate the federal set-aside plan that the Supreme Court upheld in *Fullilove*, terming the set-aside at issue in that case an inappropriate partisan political effort to give minorities "a piece of the action."[77] The four-justice conservative block, plus Justices White and Stevens, produced the 6–3 decision invalidating the *Croson* affirmative action plan.

In *Metro Broadcasting*, Justices White and Stevens switched their votes and joined the liberal affirmative action block. Justice White appears to have joined the liberal block despite his conversion to affirmative action conservatism, because his longstanding belief in deference to federal governmental regulation managed to override his conservatism.[78] Justice Stevens appears to have joined the liberal block despite his anti-affirmative action votes in cases like *Croson*[79] and *Fullilove*[80] because the F.C.C. minority preference that was involved in *Metro Broadcasting* did not utilize numerical set-asides. Rather, it gave minority broadcasters a preference in licensing proceedings that might or might not prove to be dispositive when considered in connection with the other factors that go into making broadcast licensing determinations.[81]

The distinction between federal and local programs that characterizes the current law of affirmative action is firmly established by *Croson* and *Metro Broadcasting*. Ironically, however, only one Supreme Court justice appears actually to believe in that distinction. Although the distinction accurately accounts for Justice White's recent affirmative action votes, the votes of all of the other justices have been determined by some other factor. Moreover, for all of the other justices except Justice Stevens, this other factor appears to have been simply the justice's general conservative or liberal political inclination. Because Justice White is the only member of the current Court who accords genuine weight to the distinction between federal and local affirmative action programs, that distinction may prove to be a fragile rather than a durable one.

Justices Brennan and Marshall, who were in the liberal core of the Court when the distinction between federal and local plans was articulated, are no longer on the Court. Their replacements, Justices Souter and

Thomas, have yet to vote on the constitutionality of affirmative action. However, to the extent that general political philosophy will continue to govern the development of Supreme Court affirmative action doctrine, either or both of these new conservative justices could easily upset the current law. It is true that both *Croson* and *Metro Broadcasting* are very recent decisions, issued after more than a decade of experimentation with plurality opinions. However, even the recent vintage of these cases may not be sufficient to reduce the likelihood of some imminent modification in the law of affirmative action. The new Reagan-Bush conservative majority on the Supreme Court appears willing to overrule even recent precedents when it has the votes to do so.[82] Nevertheless, the current centralized law of affirmative action may persist, simply because it serves the conservative majoritarian interests that are so well represented on the Supreme Court.

The Concrete Dangers of Centralization

The white majority currently controls the allocation of economic and political resources in the United States.[83] As a result, economic assumptions about rational wealth maximization suggest that the majority will attempt to channel as many of those resources as is practical to itself rather than to racial minorities.[84] I do not wish to suggest that an economic model provides the only acceptable model for conceptualizing affirmative action issues. However, an economic model does seem particularly appropriate in light of the underlying economic nature of the societal resources around which the affirmative action debate has centered, and in light of the pluralist conception of partisan politics that this book has advocated. Both economics and pluralist politics rest upon the assumption of rational, self-interested wealth or utility maximization. One could, of course, reject the rational wealth maximization assumption of human motivation, preferring instead to view human beings as possessing the capacity for benevolence and generosity. However, benevolence and generosity can be assimilated into the rational wealth maximization model simply by treating them as factors that even a self-interested majority would wish to advance in order to enhance the majority's sense of self-esteem.[85] In a sense, this makes the rational wealth maximization assumption tautological, but it also makes the assumption parsimonious enough to serve as a useful analytical construct.[86]

A rational wealth maximizing majority will not generally favor affirmative action, precisely because affirmative action allocates to racial minorities societal resources that would otherwise be enjoyed by the majority. However, the majority is not free to reserve all of society's economic and political resources for itself, because such short-sighted self-interest would ultimately relegate the majority to a less than optimal position. There are several reasons for this. As an initial matter, there would be unacceptable collateral consequences attendant to denying racial minorities access to all, or even most societal resources. For example, the crime, violence, and disease associated with the poverty that ensued could not successfully be confined to minority communities alone without considerable expenditures of majoritarian resources in the form of police repression, health restrictions, and the like. Some regimes, such as the antebellum slavery regime in the United States and the current apartheid regime in South Africa, have attempted to enforce the sorts of laws that are necessary to minimize minority access to societal resources. Such regimes, however, eventually collapse under the pressure of their own repression, just as American slavery collapsed after the Civil War, and just as apartheid is presently collapsing in South Africa.[87] In the contemporary United States, which has now evolved beyond its *de jure* apartheid phase, it would almost certainly be more efficient for a self-interested majority to provide racial minorities with enough resources to avoid at least the most egregious externalities associated with the majoritarian hoarding of all significant societal resources.

The refusal to allocate any significant societal resources to racial minorities would also deprive the majority of the benefits that minorities are capable of providing to the majority. These benefits can be as mundane as manual labor,[88] as lucrative as athletic or entertainment appeal,[89] or as exceptional as a lifesaving scientific discovery.[90] However, those benefits will never be available to the majority if minorities are not given the basic resources necessary to permit such benefits to come into existence. In addition, the majority will suffer reduced self-esteem and goodwill if it is perceived by itself and by others to be callous and indifferent to the subsistence needs of other human beings—even minority human beings. Charity has always been a strong component of the American Judeo-Christian ethic. Even the substantial economic benefits of slavery were eventually abolished in large part because of majoritarian perceptions of slavery as immoral and un-American.[91] Moreover, the majority's desire to preserve its own self-esteem, as well as the goodwill of others, is one of the factors that accounts for the Supreme Court's majoritarian decision to allocate educational resources to racial minorities in *Brown*.[92]

A rational wealth-maximizing majority will not attempt to allocate all significant societal resources to itself because the costs of doing so are prohibitive. Rather, the majority will strive for the optimal allocation of resources between itself and racial minorities. Stated differently, the majority will not oppose all affirmative action. Instead, it will favor just the right amount of affirmative action—not too much, but not too little either. The Supreme Court's insinuation of itself into a position of control over the affirmative action policymaking process helps the majority to achieve the optimal level of affirmative action because of the Supreme Court's inherent conservatism.[93] The way that the Court has chosen to satisfy this optimization obligation is by centralizing the law of affirmative action.

On a superficial level, the control that the Supreme Court exercises over the formulation of majoritarian affirmative action policy seems nonsensical. Whatever justification there might be for Supreme Court imposition of affirmative action responsibilities on the representative branches of government, it is difficult to find a justification for Supreme Court invalidation of affirmative action programs that the representative branches voluntarily choose to adopt. If the openly majoritarian branches of government are unconstitutionally discriminating against racial minorities, the Supreme Court is arguably justified in imposing affirmative action obligations to remedy that discrimination. The representation-reinforcement theory of constitutional law, which contains perhaps the most popular contemporary defense of judicial review, provides for such judicial intervention when necessary to counteract majoritarian exploitation of discrete and insular minorities who are underrepresented in the political process.[94] However, when an openly majoritarian branch of government has chosen to adopt an affirmative action program, it appears to make little sense for the Supreme Court to invalidate that program on constitutional grounds. Assuming that the plan actually benefits racial minorities, there is no discrete and insular minority for the Court to protect. Although affirmative action can adversely affect members of the white majority, the white majority is, by definition, adequately represented in the political process and does not, therefore, require Supreme Court intervention to protect its interests. Nevertheless, the Supreme Court now routinely reviews majoritarian affirmative action programs to assess their constitutionality, and frequently invalidates those programs as it did in *Croson*.

Supreme Court review of majoritarian affirmative action plans does not make sense as a method for protecting racial minority interests, but it does make sense as a method for protecting the majority. When the majority elects to adopt a voluntary affirmative action plan it derives certain benefits from doing so. Those benefits take the form of enhanced majoritarian self-esteem, as well as increased goodwill and tolerance on the part of

racial minorities who would otherwise resent the majority's disproportionate accumulation of societal resources. The self-esteem benefits are
very real, although they are largely intangible. The minority-goodwill benefits are more concrete, ranging from reduced minority opposition in polite
politics to reduced boycotts and riots in less-polite politics.[95] The majority,
however, must pay the costs associated with securing those benefits through
the increased minority allocations of societal resources that are entailed
in the affirmative action programs that the majority adopts.

Judicial review of majoritarian affirmative action programs permits the
majority to derive the benefits associated with the voluntary adoption of
affirmative action programs at a discounted political cost. Meaningful judicial review will necessarily result in the invalidation of some percentage
of the affirmative action programs that the majority adopts. In modern
history, the Supreme Court has invalidated the affirmative action programs
at issue in three of the eight affirmative action cases that the Court has
resolved on constitutional grounds.[96] This invalidation rate of 37.5 percent
essentially means that the majority can purchase the benefits of affirmative
action for the price of 62.5 cents on the dollar—the inverse of 37.5
percent—simply by filtering majoritarian affirmative action policies through
the process of judicial review.

The reason that Supreme Court invalidation does not also reduce the
benefits associated with voluntary affirmative action is that the Court,
rather than the majority, is viewed as the entity responsible for having
prevented the majoritarian affirmative action programs from taking effect.
Because the majority is not implicated in the Court's invalidation, the
majority is able to retain the enhanced self-esteem and minority goodwill
that was initially associated with its adoption of the invalidated affirmative
action program. As long as the perception persists that the Court operates
in a doctrinally principled manner, rather than as a disguised majoritarian
institution, judicial review will continue to make the adoption of voluntary
affirmative action programs a bargain for a rational wealth-maximizing
majority.

The political costs of affirmative action to the majority are further
reduced by the manner in which the Supreme Court has structured the
law of affirmative action. The Court not only invalidates a percentage of
the affirmative action programs that racial minorities are successful in
convincing the majority to adopt, but the programs that the Court is willing
to uphold are the very programs that minorities will typically lack the
political power to get enacted with any degree of frequency. By centralizing
the law of affirmative action, the Supreme Court has effectively forced

racial minorities to divert their affirmative action political efforts from the local level to the national level. This benefits the majority at the expense of racial minorities because it requires minorities to expend their political capital where it will pose the least threat to majority interests.

As the Richmond set-aside plan that the Supreme Court invalidated in *Croson* reveals, in some localities racial minorities will possess sufficient political power to demand the enactment of affirmative action programs. In Richmond, blacks comprised 50 percent of the population, held five of nine city council seats, and were able to secure the adoption of a set-aside plan that reserved 30 percent of the public funds expended on municipal construction contracts for minority contractors—contractors who had previously been awarded only 0.67 percent of the city's prime contracts in the absence of the set-aside plan.[97] On the national level, however, racial minorities will comprise a much smaller percentage of the electorate than they do in many localities. For example, although blacks comprise 50 percent of the population in Richmond, they comprise only 13 percent of the population nationally.[98] At the national level, racial minorities simply lack the ability to compete as effectively in the pluralist political process as they can in areas having a heavy concentration of minority voters. Nevertheless, the Supreme Court's decision to apply strict judicial scrutiny to local affirmative action plans while applying relaxed intermediate scrutiny to federal plans, creates compelling incentives for racial minorities to forego the local political battles that they could win in favor of the national battles that they are much more likely to lose.

It is true, of course, that racial minorities can sometimes secure political victories at the national level. The federal civil rights legislation that was enacted by Congress during the 1960s and 1970s illustrates the possibility of minority influence in national politics.[99] In addition, the existence of federal affirmative action programs, such as the minority enhancement program upheld in *Metro Broadcasting* and the minority set-aside upheld in *Fullilove*, indicate that racial minorities sometimes possess the political power to secure the enactment of national affirmative action programs.[100] However, minorities can also fail to secure the enactment of even mundane civil rights legislation at the national level because of their lack of political power, as they did in their initial efforts to secure enactment of the proposed Civil Rights Acts of 1990 and 1991.[101] Other issues, such as public funding for abortions, may be susceptible to minority victories at the national level, but they are much more susceptible to such victories at the local level where racial minorities possess greater political power.[102] Still other important legislative reforms are capable of advancing immeasurably the interests of racial minorities, but they are unlikely ever to be taken seriously at the national level precisely because of their potential to upset the existing allocation of resources between whites and minorities. Issues such as meaningful income redistribution[103] and proportional legislative representation fall into this category.[104] Finally, when minorities are forced to operate on the national political level, even their victories can, in a sense, become losses. This is because minorities operating on the level of national politics, where they constitute only a small percentage of the total electorate, are forced to join national political coalitions that will invariably be controlled by white interest groups rather than by racial minorities themselves. This need for minorities to join such coalitions simply enables whites to perpetuate further their control over the fates of racial minorities, and frustrates further minority efforts to achieve political self-determination.

The Reagan-Bush Supreme Court now appears to have a strong enough conservative majority to invalidate all affirmative action programs if it so desires. Chief Justice Rehnquist and Justices O'Connor, Scalia, and Kennedy consistently vote against the constitutionality of affirmative action. In addition, although Justices Souter and Thomas do not yet have voting records on the issue as Supreme Court justices, both have expressed hostility to affirmative action in other contexts. Justice Souter, while serving as the Attorney General of New Hampshire, referred to affirmative action as "affirmative discrimination," and he resisted compliance with Equal Employment Opportunity Commission requirements to provide statistical information to the federal government about the racial breakdown of New Hampshire public officials.[105] Justice Thomas has, at times, attributed his academic and political achievements to the existence of affirmative action programs, but his most recent sentiments, expressed as the head of the Equal Employment Opportunity Commission, as a Court of Appeals judge, and as a Supreme Court nominee, have all been strongly critical of affirmative action.[106] This appears to give the current Court six solid votes against affirmative action—enough to invalidate federal as well as local programs if the Court should desire across-the-board invalidation. However, if the Supreme Court were to invalidate *all* affirmative action programs, it would risk losing its representation-reinforcement reputation as the guardian of minority interests.

A Supreme Court prohibition on all affirmative action, just when popular opposition to affirmative action was at its peak in a deteriorating economy, might prompt racial minorities to come to view the Court as a surreptitiously majoritarian institution. This, in turn, could cause minorities to cease their reliance on Supreme Court adjudication as a passive alternative to more aggressive, extra-legal strategies for the pursuit of racial justice. If racial minorities were thus provoked to abandon their dependence on Supreme Court protection, the Court would no longer be able to serve its majoritarian function of subordinating minorities with rhetoric rather than coercion. The majority would then be forced to resort to more costly and less effective means of racial subordination in order to retain their present disproportionate allocation of societal resources. In order to prolong minority acquiescence in continued Supreme Court protection, therefore, the Court is likely to permit some affirmative action programs to retain their constitutional validity. For the instrumental reasons that have been discussed, the present distinction between federal and local affirmative action provides a convenient, if not Machiavellian, means of prolonging minority dependence on the Court. However, the distinction also has additional, subtle features that increase its utility to a veiled majoritarian Court.

The Subtle Dangers of Centralization

One might suspect that, as bad as the Supreme Court's centralization of affirmative action may be, it is still better than Supreme Court invalidation of all affirmative action programs, including federal as well as local plans. At least minorities can now compete for national affirmative action programs, the enactment of which they will be able to secure on at least some occasions. However, even that suspicion seems dubious after one considers the more subtle consequences of the Court's centralization of affirmative action. Conceptually, the most significant difference that exists between centralization and decentralization is that centralization connotes universalism, rational objectivity, and race neutrality, while decentralization connotes parochialism, irrational subjectivity, and racial bias. Capitalizing on those connotations, the Supreme Court's preference for centralization over decentralization reflects an ideology of colorblind race neutrality that all but guarantees the perpetuation of majority dominance over racial minorities.

In contemporary America, centralization is associated with the positive cultural attributes of universalism, rational objectivity, and race neutrality.[107] Universalism is the belief in transcendent normative truths that can serve as guideposts to lead us from the morass of cultural relativism to the high ground of moral propriety, thereby saving us from the abyss of nihilistic despair into which we will fall if we reject the call of universalist pursuits. Rational objectivity is the analytical process through which universalist norms can be ascertained in the abstract and implemented on an operational level, free from the distortions of irrational passion. Race neutrality is the virtue that results from the application of rational objectivity to universalist norms in the context of race relations. The fact that centralization is linked to these positive cultural attributes is illustrated by the history of race relations in the United States. After the regional South subjected racial minorities to the brutal afflictions of slavery and racial segregation, the centralized federal union intervened to right those regional wrongs by fighting a Civil War and enacting numerous civil rights laws that guaranteed to all oppressed minorities the right of racial equality. Accordingly, the central government, cognizant of the universalist imperative to honor the equality of human dignity, behaved in a rationally objective manner and supplanted a regional domain of racial bigotry with a national regime of race neutrality.[108]

Decentralization is associated with the negative cultural attributes of parochialism, irrational subjectivity, and racial bias.[109] Parochialism is the belief that the particularized preferences that emanate from the morass of cultural relativism can be imposed upon others who do not share those preferences, just as if the preferences in fact reflected universalist moral canons. Irrational subjectivity is the tainted analytical process through which parochial norms are mistaken for universalist norms in order to satisfy the self-interested demands of passion that could not be justified through recourse to rational objectivity. Racial bias is the vice that results from the application of irrational subjectivity to parochial preferences in the context of race relations. The fact that decentralization is linked to these negative cultural attributes is also illustrated by the history of race relations in the United States. The reason that the centralized federal union was required to wage a Civil War and to enact numerous civil rights laws was because the regional South had chosen to inflict its parochial preferences for slavery and segregation on vulnerable racial minorities who did not share those preferences. Accordingly, the regional South, blinded by the intensity of its parochial passions, behaved in an irrationally subjective manner in instituting its bigoted regime of racial bias that only the remedy of centralization could cure.[110]

The connotations of centralization and decentralization that emerge from these contrasting accounts pervade the Supreme Court's affirmative action opinions. The primary justification that the Court has offered for its affirmative action decisions relates to the importance of pursuing the cultural goal of race neutrality. This is true of both the decisions invalidating and upholding affirmative action programs. When the Court invalidates an affirmative action program, it does so because of the need to prohibit race-conscious remedies that are inconsistent with our ultimate cultural goal of achieving a colorblind society in which the allocation of societal resources is based upon merit rather than upon the color of one's skin.[111] When the Court upholds an affirmative action program, it does so only because of the need to engage in temporary race-conscious remedies that are necessary to alleviate the effects of past discrimination in a way that will advance our ultimate goal of achieving that same colorblind society.[112] Accordingly, the Supreme Court's preference for a centralized, rather than a decentralized, law of affirmative action reflects this deeper cultural preference for the virtue of race neutrality that centralization connotes. As noble as this judicial preoccupation with race neutrality may appear on a superficial level, beneath the surface it is profoundly subversive.

The problem is that we do not live in a colorblind, race-neutral society. Nor do we live in a society that is capable of becoming colorblind in the conceivable future. In the United States, race is invariably implicated in most significant societal decisionmaking.[113] Decisions about civil rights and affirmative action obviously implicate the issue of race, because those decisions directly determine how societal resources will be allocated between the white majority and racial minorities. However, societal decisions about matters that do not directly address the issue of race also affect racial interests in substantial ways.

We cannot adopt an internal revenue code without determining how societal wealth will be allocated between middle-class whites and indigent racial minorities.[114] We cannot adopt a federal budget without determining how taxpayer revenues will be redistributed between white defense contractors and minority school children.[115] We cannot commence military engagements without sentencing racial minorities to die in disproportionate numbers for whatever majoritarian interest is thought to be advanced by the military operation at issue.[116] We cannot institute capital punishment without similarly sentencing minorities to die in disproportionate numbers in our gas chambers and electric chairs.[117] We cannot abolish capital punishment without diluting whatever deterrent effect it may have in the minority communities that suffer a disproportionate share of our nation's violent crime.[118] We cannot prohibit, permit, or fund abortions without extending the costs and benefits of those decisions in a manner that has an integral impact on minority family structure.[119] We cannot even determine whether the first amendment protects "for sale" signs without affecting the patterns of residential segregation that exist in the United States.[120] If one doubts the pervasive ability of race to influence the resolution of issues that should properly have nothing whatsoever to do with race, one need only try to account for why the District of Columbia has been unable to escape its colonial status and achieve voting representation in Congress. No plausible explanation is possible without falling back on the factor of race to explain this aberration in democratic theory.[121]

It is difficult to contest the immanence of race in societal decision-making. At times, the role of race has been explicit, as in the eras of slavery, Jim Crow, and *de jure* segregation. More recently, the role of race has been implicit, with societal decisionmaking being based upon factors that correlate with race rather than on race itself. The result is the same, however, regardless of the route by which it is achieved. Racial minorities are systematically disadvantaged by majoritarian social policies that allocate societal resources to whites rather than to racial minorities. This is decidedly *not* race neutrality. It is racial discrimination pure and simple, and it continues to be racial discrimination whether it takes an explicit or a subtle form.

One could argue about the degree to which racial considerations consciously motivate the formulation of the social policies that have adversely affected racial minorities, but such arguments are likely to be unproductive. Chapter 4 has illustrated that it is always possible to deconstruct the distinction between the concepts of intent and effect in the context of disparate racial impact.[122] Even tolerance of uncertainty about the racially correlated consequences of social policies can be reconceptualized to constitute racially motivated societal decisionmaking.[123] Only a culture in which the issue of race never even entered the conscious contemplation of social policymakers could claim to be capable of colorblind race neutrality. That is not our culture. In the United States, most societal decisions have an appreciable impact on racially identifiable interests. And all of those decisions are race-conscious decisions.

Viewed as an outgrowth of our inevitably race-conscious culture, the Supreme Court's insistence on race neutrality becomes disquietingly suspicious. It ceases to resemble an admirable social panacea, but rather metastasizes into a virulent social malignancy. Because unspoken racial considerations will continue to motivate the manner in which major societal decisions are made, a judicial prohibition on explicitly race-conscious efforts to counteract that tacit race-consciousness serves only to protract the present allocation of resources—an allocation under which the majority benefits at the expense of racial minority interests. Stated more starkly, race is so intrinsic in our societal decisionmaking that the option of race neutrality is simply unavailable. Our only choice is between allocating a resource to the white majority or allocating it to a racial minority. When a resource is allocated to a racial minority, we call the process affirmative action. When that same resource is allocated to the white majority, we call it colorblind race neutrality. The only difference between the two, however, is the recipient of the resource. Both are equally race-conscious, but only affirmative action threatens the socio-economic status quo. When the Supreme Court opts for race neutrality, therefore, it is opting for continued racial discrimination in favor of whites and against racial minorities.

The problem can be illustrated by considering the affirmative action controversy that has arisen concerning the use of racial preferences as one of the criteria that are customarily used in the law school admissions process.[124] The controversy centers around the claim made by white applicants that they are sometimes denied admission in order to allocate seats to minority applicants who have lower grades or Law School Admission Test (LSAT) scores than the rejected white applicants.[125] In essence, the argument of the disappointed white applicants is that the law schools are using illegitimate, race-conscious affirmative action criteria rather than race-neutral, merits-based criteria in order to make admissions decisions. The law schools typically defend their affirmative action programs by emphasizing the need to compensate racial minorities for generations of past discrimination, and by highlighting the pedagogical benefits of diversity for white and minority students alike.[126] As has been noted, it would be pedagogically unsound to attempt case analysis of a decision about abortion or racial discrimination in the presence of white males alone.[127]

The problem with this challenge to affirmative action and with the conventional argument offered in its defense is that both accept the unstated premise that it is *possible* to make race-neutral law school admissions decisions in our contemporary cultural climate. Both positions assume that the "merits-based" criteria of grades and standardized test scores reflect something that exists independent of race. The positions differ only with respect to the legitimacy of departing from reliance on those race-neutral factors. In a multiracial admissions context, however, grades and test scores tend to be used as simply a proxy for race. Neither measures anything that is indigenous to successful legal practice, but both measure factors that correlate with race.

Grades are thought to be relevant to the law school admissions process because they predict future academic and professional success. However, the reasoning that supports these predictive claims is circular. The evidence of success on which that reasoning is based turns out to be directly dependent on, rather than independent from, the grades themselves. The suggestion that grades predict academic success comes close to being a truism. Grades do not so much predict as define academic success. Because academic success is itself judged by grades, and the honors that are derived from grades, the bare claim that grades predict academic success simply lacks content. To be coherent, the claim must be that grades earned in college will accurately predict grades earned law school. As an empirical matter, there is some correlation between college and law school grades, but the correlation coefficients are not high enough to generate much excitement.[128] Indeed, law school admissions officials appear to rely more heavily on standardized LSAT scores than upon college grades as a predictor of law school academic success precisely because LSAT scores are standardized rather than variable across undergraduate colleges.[129] In addition, the anecdotal evidence that exists concerning college luminaries who become pedestrian law students and mediocre college students who become law school successes is too plentiful to give the claim much intuitive appeal. Moreover, to the extent that a correlation between college and law school grades does exist, it still fails to establish that grades are in any sense an independent measure of academic success. It simply establishes the still-circular proposition that students who are good at getting grades in one context tend to be good at getting grades in another context. The number of not-so-bright students who receive high grades, as well as the number of obviously bright students who receive undistinguished grades, necessarily calls into question the validity of grades as a measure of intellectual ability.

In order to develop a noncircular justification for relying more heavily on college grades than upon other factors in making law school admissions decisions, one would have to establish that grades were good predictors of something other than future grades. One would have to establish that they correlated with an independent measure of professional success that existed outside of the grading context. Ironically, however, that is a showing that cannot be made, precisely because the traditional measures of professional success are also heavily dependent upon grades. One might initially be tempted to view judicial clerkships, academic appointments, or prestigious law firm affiliations as independent measures of professional success, but those positions are overwhelmingly awarded on the basis of grades. As a result, reliance on these positions as measures of professional success is as circular as reliance on grades themselves. Moreover, these positions are awarded on the basis of law school grades rather than college grades, thereby further attenuating any connection that exists between this measure of professional success and the grades that actually serve as the basis for law school admissions decisions. One can conclude from this analysis that grades have some correlation with other grades and with other factors that are themselves dependent upon grades, but one cannot justifiably conclude much of anything else. One certainly cannot conclude that grades are a more legitimate law school admissions criterion than diversity-related factors might be.

The same circularity problem arises in connection with efforts to justify the use of LSAT scores as an admissions criterion that should be favored over other possible criteria. However, the LSAT circularity reveals even more clearly how purportedly neutral selection criteria can mask majoritarian racial preferences. Like grades, LSAT scores are thought to be relevant to the law school admissions process because they too predict future academic and professional success. Although LSAT scores have proven to correlate with law school grades better than college grades do,[130] reliance on LSAT scores remains vulnerable to the problem that law school grades themselves have not been shown to correlate with any independent measure of professional success. If one strains to find a measure of professional success that is independent of LSAT scores, LSAT scores are likely to have no correlation—or even a negative correlation—with those independent measures. For example, if one were to focus on income earned as a lawyer as an independent measure of professional success, it seems intuitively unlikely that any strong correlation between LSAT scores and income would emerge. Many high-income lawyers derive their incomes from prestigious law firms that have hired them on the basis of their LSAT-correlated academic records. This deprives income of its independence as a measure of professional success for these lawyers. However, if one were to exclude prestigious law firm incomes from the sample and examine small firms or sole practitioners, whose incomes are not directly dependent upon their academic successes, it seems unlikely that any significant correlation between LSAT scores and income will be found. Moreover, an old adage declares that the "A" students will become law professors, the "B" students will become judges, and the "C" students will become rich. Assuming that LSAT scores correlate with grades, this adage suggests that the students with the highest LSAT scores will accept the lower-paying academic and judicial jobs, while the students with lower LSAT scores will engage in the more lucrative legal practices.

If professional success is gauged by the independent measure of cases won in court, it is again unlikely that any significant correlation between

LSAT scores and professional success will be found to exist. The lawyers who win the most cases in court are likely to be the lawyers who possess the most highly developed oral and dramatic skills with which to charm judges and mesmerize juries. These skills, however, are not tested on the LSAT because they are not relevant to the conception of legal practice that the LSAT is intended to foster. As a result, there is no reason to suspect that LSAT scores will correlate with these skills.

If professional success is defined in terms of the inclination and ability to help clients who most need the assistance of the legal system in order to secure food, shelter, and the other basic necessities of life, the cultural biases inherent in the LSAT will probably produce a negative correlation between LSAT scores and legal success. The LSAT has at times deemed mathematical aptitude to be relevant to high quality legal practice, and the current LSAT tests proficiency in solving logic puzzles.[131] However, I have yet to see a section of the LSAT that is designed to test for fluency in Spanish, familiarity with the technical deficiencies of various drug testing techniques, or familiarity with ghetto attitudes toward police authority, even though these areas of knowledge are crucial to certain minority conceptions of high quality legal practice.

Neither LSAT scores nor grades constitute independent measures of professional proficiency. They do not correlate with any neutral conception of high quality legal practice, but rather, they reflect a majoritarian preference about the shape that legal practice should take. This majoritarian conception of legal practice is far from preordained; it is subjective, highly contingent, and wholly normative. It is also far from being race-neutral. Although grades and LSAT scores do not correlate with any non-normative, merits-based conception of quality legal practice, they do by hypothesis correlate with race. That is why the white applicants who are disappointed by a law school's affirmative action programs choose to argue that diversity criteria should be subordinated to grades and LSAT scores in making admissions decisions. But all that they are really saying is that admissions standards should be used that favor the white majority rather than racial minorities in the allocation of the disputed law school seats. In the final analysis, those seats will either be given to whites or they will be given to racial minorities. Although the opponents of affirmative action would have us believe that an allocation to whites is an exercise of colorblind race neutrality, there is simply no way to allocate those societal resources in a race-neutral manner. Far from being race-neutral, a decision to rely on grades and LSAT scores rather than on affirmative action criteria would simply be racial discrimination in disguise.

It has always seemed curious to me that white opponents of racial affirmative action have been uncritical of affirmative action programs that are intended to favor alumni sons and daughters, even though alumni-related affirmative action deprives whites of many more seats in educational institutions than racial affirmative action does.[132] The absence of white opposition to geographical and athletic affirmative action programs is similarly puzzling. Unfortunately, the easiest way to account for this seemingly irrational behavior is to postulate that whites do not so much resent being deprived of societal resources as they resent being deprived of societal resources for the benefit of racial minorities. That postulate is, of course, consistent with the present thesis: race is such a potent force in contemporary culture that it cannot escape being a substantial factor in societal decisionmaking even with respect to issues that are seemingly unrelated to race.

Colorblind race neutrality can now be seen simply as code for white supremacy in the allocation of societal resources. Accordingly, the Supreme Court's preference for race neutrality over race consciousness in the formulation of race-related constitutional principles can be seen as Supreme Court complicity in discriminatory majoritarian desires. The Supreme Court has justified its preference for race neutrality by invoking the complex of connotations that surround our cultural preference for centralization over decentralization. That particular justification, however, has additional nonapparent majoritarian utility because it deters racial minorities themselves from pursuing the most promising strategies of resistance to majoritarian domination. Although the positive and negative connotations that contemporary culture has respectively attached to the concepts of centralization and decentralization serve to benefit the white majority, racial minorities would benefit from interchanging those connections.

Professor Peller has argued that the universalism, rational objectivity, and race neutrality that I have associated with centralization all contribute to an integrationist conception of race relations, under which the white majority and racial minorities coexist harmoniously as part of a single community characterized by mutual respect and racial tolerance.[133] The parochialism, irrational subjectivity, and racial bias that I have associated with decentralization contribute to a separatist conception of race relations, under which the disharmony that characterized the segregated South precludes mutual respect and racial tolerance.[134] However, just as the purported majoritarian preference for race neutrality masks an actual majoritarian desire for the race-conscious allocation of societal resources, the purported majoritarian preference for integrationism masks an actual majoritarian desire for separatism in the exercise of economic and political power. The most effective way for racial minorities to combat the pervasive majoritarian accumulation of societal power is to adopt the same separatist strategy that the majority used to acquire that power to begin with. The separatism that is relevant in the present context does not relate to physical separation. Rather, it relates to the cultural commitment to independence and self-sufficiency that the majority has used so successfully to resist the sharing of societal power with racial minorities. Although such a separatist strategy was embodied in the black nationalism and black power movements of the late 1960s and early 1970s, the white majority was successfully able to deflect those efforts at minority self-determination by relying on the rhetoric of integrationism to perpetuate majoritarian domination of racial minority interests.[135]

As Peller has demonstrated, the utopian rhetoric of integrationism successfully implicated racial minorities in the perpetuation of their own subordination. By accepting the majoritarian assertion that black nationalism was the analytical equivalent of the white separatism that spawned southern segregation, racial minorities were effectively taught to fear their own self-determination, believing that self-determination would both endorse the same separatist principles that had been responsible for past minority subordination and offend the integrationist principles that held the only hope of achieving durable racial equality.[136] The Supreme Court was particularly effective in disseminating this message to racial minorities through the vehicle of *Brown v. Board of Education*, which not only proclaimed the universalist benefits of integrationism but enticed minorities into believing that the Supreme Court would secure those benefits for them.[137] The majority did not emphasize, and racial minorities apparently did not notice, that the white majority had retained its separatist control over the political and economic power that is exercised in the United States even while eschewing the principle of separatism. Accordingly, racial minorities dutifully resisted the appeal of nationalist strategies for the advancement of minority interests.

The majoritarian underpinnings of integrationism have now become more visible as the rationally self-interested majoritarian preference for continued minority subordination has become more brazen. President Bush's successful political exploitation of latent white racial prejudices in his "Willie Horton" presidential campaign,[138] as well as the breadth of support for his politically expedient opposition to civil rights reform legislation,[139] has made it apparent that the national electorate no longer holds warm or cuddly feelings toward its minority competitors for societal resources. Moreover, the Supreme Court's doctrinally suspect assault on voluntary affirmative action has exposed the Court's own views about the desirability of genuine racial equality, revealing the Court to be simply a surreptitious agent for the advancement of majoritarian interests.[140] These majoritarian predispositions are not new; they are structural features of our constitutional form of government. However, postmodern analytical insights have made these structural features newly apparent, thereby providing racial minorities with a second opportunity to assert control over their own interests.

Once freed from universalist claims about the moral desirability of race neutrality and integrationism, racial minorities can unabashedly pursue the race-conscious strategy of nationalism in an effort to advance minority interests. The same deconstructive techniques that permit the analytical inversion of doctrinal hierarchies[141] also permits the inversion of the majoritarian cultural preference for centralization over decentralization. That preference is based upon the supposed association between centralization and the universalism, rational objectivity, and race neutrality that it connotes, with the goals of equality and racial justice. Decentralization, and the parochialism, irrational subjectivity, and racial bias that it connotes, is supposedly associated with inequality and racial prejudice. However, these associations can be easily interchanged.

Once centralization and its connotations are recognized to constitute mere camouflage for race-conscious majoritarian subordination, it is centralization that takes on the disfavored status in the hierarchy between centralization and decentralization. Universalism becomes a mere facade for what is actually a parochial majoritarian desire to subordinate racial minorities; rational objectivity becomes a facade for racist majoritarian passions that merely parade as detached, objective reason; and race neutrality becomes the facade for a doctrinal regime whose function is simply to perpetuate racial prejudice and discrimination. The centralized federal intervention that was initially thought to protect racial minorities from regional racial prejudice reemerges as an oppressive system of racial subordination that minorities lack the societal power to escape.

Once decentralization and its connotations are recognized to have been miscast as the villains in our ubiquitous racial conflicts, it is decentralization that actually merits the privileged status in the hierarchy between centralized and decentralized approaches to the problem of race relations. Parochialism becomes the honest recognition that adherence to local norms and values is the best that one can hope for in striving to engage in morally appropriate behavior; irrational subjectivity becomes the honest submission to felt notions of right and wrong that are often conveniently suppressed by expedient assertions of rational objectivity; and racial bias becomes the honest appreciation of cultural differences that must be accommodated rather than repressed in order to permit the eradication of racial prejudice and discrimination from contemporary culture. The decentralization of race relations that was initially thought to subject racial minorities to regional racial prejudice reemerges as the most promising minority strategy for escaping the hardships of centralized racial oppression.

Because the hierarchy between centralization and decentralization can always be inverted, there is no analytically sound manner in which racial minorities can determine the strategy that will best promote the objective of racial justice. Minorities will have to select the strategy that resonates best for them in those decisional spheres that supersede the pre-postmodern sphere in which race relations analysis has been conducted to date. In those superseding spheres, the nationalist self-determination that racial minorities have yet to experience in any meaningful way is likely to have considerably more appeal than the integrationism that has remained for so long a hollow and unfulfilled promise.

Nationalism is a very dynamic form of group identification that can induce interests groups to engage in seemingly irrational behavior. In geopolitical contexts, nationalism has proven to be a uniquely potent source of ideological motivation. The invocation of nationalist icons, such as "traditional American values" or our "vital national interests," can be used to mobilize support for political agendas that range from civil rights to foreign military intervention. President Bush's stated opposition to affirmative action has been based upon its asserted conflict with the ideals of merit and individual achievement—ideals that, of course, are core aspects of "traditional American values."[142] President Bush's stated reason for waging war against Iraq—something that seems to defy all efforts at rational justification—was similarly rooted in nationalism. Although he has been inconsistent about the details, the President chose to assert that the war was justified by the need to eliminate the Iraqi threat to our "vital national interests."[143] Even skeptical commentators intent on looking behind the President's rhetoric were forced to fall back on equally nationalist explanations of our military involvement: the most plausible account is that the war was fought in order to reassert American military superiority in a world that had witnessed the decline of American economic superiority.[144] In World War II, nationalistic passions ran so high that they not only caused the United States to intern Japanese-American citizens,[145] but they also caused the United States to become the only nation on earth ever to drop an atomic bomb on human beings. Apparently, this was done for no reason other than to celebrate nationalistic arrogance.[146] The recent disintegration of the Soviet empire and of the Soviet Union itself has generated nationalistic conflicts in eastern Europe and in the old Soviet republics that are as violent as they are difficult to comprehend.[147] The intractable Arab-Israeli conflict in the Middle East[148] and the equally intractable Catholic-Protestant conflict in Northern Ireland[149] have both been fueled by intensely nationalistic feelings of group identification and intergroup hostility. In South Africa, the majority black nation is not only struggling to wrest economic and political control from the minority white nation, but the black tribal nations are even fighting among themselves for future control of the country's resources.[150]

Nationalism is not a pretty thing. It is an extremely potent force, and it is extremely irrational. It is also dependent upon vehement acquiescence in the transcendent importance of cultural distinctions that are, at bottom, extremely arbitrary. Nationalism is the force that prompts nations to wage war against each other, that prompts religions to persecute each other, and that prompts races to discriminate against each other, all for reasons that stubbornly resist legitimate explanation. In the context of race relations, nationalism is simply racism. It is a selfish concern with the advancement of one's own interests over the interests of another solely because of one's racial group identification. It is what the white majority in the United States has been practicing since the founding of the nation, and it is what I predict racial minorities in the United States will eventually begin to practice as the strategy for escaping majoritarian subordination. Nationalism is not nice, but it is too potent a force for racial minorities to continue to ignore. In a classic race to the bottom, both the white majority *and* racial minorities will eventually become engaged in the pursuit of societal goals that are single-mindedly self-concerned. And this, ironically, will be the manner in which contemporary culture is finally able to demonstrate the fact of racial equality in the United States.

The Supreme Court's centralization of the law of affirmative action has disadvantaged racial minorities in concrete ways by requiring them to compete for majoritarian concessions in the national political arena where they are rarely likely to prevail, rather than in local arenas where they would often possess the power to prevail. More subtly, and more surreptitiously, the Supreme Court's centralization of affirmative action has helped to indoctrinate racial minorities into a value system that promotes the illusion of colorblind race neutrality over the objective of race-conscious self-determination. The brilliance of this system is not that it benefits the white majority by permitting it to amass a disproportionate share of societal resources. Rather, the brilliance of the system is that it implicates racial minorities in their own subordination by effectively precluding minority pursuit of nationalist strategies—the strategies that offer the greatest promise of promoting racial equality. As racial minorities come to recognize the ingenious nature of the system that has oppressed them, they will learn to adopt the nationalist tactics of their oppressors. But that will, at best, constitute a bittersweet victory. The Supreme Court's centralization of the law of affirmative action has incriminated the Court in this unfortunate form of racial debasement. But as invidious as the Supreme Court's involvement has been, it is not as invidious as the practice of legitimating counterproductive racial stereotypes in which the Supreme Court has also engaged.

CHAPTER 9

Legitimation

Racial minorities in the United States have suffered centuries of brutal inequality with remarkable quiescence. Slave rebellions were rare; race riots have been few and far between; and concerted minority political action has remained largely untried. Even recent minority political victories in majority voting districts have been unsuccessful at securing true minority participation in the political process, because the victorious minority candidates have had to strip their candidacies of anything other than diluted concern for racial issues in order to make themselves acceptable to majority voters.[1] As Chapter 7 has explained, minorities have become dependent upon the Supreme Court rather than upon themselves for the education of minority children in particular, and for normative and aspirational guidance in general. As Chapter 8 has explained, minorities have acquiesced in the Supreme Court's vision of colorblind race neutrality, even though that vision simply masks a system of white supremacy in the allocation of societal resources. One might well wonder why American racial minorities have been so submissive for so long. The answer is, in part at least, because American racial minorities—like the majority itself—have come to believe in the inevitability of the present legal system. This belief, however, does not derive from its accuracy; rather it derives from the manner in which the fundamental assumptions of the legal system have been legitimated. The process of legitimation is a process through which an unstated assumption comes to be accepted without scrutiny because our analytical attention has been diverted from the assumption itself to some controversy whose existence presupposes the validity of the assumption. Like the fabled post-hypnotic suggestion, a legitimated assumption derives its power from our inattention to its operation.

The Supreme Court has been especially accomplished at legitimating the assumptions on which the purported race neutrality of our legal system rests. In particular, the Court has legitimated three assumptions that account for the continued willingness of the majority to inflict, and racial minorities to tolerate, the inequalities that minorities suffer. First, the Court has legitimated the assumption that there exists a category of fundamental minority rights that the majority cannot properly infringe. Second, the Court has legitimated the assumption that the Supreme Court is the societal institution that has the final say about the content of those rights. Third, the Court has legitimated the assumption that racial minorities cannot properly make demands on the majority that exceed the scope of those judicially defined rights. This final assumption carries with it certain connotations about the industrious beneficence of the majority, as well as the indolent ingratitude of racial minorities, that further reinforce the acceptability of the present distribution of societal power and resources. If scrutinized, it is likely that these legitimated assumptions would become unacceptable, and that racial minorities would assert claims for racial equality with unprecedented vigor. The Supreme Court, however, is very good at its job, and the legitimated assumptions threaten to persist indefinitely.

Majoritarian Legitimation

One of the most significant majoritarian functions that the Supreme Court serves is the function of legitimating counterproductive assumptions about the legal system that underlie the traditional model of judicial review. The process of legitimation is the process by which a social practice or status comes to be viewed as appropriate under a set of generally agreed-upon governing criteria.[2] For example, when a criminal defendant is convicted after a fair trial, the conviction is viewed as legitimate, even if the jury was unknowingly mistaken in its conclusion about the defendant's guilt. Because we realize that ultimate accuracy is elusive, we are forced to settle for procedural regularity, seasoned with good faith and best efforts, as the basis for judging the appropriateness of a criminal conviction. The criteria governing the legitimacy of the criminal justice system emanate from a shared moral theory whose tenets are difficult to specify with precision. Despite this difficulty of precise specification, however, we tend to view the governing criteria as satisfied by the good-faith procedural regularity on which the criminal justice system insists. Indeed, it is precisely the process of legitimation that permits us to view the criminal justice system as morally appropriate even though we cannot articulate the governing criteria, and even though more careful scrutiny would almost certainly leave us skeptical about its legitimacy.[3]

The process of legitimation works best when its operation is undetected, because the results of the process can then be transmitted without ever being subjected to scrutiny. Consider the phenomenon of hypnosis. The fabled post-hypnotic suggestion derives its power from the amnesia that the hypnotist induces concerning the hypnotic process. Because the subject of the hypnosis is unaware of the process by which his or her hypnotically influenced beliefs were acquired, the subject accepts those beliefs with a degree of unthinking conviction that would never be possible if the actual origin of those beliefs were to become known. Similarly, the legitimation process owes its effectiveness to the surreptitious nature of its operation. Although my psychiatrist friends insist that the phenomenon of hypnosis is much more complex than the process I have described, my use of hypnosis in the present context is intended to be metaphorical rather than technically precise.

The manner by which the legitimation process evades detection is through the technique of distraction. Arguments always rest upon underlying assumptions. When one's analytical attention is focused on the intricacies of an argument, however, the underlying assumptions on which the argument rests may completely escape scrutiny. This is particularly true where the argument concerns a controversial topic. The controversy itself serves to increase the level of distraction, thereby also increasing the likelihood that underlying assumptions will be overlooked. The legitimating effect of rape laws provides a comprehensible example. Professors Dworkin and MacKinnon have argued that rape laws legitimate assumptions about women that reinforce their status as objects of male sexual exploitation.[4] While vigorous arguments are exchanged concerning the meaning of controversial issues such as the nature and scope of a woman's consent, the underlying assumption that male-drafted rape laws can properly determine the circumstances under which women can be forced to submit to sexual intercourse at the behest of men is simply accepted without scrutiny. The distraction legitimates the assumption by causing the assumption to be accepted without scrutiny. If the point seems trivial or artificial, consider that most of us have been distracted from the realization that the legal system *does* permit men to engage in forcible intercourse with women. As a *de jure* matter, forcible intercourse is permitted by husbands, who in most jurisdictions lack the legal capacity to commit rape.[5] As a *de facto* matter, forcible intercourse is permitted by social acquaintances, against whom rape convictions are very difficult to obtain.[6]

Simplistic versions of legitimation theory depict legitimation as a tool of the elites in power to trick the masses into permitting them to remain in power. For the same reasons that legal doctrine cannot be counted on to generate only one predictable result to the exclusion of contradictory results,[7] legitimation doctrine—assumptions about which surreptitious activities will produce which societal outcomes—cannot be counted on to generate only one predictable result either. Accordingly, descriptions of the legitimation process as conspiratorially instrumental do not have much appeal.[8]

A more sophisticated version of legitimation theory depicts legitimation as the process by which beneficiaries of the present distribution of societal resources seek to convince those who do not benefit that the social and legal systems responsible for the present distribution are basically fair and should not be replaced. Because the system is fair rather than capricious, redistribution of resources is possible within the system as a reward to those who comply with the system's norms. This theory is less crass, but it is still too conspiratorial to have ultimate appeal.[9]

A more appealing depiction of legitimation is as an essentially passive process that perpetuates the status quo largely through inertia. Although the assumptions underlying the current system could be easily scrutinized and the unacceptable assumptions rejected if anyone ever thought to scrutinize and reject them, typically no one ever does. Use of the system reinforces itself because its underlying assumptions are too commonplace to be questioned before they are used, and each use further increases the strength of the assumptions so that subsequent questioning becomes progressively less likely. Moreover, those who possess societal power are as captive to the unquestioned assumptions as those against whom societal power is exercised. Rather than creating an instrumental threat, the process of legitimation more subtly threatens the appropriateness of the ways in which we conceptualize and perceive.[10]

The traditional model of judicial review legitimates unhealthy assumptions governing the ways in which the majority thinks about racial minorities, as well as the ways in which racial minorities think about themselves.[11] The process of Supreme Court adjudication is a heavily publicized distraction that focuses national attention on the cases that are argued before the Court each Term. For lawyers, attention is focused on the complex and esoteric doctrinal issues to which the bulk of the adjudicatory process is directed. For nonlawyers, attention is focused on the controversial social issues that will be affected by the Court's decisions, as those decisions and their likely impact are popularized in the national press. For both, analytical attention is successfully deflected from important assumptions that underlie the concept of countermajoritarian judicial review. The traditional model rests on three assumptions that are necessary to the coherence of countermajoritarian review. First, it assumes the existence of a category of individual or substantive rights that the majority cannot legitimately abrogate. Second, it assumes that the Supreme Court can legitimately resolve ambiguities that inhere in the definitions of those rights. Third, it assumes that minorities cannot legitimately make demands on the majority that exceed the scope of those rights, because those additional demands would interfere with the rights of the majority. The traditional model legitimates these assumptions by placing them beyond active scrutiny. However, active scrutiny could well cause those assumptions to be rejected.

Countermajoritarian review depends upon the existence of substantive rights because without such rights, judicial invalidation of majoritarian enactments would be undemocratic.[12] For over a decade, commentators along the periphery of mainstream legal scholarship have in fact attempted to subject the substantive rights assumption to closer scrutiny through what has come to be known as "the critique of rights." Stated succinctly, the critique of rights asserts that a concept of rights can never protect a fundamental interest from political abridgement, because the contours of the fundamental interest can never be articulated in a manner that is sufficiently determinate to prevent its sacrifice for reasons of political expediency. Just as the doctrinal indeterminacy discussed in Part I undermines the traditional model of judicial review, the indeterminacy inherent in efforts to define fundamental rights undermines the ability of a political system to respect those rights in troublesome cases. Moreover, a rights-based approach to the protection of fundamental interests is counterproductive, because it legitimates the unstated assumptions on which particular claims of right necessarily rest, in a way that permits those assumptions to be used against the very party asserting the claim of right. Finally, by limiting the scope of the discourse used to discuss social problems, rights rhetoric inhibits the imagination of new ways in which social problems and solutions can be conceptualized.[13]

Despite peripheral adherence to the critique of rights, it remains the case that the substantive rights assumption has received little scrutiny by mainstream legal scholars and virtually no scrutiny by anyone outside the fields of theoretical academics to which rights theory is directly relevant. Although it is possible for a once-unquestioned assumption to be accepted rather than rejected after subsequent scrutiny, the substantive rights assumption does not seem to fit into this category. I suspect that most adherents to substantive rights theory could neither outline the basic critique of rights nor explain why they had chosen to reject the critique. These are things that one would expect adherents to be able to do if they had rejected the critique and accepted the substantive rights assumption after serious scrutiny.

Professor Carrington, who has in a sense become the victim of frustrations both felt and generated by the critical legal studies movement,[14] is often accused of having misunderstood the arguments that he has rejected.[15] Whether or not this is true with respect to Professor Carrington, the mere reflex acceptance of an assumption after only nominal scrutiny would not be sufficient to avoid the dangers associated with the process of legitimation. It is also true, however, that some of the commentators who have expressed skepticism about the critique of rights have a very sophisticated understanding of the critique.[16] Nevertheless, it seems that the continued allure of substantive rights theory is attributable more to the process of legitimation than to its acceptance after scrutiny.

If the substantive rights assumption were subjected to serious scrutiny, it is unlikely that it could survive. It would be rejected for the same fundamental reason that Part I rejected the possibility of a countermajoritarian judicial capability. It is not possible to define a substantive right in a way that precludes the possibility of majoritarian abrogation through judicial interpretation. As a result, a substantive right can only *reflect* a judicial decision about how a particular dispute should properly be resolved; it cannot *determine* that decision.

It is easy to understand why the majority would acquiesce in the substantive rights assumption without scrutiny. The history of Supreme Court judicial review indicates that judicial recognition of substantive rights has typically served to advance majoritarian interests at the expense of the minority.[17] It is more difficult to understand why minorities themselves have not been more receptive to the invitation to rethink rights. A few minority commentators now seem skeptical of the substantive rights assumption.[18] However, most minority commentators sympathize with the critique of rights to some degree, but caution against wholesale rejection of the one concept that they believe has permitted minorities to secure the few gains that have been secured to date.[19] Still other minority commentators strenuously defend the rights-based system, even against the few minority challenges that have been made to the substantive rights assumption. They advocate reform but not abandonment of the present system.[20] The fact that most members of racial minority groups embrace the concept of substantive rights, and resist efforts to abandon that concept with varying degrees of vigor, reveals how well the Supreme Court adjudicatory process has legitimated the substantive rights assumption.

The second assumption that the traditional model of judicial review legitimates is the assumption that ambiguities in the nature and scope of substantive rights are to be resolved through exposition by the Supreme Court. Once again, critical scrutiny could well cause that exposition assumption to be rejected. If a concept of substantive rights were deemed to be desirable, political enforcement of those rights through the structural safeguards established by the framers would seem to be more desirable than Supreme Court enforcement.[21] The Supreme Court is mostly white and mostly male, and as an institution it is mostly nonresponsive to fresh or innovative political thinking.[22] Moreover, its first two efforts to protect substantive rights from federal majoritarian abrogation produced *Marbury*[23] and *Dred Scott*.[24] There may have been a lesson in that. Part I of this book argues at length that the inevitable political biases and predispositions of the homogeneous Supreme Court cannot successfully be prevented from dominating the judicial decisionmaking process. As a result, scrutiny of the exposition assumption would be unlikely to result in continued acceptance of that assumption. Once again, it is easy to understand why the majority, which has typically benefitted from Supreme Court control over rights, would feel no pressing need to question the assumed appropriateness of that control. But again, even minorities often feel compelled to defend the Court against charges of racial bias or insensitivity.[25] And again, this illustrates the power of the legitimation phenomenon.

The third assumption legitimated by the traditional model is that minorities are not entitled to any more than what the Supreme Court gives them in the process of protecting their substantive rights. Because the discrete and insular nature of racial minorities renders them unable to participate effectively in the political process, the political process need not take their desires seriously. Moreover, because the Supreme Court is the specialist when it comes to determining what degree of majority deference to minority interests is appropriate, the representative branches are under no obligation to make more concessions to minorities than the Court requires them to make. As a result, any additional concessions that the political process does choose to make are gifts, emanating from majoritarian generosity, for which minorities should be grateful. However, if the representative branches become too generous and make concessions that the Court deems inappropriate, the Court itself will have to invalidate those concessions in order to prevent abrogation of the rights of members of the *majority* race. This judicial protection of majority rights is something about which racial minorities cannot complain because minorities themselves have forcefully insisted on Supreme Court protection of substantive rights.

If scrutinized, the assumption that Supreme Court concessions should constitute a ceiling on the benefits to which minorities are legitimately entitled would almost certainly be rejected. The fourteenth amendment was enacted in order to authorize legislative—not judicial—protection of minority rights, thereby making it more than a little ironic for the Court to invalidate majoritarian enactments under the fourteenth amendment in order to protect majority rights.[26] In addition, for all of the reasons that the Court proved to be a dubious expositor of substantive rights, it is also a dubious arbiter of disputes over the proper allocation of societal resources. The allocation issue is inherently political. One particular resolution cannot be more "legitimate" than another. Different resolutions simply represent different outcomes in a process of pluralist political negotiations. For the same reason, it makes little sense to view a concession secured through the pluralist negotiation process as a gift. The concession evidences no generosity, it merely reflects the point along a continuum at which particular political interests intersect.

The three assumptions legitimated by the traditional model of judicial review convey an artificial impression of the legal system. However, those assumptions also combine to project an invidious image of racial minorities that is far more troubling. As envisioned by the traditional model, racial minorities are not capable of protecting their own interests through the pluralist political process. Rather, their welfare derives from the solicitude of the Supreme Court, whose dependents they seem destined to remain.[27] Although not able to participate unaided in the political process, racial minorities nevertheless do make occasional attempts to get more than they are legally entitled to by appealing to the generosity of the representative branches. However, because the majority is in fact generous, minority requests for assistance are often granted. Racial minorities should be grateful for the protection that they have received from the Court, and for the consideration shown them by the majoritarian branches. Rather than demonstrating their gratitude, however, minorities often appear unsatisfied, unappreciative, and shameless in their perpetual ability to ask for yet another majoritarian concession.

That this legitimated vision constitutes a widely shared majoritarian view of racial minorities is unfortunate. That it also constitutes a widely shared minority view is tragic.

In this regard, perhaps the most serious danger to racial minority interests that is posed by the phenomenon of legitimation is that racial minorities will adopt the white majority as their reference group and will advance the interests of the majority at the expense of their own minority interests. This danger is more than theoretical. There have always, of course, been racial minority group members who have acquiesced in white definitions of appropriate social thought and behavior because the hegemonic capabilities of the white majority have left them with little alternative. Recently, however, some racial minority group members have *elected* to embrace the assumptions about race and race neutrality that have been legitimated by the white majority.

The new wave of minority neoconservatives that includes Stephen Carter,[28] Dinesh D'Souza,[29] Randall Kennedy,[30] Glen Loury,[31] Thomas Sowell,[32] Shelby Steele,[33] and Clarence Thomas[34] potentially harms racial minority interests in a number of ways. The absence of these neoconservatives from the struggle to reach beyond the legitimated conceptions of merit and race neutrality that have been used so successfully to subordinate racial minorities deprives that struggle of the increased skill and solidarity that it would derive from the presence of those talented individuals. In addition, minority neoconservatives almost certainly provide reassurance to the white majority by blunting the force of the more radical minority challenges that have recently been brought to bear upon the legitimated concepts of merit and neutrality. Moreover, because the defection of the minority neoconservatives has been rewarded by the bestowal of enhanced prestige from the white institutions with which the neoconservatives are associated, the efficacy of the existing system of rewards and punishments has undoubtedly been reinforced in a way that will facilitate the majoritarian seduction of future minority talent.

However, as Professor Delgado has emphasized, many of the minority neoconservatives have refused to submit to at least some of the assumptions concerning race that have been legitimated by the white majority.[35] Most notably, this refusal has encompassed serious skepticism about the continued viability of Warren Court liberalism and traditional civil rights approaches for the resolution of race-relations problems confronting the present generation of racial minorities.[36] In addition, the minority neoconservatives may share with the more radical race theorists a belief in the desirability of viewing pertinent realities as contingent social constructs, rather than as the more tangible and universal structures suggested by the white majority through its essentialist legitimation.[37] If there is a deep congruence of concern and epistemological perspective hidden beneath the doctrinal differences that exist between radical and neoconservative racial minority group members, that congruence may well be accompanied by the potential for an alliance so substantial that it will actually advance minority political power and self-determination against the wishes of the white majority. Whether the minority neoconservatives turn out to be an important catalyst in the quest for minority self-determination, or simply foot soldiers in the war of white legitimation, the legitimation phenomenon will nevertheless retain one feature that makes it particularly pernicious.

The Danger of Legitimation

At the close of a book of this type, it would be customary to emphasize that the way to escape the legitimated assumptions of the traditional model, as well as the unfortunate vision of minorities that those assumptions convey, is for minorities to embrace a political model of the Supreme Court. If the Supreme Court adjudicatory process can be viewed as simply one aspect of the larger political process, the assumptions underlying the traditional model will no longer be legitimated by minority use of the Supreme Court to advance minority interests. Rather, political use of the Court will constitute an act of minority self-determination, not an act of continued dependency. Moreover, minorities will finally have learned to place their faith in the pluralist branches of government that are institutionally capable of respecting their interests, rather than the one branch whose design compels it to retard recognition of minority claims of entitlement.

The reason that I am unable to endorse the traditional ending is that, in the present context, it is highly problematic. Political use of the Supreme Court will legitimate the assumptions underlying the traditional model as much as they are legitimated by purported countermajoritarian use. In order to be effective, political users of the Supreme Court will still have to be good litigators. They will have to invoke precedents in their briefs and pay homage to the justices in their oral arguments. Moreover, because the justices themselves will continue to adhere to the traditional model, minority advocates will also have to rely upon rights rhetoric in order to formulate winning arguments. This means that minority litigators will not only have to employ the traditional mechanisms of Supreme Court review, but they will have to feign allegiance to the traditional model as well. From the outside, political and traditional uses of the Supreme Court will look precisely the same. As a result, political use of the Court by racial minorities will do nothing to undermine the strength of legitimated assumptions in the minds of the majority. Rather, it will simply constitute additional use of the Court that will further reinforce the legitimated assumptions.

The only hope is that minorities themselves will attribute a different significance to Supreme Court litigation. However, the traditional model is deeply ingrained. The strength of that model can be experienced simply by trying to picture an acceptable social order that does not incorporate a functioning concept of rights. Without considerable practice, most members of a liberal society find it difficult even to imagine, let alone favor, such a social order. Moreover, the strength of the traditional model is ingrained in minority minds just as it is in the minds of the majority. In fact, the legitimation process has been so successful that minorities may find it even more difficult than the majority to relinquish that model. It seems that very few left-oriented political radicals are minority group members. Moreover, the dissonance generated by minority efforts to feign sympathy for countermajoritarian review while believing that the process is only political is likely to be at least substantial, if not overwhelming. Accordingly, attempted political use of the Court will pose a constant threat, even for minorities, of regression to the traditional model.

Rather than offering a prescription for remedial action, recognition of the countermajoritarian fallacy simply constitutes a cause for despair. Because Supreme Court review cannot successfully be avoided, minorities have no alternative but to participate in a process of judicial review that reinforces the traditional model. And they must do so even though the traditional model consigns them to a role of continual Supreme Court dependency. Ironically, it is as if the very structure of American constitutional government, dedicating an entire branch to the protection of minority rights, was designed in a way that would ensure ultimate majoritarian control over minority interests and preclude racial minorities from ever securing the capacity for self-determination. The truly terrifying truth that is legitimated by the Supreme Court's guarantee of countermajoritarian judicial review is that the Court's protection of racial minority interests appears to be perpetual. What an ingenious constitutional scheme.

CHAPTER 10

Summary and Conclusion

For racial minorities, judicial review has proven to be more of a curse than a blessing. Rather than protecting racial minority interests from the tyranny of the majority, the Supreme Court has done just the opposite. It has protected the majority from claims of equality by racial minorities. During the early history of the Supreme Court, the Court was fairly explicit in its sacrifice of minority interests for majoritarian gain. Whether the Court was abandoning the Cherokee Tribe in the face of majoritarian hostility as it did in *Cherokee Nation v. State of Georgia*,[1] denying citizenship to blacks in gratuitously demeaning terms as it did in *Dred Scott*,[2] invalidating Reconstruction civil rights legislation as it did in *The Civil Rights Cases*,[3] or proclaiming the virtues of *de jure* segregation as it did in *Plessy*,[4] the nineteenth-century Supreme Court was fairly transparent in the implementation of its mission to protect white majority interests. In the post-*Brown* twentieth century, the Court has been more opaque in the implementation of its mission, but the mission has remained the same. Racial minority interests have still been sacrificed to majoritarian desires, but the doctrinal mechanisms on which the Court has relied to effect the sacrifice have been more sophisticated, lurking in the interstices of complex and esoteric constitutional rules. The Court has even mastered the extremely sophisticated strategy of dressing minority losses in the attire of minority gains when it serves majoritarian ends to grant such apparent concessions, as the Court did in *Brown v. Board of Education*.[5] The structural reasons for which the Court is destined to serve majoritarian rather than countermajoritarian ends have been discussed in Part I, and they are summarized below. The ways in which the Court's veiled majoritarianism have contributed to the perpetuation of minority subordination in contemporary culture have been discussed in Part II, and they too are summarized below. Despite the sense of hopelessness that continued Supreme Court "protection" portends, all of this suggests a rather intriguing conclusion for racial minorities who are seemingly trapped in the predicament of judicial review. The efficacy of this conclusion, however, depends upon a subtle appreciation of the precise locus of the contest that presently exists between the Supreme Court and racial minorities in America.

Summary of Part I

Part I of this book has described how Supreme Court adjudication fails to serve the countermajoritarian judicial function that is traditionally ascribed to it. The framers initially designed a system of government in which individual liberty and property rights were to be protected by the political safeguards of federalism and separation of powers. During the New Deal, however, those safeguards were largely eviscerated, in accordance with majoritarian political preferences. As a result, the task of protecting individual rights has fallen to the Supreme Court. Under the *Marbury*-based traditional model of judicial review, the Court is an appropriate guardian of individual rights because it possesses institutional advantages over the representative branches that promote sensitivity to politically impotent interests. Because of this sensitivity, the Court is able to honor rights that an unconstrained political branch of government would prefer to exploit for majoritarian purposes. The rights of racial minorities, like the rights of individuals, are subject to similar majoritarian exploitation because of the relative political powerlessness that racial minorities have historically been forced to endure. Accordingly, the traditional model of judicial review requires the Court to protect the interests of racial minorities from majoritarian abrogation, just as it requires the Court to protect the rights of individuals. Under the traditional model, the ability of the Supreme Court to operate in a countermajoritarian manner is essential. Although the Court is commonly perceived to be performing its prophylactic function in an acceptable manner, the Court in fact does not possess the countermajoritarian capacity that the traditional model attributes to it. Moreover, the Court not only lacks the ability to serve as a guardian against majority preferences, it actually advances those preferences through its adjudications.

The Supreme Court as currently conceived cannot possess the countermajoritarian capacity required for traditional judicial review because the membership of the Court consists of socialized justices who possess the values and predispositions of the same elite political majority that controls the representative branches. As a statistical matter, therefore, those majoritarian-influenced jurists will exercise judicial discretion in the same way that the members of the representative branches exercise political discretion, unless unique features of the judicial process successfully constrain the exercise of judicial discretion. Although both formal and operational safeguards have been built into the judicial process in order to guarantee its countermajoritarian capabilities, those safeguards are ineffective.

The formal safeguards of life tenure and salary protection are designed to protect the judiciary from overt political pressures that might be exerted by the representative branches in order to affect the outcome of particular cases. It is unlikely that these safeguards are effective in attaining this limited objective, but more important, they are not even addressed to the majoritarian influences that the process of socialization has exerted over judicial attitudes and values. The operational safeguard of principled adjudication, which arguably *is* addressed to the problem of socialized judicial preferences, cannot ultimately serve the desired insulating function, because the legal principles on which the adjudicatory process relies themselves depend upon unconstrained discretionary input in order to derive their operative meanings.

Many legal principles expressly incorporate majoritarian preferences into their meanings, because the governing legal standard is defined to coincide with whatever meaning a majoritarian branch has given it. More subtly, the same result is often accomplished through deferential standards of review, which permit majoritarian preferences to govern the content of a principle because the Court will not intervene to alter its majoritarian meaning. Although not all legal principles incorporate majoritarian preferences into their meanings, it is the Supreme Court that must decide which principles do and which do not. This decision requires an act of judicial discretion, and it poses all of the dangers associated with the exercise of such discretion.

Even when a legal principle does not itself incorporate majoritarian preferences into its meaning, the dangers of majoritarian influence remain, because there are two additional aspects of the adjudicatory process from which judicial discretion cannot be eliminated. The Court must identify the legal principle that controls resolution of a particular case, and it must apply that principle to the facts of the case. Both of these activities ultimately rest upon purely discretionary determinations.

In order to identify a governing principle of law, the Court must choose between the competing principles that are potentially applicable. The Court's decided cases reveal that identification of the governing legal principle is largely unconstrained. The arguments favoring choice of one potential principle are likely to be as strong as the arguments favoring another, thereby giving the Court little guidance in selecting among the competitors. Moreover, provisions of law that make a particular principle expressly applicable are often honored by the Court, but they are also often ignored. Even when the Court's own precedents require application of a principle, the precedents fail to provide effective constraint, because under the doctrine of stare decisis, the Court's own precedents can always be overruled. In addition, the Court can rely upon legal fictions to circumvent an explicitly applicable principle while pretending that the principle is actually being applied. Not even the fundamental nature of the case at issue can be relied upon to ensure that the Court will select the governing principle designed for cases of that type, because characterizing the nature of a case is itself a highly discretionary activity.

Once a governing principle has been selected, application of that principle to the facts of a particular case also requires heavy reliance on judicial discretion. Legal principles contain inevitable ambiguities that make them vulnerable to deconstruction. That is, legal principles can be detached from the policy objectives with which they are initially thought to be associated and then reattached to conflicting policy objectives. As a result, a single legal principle can be shown to generate contradictory outcomes. This makes it unclear which application of a principle best serves the policy functions for which the principle was adopted. Again, the only way to choose between competing applications is through the unconstrained exercise of judicial discretion. Not surprisingly, the race cases in which the Supreme Court has applied particular principles of law exhibit a notable lack of consistency when examined from a policy perspective.

If the present thesis concerning the necessary correspondence between majoritarian and countermajoritarian dispositions of minority interests is correct, one would expect the Supreme Court to preserve for itself opportunities to submit to majoritarian desires. Whether done intentionally or unconsciously, the formulation of doctrinal rules whose applications require significant amounts of judicial discretion has ensured the continued presence of enough doctrinal latitude for majoritarian influences to operate effectively within the judicial process. Without imputing improper motives to the Court, it is sufficient to note that if one were to design a sophisticated judicial system that would optimize the protection of majority interests in the face of minority demands for better treatment, it would look very much like our present judicial system. Accordingly, it is unrealistic to conceive of the Supreme Court as anything other than a veiled majoritarian institution. And because it is a majoritarian institution, one of the primary tasks that has tacitly been assigned to the Supreme Court is to effectuate the majoritarian preference for the continued subordination of racial minorities.

Summary of Part II

Part II of this book has described how the Supreme Court developed the legal doctrines that govern race relations in a way that permits the subtle perpetuation of minority subordination. Because the Supreme Court operates in a veiled majoritarian manner, racial minorities could rationally prefer the overt political process to the Supreme Court adjudicatory process as the most promising means for advancing racial minority interests. The process of positive politics is pure in the sense that it purports to be nothing more than what it is—a process for generating outcomes in a pluralist political environment. Unlike the process of Supreme Court adjudication, which purports to have normative content that places it above the realm of mere crass political exchange, the positive political process has no doctrinal pretensions behind which the majority can hide as it extracts resources from racial minorities.

Contemporary racial minorities possess a degree of political power that enables them to operate effectively in the pluralist political process. By pooling their political resources, individual minority groups can increase their inherent political strength. Minorities can further enhance their political strength by forming political coalitions with sympathetic majority interest groups on both short and long term bases. The fact that racial minority interests have historically fared better before the representative branches of government than before the Supreme Court not only illustrates the viability of such a political strategy, but suggests that the simplicity of the overt political process is more advantageous to minorities than the complexities of Supreme Court politics.

Because life tenure gives Supreme Court justices longer terms of office than the terms held by members of the representative branches, the Supreme Court tends to be an inherently conservative proponent of the status quo, rather than a proponent of the social progress that is required for the advancement of racial minority interests. Nevertheless, the nature of the American legal system is such that minorities do not have the option of avoiding the Supreme Court in favor of ordinary politics. Minorities will have to appear before the Court in order to implement the gains that they secure through the overt political process, and to defend those gains when they are challenged by disappointed members of the white majority. As a result, racial minority interests cannot escape the protective custody of the Supreme Court.

The fact that the Supreme Court will inevitably be involved in the formulation of social policies that affect racial minority interests means that minority interests will be subject to surreptitious sacrifice for the benefit of the white majority. There are three ways in which the Supreme Court places minorities at a systemic disadvantage in their quest to secure racial justice. The first is by promoting continued belief in the counter-majoritarian model of judicial review, which has lulled racial minorities into a dependency relationship with the Supreme Court under which minorities have come to rely on judicial review rather than on minority political strength for the protection of minority interests. The second is by centralizing the law of affirmative action in a way that makes it difficult for minorities to capitalize on the local political power that they do possess. The third is by legitimating a set of counterproductive assumptions about the operation of the legal system, and the worth of racial minorities, that can reduce the will of even minorities themselves to achieve equal status with whites.

The first way in which the Supreme Court has systemically disadvantaged racial minorities is by successfully consigning minorities to the status of Supreme Court dependents. The Court accomplished this through issuance of its decision in *Brown v. Board of Education*. Although *Brown* promised to desegregate the schools and to eliminate race-based governmental classifications, it did neither. *Brown* merely replaced *de jure* segregation with *de facto* segregation in a way that simply prompted governmental policymakers to rely on racial correlates rather than race itself when they wished to utilize a race-based classification. *Brown* is better understood as a majoritarian decision that inflicted national foreign policy preferences on the regional south than as a countermajoritarian decision that imposed the rule of law on a massively resistant majority.

Notwithstanding its true majoritarian nature, *Brown* has come to be viewed as proof of the Supreme Court's countermajoritarian capabilities. Because racial minorities have come to share this view of *Brown* they have permitted the Court to dictate *minority* political policy to them. Racial minorities have disregarded their own progressive political and intellectual leaders and have manifested their dependence upon the Supreme Court in electing to pursue the elusive goal of integrated education, rather than the goal of high quality education in minority-controlled schools. Moreover, they continue to do so even though this strategy has resulted in nearly forty post-*Brown* years of inferior education for minority school children.

This submissiveness on the part of racial minorities reflects a deeper minority dependence on the Supreme Court as the institution that prescribes the ways in which minorities conceptualize the problems associated with race. Most notably, this dependence has prompted minority acceptance of the Court's prescription for assimilation rather than self-determination as the aspirational goal for right-thinking racial minority groups to pursue. On an even deeper level, it is dependence upon Supreme Court paternalism that has led minorities to eschew aggressive, self-determined political action in favor of the safety inherent in continued minority status as wards of the Supreme Court.

The second way in which the Supreme Court has systemically disadvantaged racial minorities is by centralizing the law of affirmative action. With the demise of *de jure* segregation, the law of affirmative action has become the most significant area of the law affecting racial minority interests. The statistical nature of contemporary racial discrimination means that only statistical allocations of societal resources offer any hope of promoting racial equality. However, it is in the interest of members of the white majority as rational wealth maximizers to allocate to themselves as large a share of societal resources as possible without either provoking minorities to adopt extra-legal strategies of resistance or causing the majority to view itself in unflatteringly selfish terms. The Supreme Court has served the function of advancing this majoritarian interest by upholding the constitutionality of only those affirmative action programs that are adopted at the national rather than the local level.

By centralizing the law of affirmative action to permit national but not local affirmative action programs, the Court has permitted the majority to retain its goodwill and positive self-image by allowing it to adopt *some* affirmative action programs. However, racial minorities possess more political power at the local level, where there can be heavy concentrations of minority voting strength, than at the national level, where minorities will comprise only a small percentage of the total electorate. As a result, Supreme Court validation of only centralized affirmative action programs turns out to be a political bargain for the white majority, because it will not result in *many* affirmative action programs actually taking effect.

More subtly, the Supreme Court's centralization of the law of affirmative action reflects our prevailing cultural preferences for universalism, rational objectivity, and race neutrality over the parochialism, irrational subjectivity, and racial bias that have come to be associated with decentralization. In a culture that is as inescapably race-conscious as contemporary American culture, allocations of societal resources are significantly dependent upon race. It is implausible to suggest that some race-neutral concept such as merit could override the racial factors that go into making resource allocation determinations. However, the Supreme Court's centralization of the law of affirmative action ultimately permits the white majority to view the race-conscious allocation of resources to racial minorities as a suspect racial preference while viewing the equally race-conscious allocation of resources to itself as the commendable exercise of race neutrality. This not only helps the majority to feel comfortable with its disproportionate allocation of societal resources, but it deters minorities from embracing nationalist strategies for the advancement of racial interests that offer the greatest hope for promoting racial equality and self-determination.

The third way in which the Supreme Court has systemically disadvantaged racial minorities is by legitimating a set of counterproductive assumptions about the nature of the legal process, and ultimately about racial minorities themselves. The process of legitimation operates by causing an unstated assumption to be accepted without scrutiny while analytical attention has been diverted to a more salient consequence of the legitimated assumption. Using this technique, the Supreme Court has legitimated three unstated assumptions that are relevant to the minority struggle for racial equality. It has legitimated the liberal assumption that there exists a category of fundamental rights that the government cannot abridge. It has also legitimated the assumption that the Supreme Court is the final expositor of the content of those rights. Finally, it has legitimated the assumption that minorities cannot properly make demands upon the majority that exceed the scope of the fundamental rights as expounded by the Court.

All of these assumptions serve the interests of the white majority, but they do not serve the interests of racial minorities. The liberal rights assumption is counterproductive because it tends to backfire on racial minorities. Its most frequent historic use has been in the protection of white property interests. Similarly, its contemporary majoritarian value lies in its use to invalidate affirmative action programs on the grounds that they interfere with majoritarian interests. The assumption that the Supreme Court is the final expositor of the content of rights is counterproductive because it authorizes the mostly white, mostly male Supreme Court to referee disputes between the majority and racial minorities over the proper allocation of resources in a way that is largely immune from political modification. Historically, this has been an arbitration system that favors the majority over racial minorities, and there is no reason to believe that this built-in bias is about to change. The assumption that minorities are not entitled to anything more than what the Supreme Court grants them not only solidifies the dependency relationship that racial minorities have with the Supreme Court, but it conveys negative connotations about the indolent ingratitude of racial minorities that perpetuate perceptions of racial minorities as inferior. To the extent that these perceptions are shared by racial minorities themselves, legitimation of this assumption frustrates minority perceptions of self-worth and inhibits the aggressiveness with which minorities will pursue their claims for racial justice.

Conclusion

The traditional model of judicial review is hopelessly disingenuous. Not only is the Supreme Court precluded from protecting minority interests by its veiled majoritarian nature, but it seems that the Court's true institutional function is to perpetuate the subordination of racial minorities for majority gain. As a matter of constitutional theory, this leads to a rather paradoxical conclusion. Although contemporary constitutional debate centers around the continued viability of the *Marbury* model, in the final analysis, it simply does not much matter whether the traditional model of judicial review is valid or not. The Supreme Court has cast far too strong a spell of necessity over the constituents of judicial review to be thwarted by mere insights into its operational deficiencies. The legal academics, operating in the name of constraining scrutiny, have also provided their share of aid and comfort to the endeavor. The more transparent the Court's deficiencies have become, the more abundant has become the flow of theory to obfuscate the transparency. And racial minorities themselves, wanting desperately to become a part of the whole, have chosen to root for the success of the undertaking. They have viewed the recurrence of judicial betrayal as an unsightly blemish upon an otherwise noble aspiration. Like the white majority, racial minorities have resisted the inference that persistent perfidy reveals a flaw at the inception of the enterprise. Everyone seems to want the system to work, no matter how unworkable the system seems to become.

In this environment, racial minorities armed with insights about the inescapable majoritarianism of the Supreme Court could do no more than treat the Court as an antagonistic political institution rather than as a hospitable benefactor. But to be effective in their political treatment, minorities would still have to file the same briefs before the Court, offer the same oral arguments, and pronounce the words "Your Honor" with the same degree of deference. No matter how enlightened it were to become, political use of the Court would still legitimate the countermajoritarian assumptions on which the traditional model is based, thereby perversely implicating racial minorities in the perpetuation of their own subordination. Sadly, the assumption that racial minorities are Supreme Court dependents who are incapable of political self-determination seems to be self-fulfilling. This poses an inescapable dilemma for minorities in search of racial justice.

Thankfully, the dilemma is only syllogistic. It is an artifact of the same sorts of rational discourse and logical analysis that could permit a social institution as regressive as the Supreme Court to become recognized as the champion of oppressed minorities. Once freed from the epistemological constraints of syllogistic analysis, racial minorities could also free themselves from the constraints of Supreme Court protection. Consider that the vision of an omnipotent God exerts enormous influence over the attitudes and behavior of the adherents to that vision. But it is of no consequence whatsoever to those for whom the vision holds no attraction. Similarly, Freud's conception of unconscious determinism is of paramount importance to those who have chosen to pursue psychoanalytic strategies for self-realization. But it is little more than a source of amusement to those for whom hard-edged conceptions of freewill offer a more comfortable account of human behavior. Even assuming that an external reality remains constant across epistemological perspectives, it is the perspectives themselves—not the underlying reality—that give life and meaning to experience. It follows that the way for racial minorities to escape the reality of Supreme Court subordination is to think about that reality differently. . . .

Thought about differently, it is not at all surprising that a Supreme Court nominally committed to the protection of minority interests would resist the escape of racial minorities from its protective custody. While it is true that under the *Marbury* model of judicial review, minorities are consigned to a role of perpetual Supreme Court dependency, minority dependence is the lesser of the two dependencies that are created by the traditional model. Under the *Marbury* model, if there were no politically impotent minorities for the Supreme Court to protect, there could be no judicial review. And without judicial review, the Supreme Court would be deprived of its distinctive significance in the American political system. Ironically, it is the Supreme Court that is actually dependent upon the continued vulnerability of minorities in order to sustain its own constitutional legitimacy. This, of course, gives racial minorities an enormous source of power over the Court. By choosing to relinquish their vulnerability, racial minorities would also terminate the traditional utility of the Supreme Court.

To date, racial minorities have charitably served as sacrificial recipients of Supreme Court largess in a way that has protected the fragile esteem of this governmental institution—an institution whose only real power lies in the continued obeisance of its minority charges. But that has proven to be a counterproductive endeavor. The society has remained unjust despite its invocation of judicial review as the symbol for its commitment to inchoate equal justice. Racial minorities have demonstrated remarkable tolerance with the shortcomings of the Court. They have treated its decisions with the patience and restraint that one would accord the misdeeds of a wayward child whose deficient parenting was properly to blame for the child's poor conduct. Nevertheless, even racial minority tolerance must eventually come to an end. The adjudicatory path to racial justice has proven unworkable, and it is now time for minorities to cease their protection of the Supreme Court. It is time to leave the Court to its fate. The continued self-sacrifice of minority interests solely to shore up the institutional importance of the Supreme Court, and the unworkable approach to justice that it represents, would serve no useful purpose. The era of the Court has come, and it has gone. And minorities must now show concern for themselves rather than continuing to protect this obsolete institution and the social order for which it stands.

Although minorities may not ultimately possess the power to control the manner in which the legal process deals with their welfare, they do possess the power to control their conception of that process. Which may be every bit as good.

Notes

INTRODUCTION

1. *Review of Supreme Court's Term: Labor and Employment Law*, 58 LW 3065 (Aug. 8, 1989). The 1988–89 Term has become infamous because the conservative civil rights decisions that the Court issued that Term served as the focus of highly publicized and racially charged legislative proceedings that ultimately led to the congressional reversal of many of those decisions. *See* Introduction, note 4 (discussing political divisiveness surrounding legislative efforts to enact proposed Civil Rights Acts of 1990 and 1991).

2. *Id.* During the 1988 Term, the Court first invalidated a minority set-aside program for government contractors and imposed a heavy burden of proving past discrimination as a prerequisite to the use of affirmative action remedies. *See* City of Richmond v. J.A. Croson Co., 488 U.S. 469 (1989). The burden of proof imposed by the case is so heavy that it was not satisfied by the well-known history of racial discrimination in Richmond, Virginia, *see id.* at 498–500, or by the fact that in a city whose population was 50 percent black, only .67 percent of the city's construction contracts had been awarded to black contractors. *See id.* at 484–85.

   Second, the Court permitted an affirmative action consent decree to be collaterally attacked by white workers who had chosen not to intervene in the Title VII action giving rise to the consent decree despite their knowledge that the Title VII action was pending. *See* Martin v. Wilkes, 490 U.S. 755 (1989).

   Third, the Court increased the burden of proof imposed on minorities who assert Title VII claims by requiring minority employees both to focus their challenges on specific rather than aggregate employment practices and to disprove employer assertions of legitimate job relatedness. *See* Wards Cove Packing Co. v. Atonio, 490 U.S. 642 (1989).

Fourth, the Court adopted a narrow interpretation of the Reconstruction civil rights statute now codified in 42 U.S.C. § 1981, holding that the statute did not prohibit racial harassment of minority employees by their employers. *See* Patterson v. McLean Credit Union, 491 U.S. 164 (1989).

Fifth, the Court held that discrimination claims filed against municipalities under 42 U.S.C. § 1981 could not be based upon a theory of respondeat superior. *See* Jett v. Dallas Independent School District, 491 U.S. 701 (1989). *Jett* was a discrimination suit in which a white employee challenged his discharge by a black employer, *id.*, but the holding applies to suits filed by minority plaintiffs as well. In a separate decision, the Court also held that 42 U.S.C. § 1983, another Reconstruction civil rights statute, did not permit race discrimination suits to be maintained against states as employers because states were not "persons" within the meaning of the § 1983 prohibition on discrimination occurring under "color" of state law. *See* Will v. Michigan Department of State Police, 491 U.S. 58 (1989).

Sixth, the Court held that the statute of limitations for Title VII challenges to discriminatory seniority systems began to run when a seniority system was first adopted rather than when its discriminatory impact later materialized in the form of subsequent seniority-based demotions. *See* Lorance v. AT&T Technologies, 490 U.S. 900 (1989). Although *Lorance* involved a Title VII claim of gender discrimination, its holding applies with equal force to race-based discrimination claims asserted under Title VII.

Seventh, the Court held that attorneys' fees for a prevailing plaintiff in a Title VII case could not be assessed against a union that intervened in order to defend the discriminatory practice being challenged. *See* Independent Federation of Flight Attendants v. Zipes, 491 U.S. 754 (1989). This adversely affects minority interests by decreasing the sources of funding available to compensate victorious minority litigants for their attorneys' fees and by increasing the sources of opposition to minority interests that may be represented in particular suits through the elimination of a potential cost of participation.

In addition to the seven decisions cited by U.S. LAW WEEK, the Court also held in another case that discriminatory employment decisions did not violate Title VII if the employer could demonstrate that the same employment decision would have been made in the absence of the impermissible discrimination. *See* Price Waterhouse v. Hopkins, 490 U.S. 228 (1989). Like *Lorance, Price Waterhouse* was a gender discrimination case, but its holding too applies with equal force to Title VII race discrimination claims.

Congress took steps to overrule many of these decisions in the proposed Civil Rights Acts of 1990 and 1991. *See* Introduction, note 4.

3. *See* Civil Rights Act of 1991, Pub. L. 102–166; 105 Stat. 1071 (1991) (to be codified).

4. After the series of conservative civil rights decisions that were issued by the Supreme Court during its 1988–89 Term, the proposed Civil Rights Act of

1990 was introduced in the Senate to overturn many of the 1988–89 Term decisions, as well as some of the other conservative civil rights decisions that the Court had issued since 1985. *See* Eskridge, *Reneging on History? Playing the Court/Congress/President Civil Rights Game* 79 CALIF. L. REV. 613, 613–17 (1991). President Bush opposed enactment of the proposed legislation on the grounds that it called for the utilization of racial quotas in hiring and promotion. Although the proposed Civil Rights Act of 1990 passed both Houses of Congress, it was vetoed by the President in October 1990. The Senate failed by one vote to override the President's veto.

In January 1991 the proposed Civil Rights Act of 1991 was introduced in the House of Representatives. That bill passed the House in June 1991, and after a compromise was worked out between the President and Senate Republicans who supported the legislation, the Civil Rights Act of 1991 was signed into law by President Bush on November 21, 1991. The Act overruled most of the conservative civil rights decisions that had been issued by the Supreme Court during the 1988–89 Term, as well as some earlier and later conservative civil rights decisions that had also been issued by the Rehnquist Court. The provisions of the Act, as well as a description of the political process leading to its enactment, are described in Alfred and Knowlton, *Civil Rights Act Will Encourage Federal Claims: The Civil Rights Act Of 1991,* MASSACHUSETTS LAWYERS WEEKLY, Dec. 9, 1991, at p. 5.

The President's actions during the two-year political struggle that led to enactment of the statute have been criticized by both civil rights leaders and moderate Republicans as divisive efforts to exploit the issue of race for partisan political gain. *See, e.g.,* Broder, *Bush's Favorite Victim,* WASH. POST, June 9, 1991, at p. D7; Raspberry, *Bush, Civil Rights and the Specter of David Duke,* WASH. POST, Oct. 30, 1991, at p. A23; Schneider, *For Danforth & Co., An Uncivil Snub,* NATIONAL JOURNAL July 6, 1991, at p. 1716. For an argument that President Bush has, throughout his career, sporadically sought to exploit racial divisiveness in his political activities, see T. EDSALL, with M. EDSALL, CHAIN REACTION: THE IMPACT OF RACE, RIGHTS, AND TAXES ON AMERICAN POLITICS (New York: Norton 1991); Morley, *Bush & the Blacks: An Unknown Story,* N.Y. REVIEW OF BOOKS, Jan. 16, 1991, at p. 19.

For an argument that the Supreme Court decisions overruled in the Civil Rights Act of 1991 exemplified a novel form of judicial activism practiced by the Rehnquist Supreme Court, pursuant to which the Court is willing to override the political preferences of both the Congress that enacts a particular piece of legislation as well as the preferences of the current Congress in order to advance the Court's own political preferences, see Eskridge, *Reneging on History?.*

5. 347 U.S. 483 (1954).
6. *Id.*

Part I

CHAPTER 1

1. For a general discussion of the historical and political context out of which the Constitution emerged and the objectives of the framers, see J. ELY, DEMOCRACY AND DISTRUST: A THEORY OF JUDICIAL REVIEW 77–88 (Cambridge: Harvard University Press 1980); THE FEDERALIST (H. Lodge ed.) (New York: G.P. Putnam's Sons 1888); G. GUNTHER, CONSTITUTIONAL LAW 10–21 (Mineola, N.Y.: Foundation Press, 11th ed. 1985); G. STONE, L. SEIDMAN, C. SUNSTEIN, and M. TUSHNET, CONSTITUTIONAL LAW 1–17 (Boston: Little, Brown, 1986); L. TRIBE, AMERICAN CONSTITUTIONAL LAW 1–17 (Mineola, N.Y.: Foundation Press, 2d ed. 1988); Eskridge, *Politics Without Romance: Implications of Public Choice Theory for Statutory Interpretation*, 74 VA. L. REV. 275, 280–83 (1988); Sunstein, *Beyond the Republican Revival*, 97 YALE L.J. 1539 (1988); Sunstein, *Interest Groups in American Public Law*, 38 STAN. L. REV. 29, 31–48 (1985).

2. *See generally* G. STONE, *et al.*, CONSTITUTIONAL LAW at 1–18.

3. *See generally id.*; Sunstein, *Republican Revival*; *Symposium: The Republican Civic Tradition*, 97 YALE L.J. 1493–1851 (1988).

4. *See* P. BATOR, D. MELTZER, P. MISHKIN, and D. SHAPIRO, HART AND WECHSLER'S THE FEDERAL COURTS AND THE FEDERAL SYSTEM 8–9 n.34 (Mineola, N.Y.: Foundation Press, 3d ed. 1988).

5. *See id.* at 8–9; A. BICKEL, THE LEAST DANGEROUS BRANCH: THE SUPREME COURT AT THE BAR OF POLITICS 15–16 (New Haven: Yale University Press 1962); G. STONE, *et al.*, CONSTITUTIONAL LAW at 30.

6. *See* G. STONE, *et al.*, CONSTITUTIONAL LAW at 31–33.

7. United States v. Butler, 297 U.S. 1, 62–63 (1936), *quoted and characterized* in G. STONE *et al.*, CONSTITUTIONAL LAW at 32.

8. *See, e.g.*, Bennett, *Constitutional Interpretation and Judicial Self-Restraint*, 39 MICH. L. REV. 213, 227 (1940).

9. *See* Currie, *The Constitution in the Supreme Court: The New Deal, 1931–1940*, 59 U. CHI. L. REV. 504, 531 (1987).

10. *See* G. STONE, *et al.*, CONSTITUTIONAL LAW at 31–38 (presenting several such theories).

11. *See* G. GUNTHER, CONSTITUTIONAL LAW at 406; L. TRIBE, AMERICAN CONSTITUTIONAL LAW at 4 n.7.

12. THE FEDERALIST 84 (Hamilton) at 537. *See also* L. TRIBE, AMERICAN CONSTITUTIONAL LAW at 4 n.7; G. STONE, *et al.*, CONSTITUTIONAL LAW at 115–22.

13. *Cf.* A.L.A. Schechter Poultry Corp. v. United States, 295 U.S. 495 (1935) (last Supreme Court decision to invalidate grant of agency power under nondelegation doctrine).

14. *See* Commodity Futures Trading Commission v. Schor, 478 U.S. 833 (1986) (upholding power of CFTC to adjudicate state law debt claims); Weiner v. United States, 357 U.S. 349 (1958) (upholding adjudicatory power of War Claims Commission).

15. *See* Morrison v. Olson, 487 U.S. 654 (1988) (upholding constitutionality of statute creating independent counsel to investigate high level executive misconduct free of presidential control); Humphrey's Executor v. United States, 295 U.S. 602 (1935) (upholding congressional restrictions on President's power to remove independent agency officials).

16. *See* United States v. Curtiss-Wright, 299 U.S. 304 (1936) (upholding authority of President to impose fines for selling arms to foreign government). *See generally* Sunstein, *Constitutionalism after the New Deal,* 101 HARV. L. REV. 421, 430–52 (1987).

17. *See* Wickard v. Filburn, 317 U.S. 11 (1942).

18. *See* Sunstein, *Constitutionalism,* 101 HARV. L. REV. at 430–52.

19. Marbury v. Madison, 5 U.S. (1 Cranch.) 137 (1803).

20. *Id.* at 163, 170.

21. *Id.* at 177–78.

22. *See generally* G. STONE, *et al.,* CONSTITUTIONAL LAW at 25–31.

23. *Cf.* Cooper v. Aaron, 358 U.S. 1, 18 (1958) (citing *Marbury* for proposition that Supreme Court "is supreme in the exposition of the law of the Constitution"). By reserving the right to have the final say over the meaning of the Constitution, the Supreme Court has also reserved the right to have the final say over the content of constitutional rights.

24. *See* U.S. CONST. amends. XIII, XIV, & XV.

25. *See generally* J. ELY, DEMOCRACY AND DISTRUST.

26. Supreme Court invalidation of coordinate branch actions has been emphasized for the sake of simplicity. Much of the Court's work admittedly involves the interpretation of federal and state statutes and common law rules. Theories of judicial review that are relevant to Supreme Court constitutional adjudication can also have an important impact on the Court's statutory and common law interpretations. For present purposes, however, Supreme Court invalidation of the acts of representative branches serves as an adequate foundation for the thesis that I wish to present.

Similarly, I do not dwell upon the differences between the role of the Supreme Court and the role of the lower federal courts. There are differences, and for many purposes the differences are significant. Again, however, I have focused on the Supreme Court for purposes of simplicity and because Supreme Court adjudication is sufficient to illustrate the points that I wish to make.

27. *See* U.S. CONST. art. III, sec. 1. The framers rejected a proposed constitutional prohibition on judicial salary increases. *See* THE FOUNDERS' CONSTITUTION, VOL. 4, 133–37 (P. Kurland and R. Lerner eds.) (Chicago: University of Chicago Press 1987).

28. While it may be relatively easy to imagine a situation in which a particular legislator has an interest in the outcome of private litigation—as where a friend, relative, or major campaign contributor is a party—it is more difficult to imagine private litigation in which the representative branch as a whole would have an interest. But even this is not impossible to imagine. For example, if a member of Congress sued for libel or slander raises a Speech and Debate Clause defense, Congress as a body, in addition to its members as individuals, will be interested in the outcome of the suit. To the extent that the representative branches do have an interest in the outcome of private litigation, the formal safeguards are as relevant as they are in public litigation that raises policy or structural issues.

There are many examples of Supreme Court cases raising policy or structural issues that directly affect the representative branches. See, e.g., Mistretta v. United States, 488 U.S. 361, 390–99 (1989) (upholding placement of Sentencing Commission within judicial branch after separation of powers challenge); Morrison v. Olson, 487 U.S. 654, 685–96 (1988) (upholding constitutionality of special counsel appointed under Ethics In Government Act to investigate alleged crimes by high-level executive officials after separation of powers challenge); Bowsher v. Synar, 478 U.S. 714, 721–34 (1986) (invalidating Gramm-Rudman-Hollings Deficit Reduction Act on separation of powers grounds because Act vested executive authority in Comptroller General who was subject to congressional removal and control); INS v. Chadha, 462 U.S. 919, 951–59 (1983) (invalidating one-House veto provision of Immigration And Nationality Act on what are essentially separation of powers grounds for authorizing one House of Congress to take legislative actions without complying with art. I, sec. 7 procedures prescribed for enacting legislation); Powell v. McCormack, 395 U.S. 486, 550 (1969) (limiting autonomous congressional power to exclude duly elected Members of House of Representatives for reasons other than those relating to defects in age, citizenship, and residence qualifications specified in Constitution); cf. United States v. Nixon, 418 U.S. 683, 706 (1973) (rejecting presidential claim of absolute immunity from judicial process based upon separation of powers claim in which Congress had possible indirect interest relating to potential exercise of congressional impeachment power).

29. Impeachment is an available form of retaliation by the representative branches, but its use may be politically too difficult to permit it to serve as the basis of a credible threat in typical cases. See Chapter 6, note 85.

30. See U.S. CONST. art. I, sec. 9, cl. 3.

31. This representation-reinforcement, separation-of-powers conception of the bill of attainder clause was developed by Professor Ely as a law student in an unattributed law review note. See Note, *The Bounds of Legislative Specification: A Suggested Approach to the Bill of Attainder Clause*, 72 YALE L.J. 330, 343–60 (1962) (criticizing *inter alia* Supreme Court's limitation of bill of attainder prohibition to penal legislation).

32. *See* G. GUNTHER, CONSTITUTIONAL LAW at 10–11.
33. *See Race Is On for 152 New Judgeships*, U.S. NEWS & WORLD REPORT, Oct. 9, 1978, at p. 54.
34. *See* U.S. CONST. art. III, sec. 2, cl. 2.
35. *See generally* G. STONE, *et al.*, CONSTITUTIONAL LAW at 70–74, 493 (discussing threatened use of power to regulate jurisdiction in various substantive areas including school prayer, reapportionment, school desegregation, and abortion).
36. *See* Leuchtenberg, *The Origins of Franklin D. Roosevelt's "Court-Packing" Plan*, 1966 SUP. CT. REV. 347.
37. *See* G. GUNTHER, CONSTITUTIONAL LAW at 22.
38. *See* Chapter 6, note 32 and accompanying text (discussing Missouri Compromise and *Dred Scott* decision).
39. *See* G. GUNTHER, CONSTITUTIONAL LAW at 23–24.
40. *See id.* at 24, 25.
41. 330 U.S. (5 Pet.) 1 (1831).
42. *Id. See* R. CHUSED, CASES, MATERIALS AND PROBLEMS IN PROPERTY 109–112 (New York: Matthew Bender 1988); G. GUNTHER, CONSTITUTIONAL LAW at 25; Burke, *The Cherokee Cases: A Study in Law, Politics and Morality*, 21 STAN. L. REV. 500 (1969).
43. *See* G. WHITE, TORT LAW IN AMERICA 20–37 (New York: Oxford University Press 1980); *see generally* Schauer, *Formalism*, 97 YALE L.J. 509 (1988).
44. *See* THE FEDERALIST 78 (Hamilton) at 482 (discussing importance of judicial judgment and adherence to precedent).
45. *See* Patterson v. McLean Credit Union, 491 U.S. 164, 172 (1989) (discussing doctrine of stare decisis).
46. *Compare* Londoner v. Denver, 210 U.S. 373 (1908) (due process requires hearing with respect to executive determinations, which affect small number of individuals) *with* Bi-Metallic Investment Co. v. State Board of Equalization of Colorado, 239 U.S. 441 (1915) (due process does not require hearing with respect to legislative determinations, which affect large number of individuals).
47. An example of the haste with which legislative "adjudication" can be conducted is provided by the House of Representatives' deportation resolutions that served as the basis for the Supreme Court's invalidation of the legislative veto device in INS v. Chadha, 462 U.S. 919 (1983). After taking no action for a year and a half, the House vetoed an Immigration and Naturalization order suspending the deportation of Mr. Chadha only a few days before the end of the last legislative session during which such a veto could have been issued. The House acted so rapidly that it did not even have time to print the veto resolution. Rather, the resolution was simply read orally on the floor of the House immediately prior to the vote that adopted it. The floor debate

was very brief; it was characterized by inaccurate statements and misunderstandings by some of the speakers; and no reason was ever given to justify the veto. The resolution passed without debate by voice vote. *See Chadha,* 462 U.S. at 923-28. Such proceedings are hardly characteristic of exemplary adjudication.

CHAPTER 2

1. The nomination by President Reagan of D.C. Circuit Judge Robert Bork to the Supreme Court was not confirmed by the Senate largely because the nominee's political views were not sufficiently within the mainstream of contemporary American political thought. *See* Greenhouse, *Bork's Nomination is Rejected, 58-42; Reagan "Saddened,"* N.Y. TIMES, Oct. 24, 1987 at p. 1. Douglas Ginsburg, the successor nominee to Judge Bork, was forced to withdraw his name from consideration during the confirmation process when it was revealed that his past recreational drug use was not sufficiently within the mainstream of contemporary American views about the appropriateness of recreational drug use. *See* Roberts, *Ginsburg withdraws Name as Supreme Court Nominee, Citing Marijuana "Clamor,"* N.Y. TIMES, Nov. 8, 1987 at p. 1. The recreational drug use in which Clarence Thomas engaged while a student, however, was not sufficiently outside the mainstream to preclude Thomas's appointment to the Supreme Court. *See* Labaton, *Thomas Smoked Marijuana But Retains Bush Support,* N.Y. TIMES, July 11, 1991, at p. A17.

2. *See* Apple, *The Thomas Confirmation; Senate Confirms Thomas, 52-48, Ending Week of Bitter Battle; 'Time for Healing,' Judge Says,* N.Y. TIMES, Oct. 16, 1991, at p. A1 (Justices Marshall and Thomas were respectively first and second blacks on Supreme Court).

3. Many of the acts of racial discrimination to which Justice Marshall has been subjected are detailed in R. KLUGER, SIMPLE JUSTICE: THE HISTORY OF *BROWN V. BOARD OF EDUCATION* AND BLACK AMERICA'S STRUGGLE FOR EQUALITY (New York: Knopf 1976), and in M. TUSHNET, THE NAACP'S LEGAL STRATEGY AGAINST SEGREGATED EDUCATION, 1925-1950 (Chapel Hill: University of North Carolina Press 1987). Acts of racial discrimination to which Justice Thomas has been subjected are discussed in Lancaster and LaFraniere, *Thomas: Growing Up Black in a White World,* WASH. POST, Sept. 8, 1991, at A1; LaFraniere, *Despite Achievement, Thomas Felt Isolated; Rebuffs Stung Emerging Conservative,* WASH. POST, Sept. 9, 1991, at p. A1; Williams, *A Question of Fairness; Clarence Thomas, a Black, is Ronald Reagan's Chairman of the Equal Employment Opportunity Commission,* ATLANTIC, Feb. 1987, at p. 70.

4. *See* G. STONE, *et al.,* CONSTITUTIONAL LAW at lxvi-lxvii.

5. *See* LaFraniere, *Despite Achievement, Thomas Felt Isolated* at A1.

6. *See id.* Justice Thomas, however, did flirt with Black Nationalism as a student. *See id.*; Williams, *A Question of Fairness.* In addition, he also engaged in minor recreational drug use as a college student. *See* Labaton, *Thomas Smoked Marijuana But Retains Bush Support* at p. A17.
7. *See* Chapter 2, note 1.
8. *See* page 10 (discussing framers' safeguards against political factions).
9. It is the danger of discounting minority interests in these ways that serves as the basis for Professor Ely's elaboration of the representation-reinforcement model of judicial review. *See* J. ELY, DEMOCRACY AND DISTRUST at 155–70.
10. *See* Lawrence, *The Id, the Ego, and Equal Protection: Reckoning with Unconscious Racism,* 39 STAN. L. REV. 317 (1987).
11. *See* page 15 (discussing methods for circumventing formal safeguards).
12. *See* Tushnet, Kovner, and Schneider, *Judicial Review and Congressional Tenure: A Research Note,* 66 TEXAS L. REV. 967 (1988).
13. *Id.* at 973, 975 n.45.
14. *Id.* at 973–75.
15. *Id.* at 977–79, *citing* M. FIORINA, CONGRESS: KEYSTONE OF THE WASHINGTON ESTABLISHMENT (New Haven: Yale University Press 1977).
16. *Id.* at 978.
17. *Id.* at 979–80, 990–91.
18. *See id.* at 980–81, 984–85.
19. *Cf. id.* at 990–91.
20. *See* Cover and Mayhew, *Congressional Dynamics and the Decline of Competitive Congressional Elections* in CONGRESS RECONSIDERED 55–56 (L. Dodd and B. Oppenheimer, eds.) (New York: Praeger Publishers 1977).
21. *See* page 26 (discussing unconscious nature of many personal attitudes).
22. *See* Chapter 2, note 10.
23. This danger of prejudice in the adjudicatory process has prompted Professor Delgado to favor the formalities of traditional adjudication over more informal alternative dispute resolution techniques as a means of protecting minority interests, in the hope that formalities will serve as a safeguard against the prejudicial attitudes of the adjudicators. *See* Delgado, Dunn, Brown, Lee, and Hubbert, *Fairness and Formality: Minimizing the Risk of Prejudice in Alternative Dispute Resolution,* 1985 WIS. L. REV. 1359.

CHAPTER 3

1. 469 U.S. 528 (1985).
2. *See id.* at 547–48.
3. *See id.* at 550–52. The Court left open the possibility that judicially enforceable limits might later be developed to govern unanticipated future circumstances. *See id.* at 554.

4. 481 U.S. 279, *rehearing denied*, 482 U.S. 920 (1987).

5. *See id.* A more recent study has also demonstrated drastic differences in the percentages of capital cases that are prosecuted depending upon the race of the victim, with the death penalty being sought in one of three cases involving white victims but only one in seventeen cases involving black victims. *See* Margolick, *In Land of Death Penalty, Accusations of Racial Bias*, N.Y. TIMES, July 10, 1991, at p. A1.

6. Justice Powell did not discuss either the source or the content of the constitutional limits. According to Justice Powell's reasoning, it may be that *no* punishment the majority views as acceptable for a particular crime will be invalidated on proportionality grounds because the very fact of majority endorsement ensures the requisite proportionality. *See* 481 U.S. at 299–300.

7. *Id.* at 300.

8. *Id.* at 310.

9. *See* 391 U.S. 145, 155–57 (1968).

10. *See* Strauder v. West Virginia, 100 U.S. 303, 305, 309–10 (1880); *cf.* Batson v. Kentucky, 476 U.S. 79, 84–88 (1986).

11. *See* 481 U.S. at 366–67 (Stevens, J., dissenting).

12. *See* Kennedy, McCleskey v. Kemp: *Race, Capital Punishment, and the Supreme Court,* 101 HARV. L. REV. 1388, 1390–95 (1988).

13. *See* Chapter 3, note 5. Another example of Supreme Court deference to majoritarian preferences in the imposition of capital punishment is provided by the Court's recent treatment of the legal issues surrounding execution of the mentally retarded. In Penry v. Lynaugh, 492 U.S. 302 (1989), Justice O'Connor, writing for the Court, stated that the eighth amendment prohibition on cruel and unusual punishment applied to practices that offend society's evolving standards of decency as expressed by "objective" evidence, such as the conduct of legislatures and sentencing juries. *Id.* at 330–31. Rather than establishing a judicial standard for what constitutes cruel and unusual punishment, therefore, the Court chose to defer to majoritarian preferences, even when those preferences adversely affected the mentally retarded—a discrete and insular minority with an immutable characteristic separating it from the majority. *Cf.* City of Cleburne v. Cleburne Living Center, 473 U.S. 432 (1985) (refusing to apply strict scrutiny equal protection standard to zoning ordinance that adversely affected mentally retarded).

14. *See, e.g.,* San Antonio Independent School District v. Rodriguez, 411 U.S. 1, 40 (1973) (rejecting equal protection challenge to public school financing scheme based upon property taxes).

15. *See, e.g.,* New Orleans v. Dukes, 427 U.S. 297 (1976) (upholding differential treatment of particular vendors in New Orleans French Quarter merely to preserve distinctive charm of area).

16. *See, e.g.,* City of Cleburne v. Cleburne Living Center, 473 U.S. 432 (1985) (invalidating municipal zoning ordinance under rational basis standard because ordinance discriminated against discrete and insular mentally retarded

even though Court was nominally unwilling to apply strict scrutiny); *id.* at 456 (Marshall, J., concurring in part and dissenting in part) (suggesting that ordinance would be valid under traditional rational basis standard); Plyler v. Doe, 457 U.S. 202 (1982) (invalidating state denial of free public education to children of illegal aliens under rational basis test because of importance of education and relationship of classification to alienage even though Court was nominally unwilling to apply strict or intermediate scrutiny).

17. *See* Korematsu v. United States, 323 U.S. 214, 216 (1944).

18. *See* G. STONE, *et al.*, CONSTITUTIONAL LAW at 541–43.

19. *See generally* J. ELY, DEMOCRACY AND DISTRUST (describing representation-reinforcement theory of judicial review).

20. 304 U.S. 144, (1938).

21. *Id.* at 152–53 n.4.

22. *See* J. ELY, DEMOCRACY AND DISTRUST. *But see* Balkin, *The Footnote*, 83 NW. UNIV. L. REV. 275 (1989).

23. *See* Washington v. Davis, 426 U.S. 229 (1976).

24. *See id.* at 242–45. Justice White's opinion for the Court discussed but disregarded earlier cases that *had* applied strict scrutiny to disparate impact claims. *See id.*

25. 323 U.S. 214 (1944).

26. *See id.* at 216. The Court upheld only the exclusion of Japanese-American citizens from certain areas of the West Coast, holding that the practice of detaining these citizens in relocation centers was not before the Court. *See id.* at 222. *See also* Hirabayshi v. United States, 320 U.S. 81 (1943) (upholding constitutionality of military curfew on West Coast Japanese-American citizens); *cf.* Ex Parte Endo, 323 U.S. 283 (1944) (imposing saving construction on governing statute and executive orders in order to invalidate detention in relocation centers of Japanese-Americans conceded to be loyal).

27. *See, e.g.*, R. DANIELS, CONCENTRATION CAMPS, NORTH AMERICA: JAPANESE IN THE UNITED STATES AND CANADA DURING WORLD WAR II (Malabar, Fla.: R.E. Krieger Publishing, rev. ed. 1981); J. TEN BROEK, E. BARNHART, and F. MATSON, PREJUDICE, WAR AND THE CONSTITUTION (Berkeley: University of California Press 1954).

28. 350 U.S. 891 (1955) (per curiam) and 350 U.S. 895 (1956) (per curiam).

29. 347 U.S. 483 (1954).

30. *Naim v. Naim* is discussed more fully in Chapter 7 as a case that challenges the countermajoritarian account of *Brown v. Board of Education*. *See* page 106.

31. 422 U.S. 490 (1975).

32. *See id.* at 502–08.

33. 429 U.S. 252 (1977).

34. *See, e.g.*, Tushnet, *The New Law of Standing: A Plea for Abandonment*, 62 CORNELL L. REV. 663, 699–700 (1977).

35. *See* City of Los Angeles v. Lyons, 461 U.S. 95 (1983); Rizzo v. Goode, 423 U.S. 362 (1976); Spomer v. Littleton, 414 U.S. 514 (1974); O'Shea v. Littleton, 414 U.S. 488 (1974).
36. For a description of the beating of a black motorist by several white police officers in the Los Angeles Police Department, which was captured in a home video recording, see Mydans, *Seven Minutes in Los Angeles—A Special Report; Videotaped Beating by Officers Puts Full Glare on Brutality Issue,* N.Y. TIMES, Mar. 18, 1991, at p. A1.
37. 491 U.S. 58 (1989).
38. *See id.* at 62–71.
39. *See id.* at 70–71.
40. 468 U.S. 737 (1984).
41. *See id.* at 753–61.
42. *Id.* at 761 [citations omitted].

CHAPTER 4

1. The process of principle selection, and the process of principle application that is discussed in Chapter 5, tend to be treated as distinct. Ultimately, however, the problems associated with each turn out to be precisely the same. This is because the only way that the selection of a governing principle can be constrained is by some other principle that controls the selection process. As a result, selection of the immediate principle, if not arbitrary, necessarily entails application of the meta-principle.
2. The literature favoring each of the two positions is cited in Lawrence, *The Id, the Ego, and Equal Protection,* 39 STAN. L. REV. at 319–21. Professor Lawrence himself favors an alternative approach that recognizes the unconscious nature of much racial discrimination and seeks to invalidate governmental acts having either conscious or unconscious discriminatory motivation as revealed by what he terms the "cultural meaning" of those acts. *See id.* at 355–81.
3. *See id.* at 319–21.
4. 426 U.S. 229 (1976).
5. *See id.* at 238–48. The holding of Washington v. Davis, 426 U.S. 229 (1976), has been reaffirmed in a number of cases including Village of Arlington Heights v. Metropolitan Housing Development Corp., 429 U.S. 252 (1977) and Hunter v. Underwood, 471 U.S. 222 (1985).
6. *See* 426 U.S. at 248.
7. *See id.*
8. 401 U.S. 424 (1971).
9. *See id.* at 242–44.
10. *See id.* at 244–45. The Court cites 13 courts of appeals decisions and four additional district court decisions. *See id.* at n.12.

11. Title VII is codified at 42 U.S.C. §§ 2000e–2000e–15.
12. 401 U.S. 424 (1971).
13. *See id.* at 429.
14. *See id.* at 429–30.
15. *See id.* at 424.
16. 42 U.S.C. § 2000e–2 [emphasis added].
17. *See* 401 U.S. at 428–29.
18. *See* page 37 (discussing policies on which the intent and effects principles are based).
19. 487 U.S. 977 (1988).
20. *See id.* at 987–89.
21. *See id.* at 989–91.
22. *See id.* at 991–99.
23. 490 U.S. 642 (1989).
24. *See id.* at 649–50.
25. *See id.* at 650–55.
26. *See id.* at 655–58.
27. *See id.* at 658–60.
28. *See id.* at 664–73 (Stevens, J., dissenting) (arguing that even under the intent test, the employer bears the burden of proving business justification as an affirmative defense).
29. *Id.* at 663–64 n.4 (Stevens, J., dissenting). *See also id.* at 662 (Blackmun, J., dissenting).
30. *Cf.* City of Richmond v. J.A. Croson Co., 488 U.S. 469 (1989), which is discussed in Chapter 8. *See* page 127.
31. *See* page 10 (discussing framers' use of federalism and separation-of-powers safeguards).
32. Although there is no particular phrase in the Constitution that imposes federalism and separation of powers requirements, it nevertheless makes sense to treat those requirements as "explicit" because, nominally at least, they are universally conceded to operate as limits on the scope of federal power.

   The death knell for the doctrine of federalism appears to have been sounded in Garcia v. San Antonio Metropolitan Transit Authority, 469 U.S. 528 (1985), where the Court held that there were no judicially enforceable federalism-based restrictions on the scope of congressional power. *See* page 27 (discussing *Garcia*).

   Some recent Supreme Court decisions have invalidated congressional enactments on separation of powers grounds. *See, e.g.,* Metropolitan Washington Airports Authority v. Citizens for the Abatement of Aircraft Noise, 111 S.Ct. 2298 (1991) (invalidating transfer of control over Washington D.C. airports from federal to local authorities on the grounds that transfer either impermissibly authorized Congress to exercise executive power, or authorized Congress to exercise legislative power in derogation of the bicameralism and presentment provisions of article I); Bowsher v. Synar, 478 U.S. 714 (1986) (invalidating Gramm-Rudman-Hollings Deficit Reduction Act); INS v. Chadha, 462 U.S. 919 (1983) (invalidating one-House veto provision of Immigration and Nationality Act). Other recent decisions, however, have upheld congressional enactments despite rather serious separation of powers problems. See, e.g., Mistretta v. United States, 488 U.S. 361, 371, 383–84 (1989) (upholding constitutionality of United States Sentencing Commission authority to prescribe binding sentencing "guidelines," despite existence of judicial members and placement in judicial branch); Morrison v. Olson, 487 U.S. 654, 692–93 (1988) (upholding independent counsel provision of Ethics in Government Act despite absence of presidential control). Notwithstanding the Court's occasional invalidations on separation of powers grounds, Supreme Court endorsement of the modern administrative state—with independent agencies exercising legislative, executive, and adjudicatory power in the absence of direct presidential control—makes it difficult to take contemporary separation of powers arguments very seriously. See, e.g., Weiner v. United States, 357 U.S. 349 (1958); Humphrey's Executor v. United States, 295 U.S. 602 (1935).

One could, of course, argue that the existence of cases like *Bowsher* and *Chadha* indicates that the Court does not ignore separation of powers requirements but merely "construes" them. This raises an intractable issue concerning the difference between application and interpretation of legal principles. When the Court holds, for example, that the first amendment does not apply to obscenity, see Roth v. United States, 354 U.S. 476 (1957), debate about whether the Court is avoiding or construing the principle of free speech may well be semantic. For present purposes, the important point is that the Court has two distinct opportunities to exercise discretion. A Court inclined to limit the scope of protected speech can either decide that the first amendment principle does not apply, or that it applies but does not prohibit the particular limitation at issue. The present discussion concerns the first opportunity. Problems attendant to the second opportunity are discussed in Chapter 5.

33. See U.S. CONST. art. I, sec. 10, cl. 1. Early nineteenth-century cases treated the contracts clause as an important limitation on the scope of governmental power. See, e.g., Green v. Biddle, 21 U.S. (8 Wheat.) 1 (1823) (invalidating state law making it difficult for landowners to eject squatters); Sturges v. Crowninshield, 17 U.S. (4 Wheat.) 122 (1918) (invalidating state law that discharged debtors from their obligations upon surrender of property). When the New Deal Court expanded its conception of permissible legislative power, it largely eliminated use of the contracts clause as a tool for restricting governmental activities. See Home Building & Loan Association v. Blaisdell, 290 U.S. 398 (1934) (upholding state depression era law imposing moratorium on mortgage foreclosures). Then, in the late 1970s, the Court seemed to begin a revival of the contracts clause. See Allied Structural Steel Co. v.

Spannaus, 438 U.S. 234 (1978) (invalidating state law increasing employer pension obligations above obligations specified in employment contract); United States Trust Co. v. New Jersey, 431 U.S. 1 (1977) (invalidating state law that repealed certain anticompetitive assurances promised to government bondholders). More recent cases, however, suggest that the contracts clause has reassumed its New Deal level of insignificance. *See* Exxon Corp v. Eagerton, 462 U.S. 176 (1983) (upholding state law that invalidated automatic tax increase pass-through in oil and natural gas contracts); Energy Reserves Group v. Kansas Power & Light, 459 U.S. 400 (1983) (upholding state law that invalidated automatic price-escalator clause in natural gas contracts). *See generally* G. STONE, *et al.*, CONSTITUTIONAL LAW at 1427–45.

34. *See* U.S. CONST. art. IV, sec. 2. The Supreme Court has not decided many privileges and immunities cases. *See* Baldwin v. Montana Fish and Game Commission, 436 U.S. 371, 379 (1978); *id.* at 395 (Brennan, J., dissenting). The cases that have been decided reflect conceptual approaches that have varied over time. Initially, the privileges and immunities clause was construed to be a device permitting the federal constitutional protection of natural rights. *See, e.g.,* Corfield v. Coryell, 6 Fed. Cas. 546 (No. 3230) (C.C.E.D. Pa. 1823) (upholding state prohibition on noncitizen collection of shellfish in New Jersey waters). As the natural rights conception of the Constitution faded, the clause reemerged as an antidiscrimination provision that required states to accord equal treatment to residents and nonresidents where important interests were involved. *See, e.g.,* Toomer v. Witsell, 334 U.S. 385 (1948). After a period of inactivity, recent cases have rejuvenated the nondiscrimination version of the clause. *See, e.g.,* Supreme Court of New Hampshire v. Piper, 470 U.S. 274 (1985) (invalidating New Hampshire rule limiting bar admission to state residents); Hicklin v. Orbeck, 437 U.S. 518 (1978) (invalidating Alaska law giving hiring preference to state residents for certain natural resource-related employment). Discriminatory laws affecting interests that were not sufficiently fundamental have been upheld, however. *See, e.g.,* Baldwin v. Montana Fish and Game Commission, 436 U.S. 371 (1978) (upholding Montana law charging higher fees to nonresidents for elk hunting licenses). The most recent privileges and immunities cases treat the clause as a limitation on the scope of the market participant exception to the dormant commerce clause. *See* United Building & Construction Trades Council v. Mayor of Camden, 465 U.S. 208 (1984) (suggesting invalidation of municipal ordinance requiring contractors awarded municipal public works contracts to give hiring preference to city residents). *See generally* L. TRIBE, AMERICAN CONSTITUTIONAL LAW at 528–45.

35. *See* U.S. CONST. art. I, sec. 6, cl. 2.

36. The Supreme Court has utilized justiciability devices such as the doctrine of standing to dismiss challenges based upon the Incompatibility and Ineligibility Clauses of article I, section 6, clause 2 of the Constitution, despite the apparent validity of those challenges on the merits. *See* Schlesinger v. Re-

servists Committee to Stop the War, 418 U.S. 208 (1974) (dismissing on standing grounds Incompatibility Clause challenge to simultaneous membership in Congress and armed forces reserves); Ex Parte Levitt, 302 U.S. 633 (1937) (dismissing on standing grounds Ineligibility Clause challenge to Supreme Court appointment of Justice Black, who while member of Senate had voted to increase retirement benefits for Supreme Court justices); cf. McClure v. Carter, 513 F. Supp. 265 (D. Idaho) (three-judge court), aff'd mem., 454 U.S. 1025 (1981) (dismissing on standing grounds Ineligibility Clause challenge to Court of Appeals appointment of Judge Mikva, who was member of House of Representatives when salaries of federal judges were increased).

37. See U.S. CONST. amend. II (guaranteeing the right to bear arms).
38. U.S. CONST. amend. IX (reserving unenumerated rights to the people).
39. See U.S. CONST. amend. XI. Eleventh amendment jurisprudence has become extremely complex. In part this is because, in interpreting the eleventh amendment bar on unconsented-to federal court suits against states, the Supreme Court has disregarded the language of the amendment, sometimes giving it a construction that is broader than its language and sometimes giving it a construction that is narrower than its language. See H. FINK and M. TUSHNET, FEDERAL JURISDICTION: POLICY AND PRACTICE, 126–30 (Charlottesville, Va.: Michie 1984); Jackson, The Supreme Court, the Eleventh Amendment, and State Sovereignty, 98 YALE L.J. 1 (1988).
40. The chronology that follows is adapted from G. STONE, et al., CONSTITUTIONAL LAW at 444–51.
41. The thirteenth amendment states:

> Sec. 1—Neither slavery nor involuntary servitude, except as a punishment for crime whereof the party shall have been duly convicted, shall exist within the United States, or any place subject to their jurisdiction.
> Sec. 2—Congress shall have power to enforce this article by appropriate legislation.

U.S. CONST. amend. XIII.

42. Act of April 9, 1866, 14 Stat. 27.
43. The fourteenth amendment states in pertinent part:

> Sec. 1—All persons born or naturalized in the United States, and subject to the jurisdiction thereof, are citizens of the United States and of the State wherein they reside. No State shall make or enforce any law which shall abridge the privileges or immunities of citizens of the United States; nor shall any State deprive any person of life, liberty or property, without due process of law; nor deny to any person within its jurisdiction the equal protection of the laws.
> *   *   *
> Sec. 5—The Congress shall have power to enforce, by appropriate legislation, the provisions of this article.

U.S. CONST. amend. XIV [emphasis added].

44. Act of May 31, 1870, 16 Stat. 140, 144.

45. 42 U.S.C. §§ 1981 & 1982.

46. That section states:

> All persons within the jurisdiction of the United States shall have the same right in every State and Territory to make and enforce contracts, to sue, be parties, give evidence, and to the full and equal benefit of all laws and proceedings for the security of persons and property as is enjoyed by white citizens, and shall be subject to like punishment, pains, penalties, taxes, licenses, and exactions of every kind, and to no other.

> 42 U.S.C. § 1981.

47. That section states:

> All citizens of the United States shall have the same right, in every State and Territory, as is enjoyed by white citizens thereof to inherit, purchase, lease, sell, hold, and convey real and personal property.

> 42 U.S.C. § 1982.

48. *See generally* G. STONE, *et al.,* CONSTITUTIONAL LAW at 444–51.

49. *See* Chapter 4, note 43.

50. *See* Chapter 4, note 41.

51. 109 U.S. 3 (1883).

52. *See id.* at 14–15.

53. *See id.* at 27–28.

54. *See, e.g.,* United States v. Cruikshank, 92 U.S. 542 (1875) (Reconstruction statutes did not reach actions of private lynch mob); Slaughter-House Cases, 83 U.S. (16 Wall.) 36 (1873) (Reconstruction amendments limited to certain rights with strong federal nexus, thereby having practical effect of leaving states as primary guarantors of most civil rights); *cf.* United States v. Harris, 106 U.S. 629 (1882) (congressional power under related Ku Klux Klan Act of 1871 insufficient to reach actions of private lynch mob).

The contemporaneous cases are somewhat more complicated than has been suggested in the text because certain decisions appear to contemplate the existence of at least some congressional power to prohibit private actions that interfere with uniquely federal rights. *See, e.g.,* United States v. Cruikshank, 92 U.S. at 555–56 (suggesting that Reconstruction statutes did not reach private actions of lynch mob because victims were not attempting to petition *federal* government in violation of right of national citizenship); *see also* Logan v. United States, 144 U.S. 263 (1892) (congressional authority extends to criminal punishment of private violence directed at individuals in custody of U.S. marshal); Ex Parte Yarbrough, 110 U.S. 651 (1884) (congressional power under Ku Klux Klan Act of 1871 sufficient to reach private violence directed at blacks voting in *congressional* election). However, the class of uniquely federal rights so protected was quite narrow, never amounting to a general prohibition on private acts of racial discrimination. It is likely that this class of rights corresponded to the "badges and incidents" of slavery with respect to which the Court contemplated congressional prohibition of private action in the *Civil Rights Cases*. *See* page 44. *See generally* G. STONE, *et al.*, CONSTITUTIONAL LAW at 444-51.

55. 392 U.S. 409 (1968).
56. *See id.* at 413.
57. 427 U.S. 160 (1976).
58. *See id.* at 167-79.
59. 485 U.S. 617 (1988).
60. 491 U.S. 164 (1989). The Court held that although § 1981 prohibited private discrimination in contracting, the statute did not reach acts of racial harassment in the performance of a contract. *See id.* at 175-85; *see also* page 99 (describing *Patterson* holding).
61. *See id.* at 164-65.
62. *See id.* at 189-90 (Stevens, J., concurring) (arguing that the legislative history disclosed an intent not to outlaw segregated public, let alone private, schools).
63. Civil Rights Act of 1964, Pub. L. 88-352; 78 Stat. 241, 243 (1964) (codified at 42 U.S.C. § 2000a (1982)).
64. Fair Housing Act of 1968, Pub. L. 90-284; 82 Stat. 73, 81 (1968) (codified as amended at 42 U.S.C. §§ 3601-3619 (1982 & Supp. IV 1986)).
65. *See* U.S. CONST. art. I, sec. 8, cl. 3.
66. *See* U.S. CONST. art. I, sec. 8, cl. 1.
67. *See, e.g.,* Katzenbach v. McClung, 379 U.S. 294 (1964); Heart of Atlanta Motel v. United States, 379 U.S. 241 (1964) (upholding commerce power as source of congressional authority for Title II of Civil Rights Act of 1964).
68. *See* page 12 (discussing erosion of framers' structural safeguards during New Deal).
69. 491 U.S 164, 172-75, *quoting Runyon*, 427 U.S. at 191 (Stevens, J., concurring, *quoting* B. CARDOZO, THE NATURE OF THE JUDICIAL PROCESS 149 (New Haven: Yale University Press 1921)).
70. *See* page 42 (discussing Reconstruction amendments and Civil Rights Act of 1866).
71. *See* Jones v. Alfred H. Mayer Co., 392 U.S. at 424 n.32.
72. The provision states in pertinent part:

> Every *person* who, under color of any statute, ordinance, regulation, custom, or usage, of any State or Territory or the District of Columbia, subjects, or causes to be subjected, any citizen of the United States or other person within the jurisdiction thereof to the deprivation of any rights, privileges, or immunities secured by the Constitution and laws, shall be liable to the party injured in an action at law, suit in equity, or other proper proceeding for redress. . . .

> 42 U.S.C. § 1983 [emphasis added].

73. *See* Will v. Michigan Department of State Police, 491 U.S. 58 (1989), *citing* Felder v. Casey, 487 U.S. 131 (1988); Patsy v. Board of Regents of Florida, 457 U.S. 496, 503 (1982).

> The jurisdictional analogue to § 1983 is contained in 28 U.S.C. § 1343(3), which

extends federal court jurisdiction to any civil action that seeks [t]o redress the deprivation, under color of any State law, statute, ordinance, regulation, custom or usage, of any right, privilege or immunity secured by the Constitution of the United States or by any Act of Congress providing for equal rights of citizens or of all persons within the jurisdiction of the United States;

28 U.S.C. § 1343(3). *See* Hagans v. Lavine, 415 U.S. 528, 535–36 (1974); Lynch v. Household Finance Corp, 405 U.S. 538, 542–46 (1972).

74. *See* Lugar v. Edmondson Oil Co., 457 U.S. 922, 926–29 (1982); *see also* Flagg Brothers v. Brooks, 436 U.S. 149, 155–57 (1978); Jackson v. Metropolitan Edison, 419 U.S. 345, 347–49 (1974); Adickes v. Kress & Co., 398 U.S. 144, 150–52 (1970).

75. The eleventh amendment states:

The Judicial power of the United States shall not be construed to extend to any suit in law or equity, commenced or prosecuted against one of the United States by citizens of another State, or by Citizens or Subjects of any Foreign State.

U.S. CONST. amend. XI.

As noted above, *see* Chapter 4, note 39, eleventh amendment jurisprudence is quite complex. The Court has simultaneously given the eleventh amendment both a broader and a narrower interpretation than one could derive from a literal reading of its language alone. Under the contemporary formulation, most suits in which the State is actually named as a defendant are barred, unless the state has waived or Congress has abrogated the immunity. *See generally* Jackson, *Eleventh Amendment*, 98 YALE L.J. at 8–13. Nevertheless, the eleventh amendment presumably permits at least some suits in which the Supreme Court is granted original jurisdiction. *See* U.S. CONST. art. III, sec. 2.

76. 209 U.S. 123 (1908).

77. *See id.* at 159–60.

78. *See* Chapter 4, note 72.

79. *See* Fitzpatrick v. Bitzer, 427 U.S. 445, 452 (1976).

80. 365 U.S. 167, 187–91 (1961).

81. *See* Fitzpatrick v. Bitzer, 427 U.S. at 452.

82. *See id.*

83. 438 U.S. 658 (1978).

84. *See id.* at 690–95.

85. *See* Will v. Michigan Department of State Police, 491 U.S. 58, 63 n.4 (1989). This, of course, suggests yet another way in which a court can avoid application of an explicitly applicable principle of law; it can simply decline ever to mention it.

86. 491 U.S. 58 (1989).

87. *See id.* at 62–71.

88. *See id.* at 71.

89. *See id.* at 71 n.10.

90. *See* Quern v. Jordan, 440 U.S. 332 (1979); Edelman v. Jordan, 415 U.S. 651 (1974).

91. It is true that this would have provided a substantive federal cause of action against such "persons" in state court cases which would not be subject to eleventh amendment protections—cases like *Will* itself, which was filed in the Michigan state court system. *See Will* 491 U.S. at 60. However, it is difficult to find anything objectionable about this result because the state courts are themselves free to invoke the common law doctrine of sovereign immunity to the extent that they wish to protect their state treasuries. Stated somewhat differently, it is difficult to see why the Supreme Court has an interest in constricting the substantive scope of § 1983 to preclude state court suits against states and state officials if the state courts themselves choose not to preclude such suits.

92. *See* page 28 (discussing *McCleskey* decision).

93. 380 U.S. 202 (1965).

94. *See* Swain v. State, 275 Ala. 508, 509-11, 156 So. 2d 368, 369-71 (1963).

95. *See, e.g.,* Strauder v. West Virginia, 100 U.S. 303, 308, 309-10 (1880); *see also* Norris v. Alabama, 294 U.S. 587, 596-99 (1935).

96. *See Swain,* 380 U.S. at 221-24.

97. *Id.* at 221-22.

98. *See id.*

99. *See* Batson v. Kentucky, 476 U.S. 79, 122-23 (1986) (Burger, C.J., dissenting), *quoting,* United States v. Leslie, 783 F.2d 541, 544 (5th Cir. 1986) (en banc).

100. 481 U.S. 279 (1987).

101. *See* page 28 (discussing *McCleskey* decision).

102. *See Swain,* 380 U.S at 222-26.

103. *See id.*

104. *See id.* at 222-28.

105. 476 U.S. 79 (1986).

106. *See id.* at 82, 100 n.25.

107. *See id.* at 134 (Rehnquist, J., dissenting).

108. *See id.* at 100-01 (White, J., concurring).

109. *See id.* at 89 n.12.

110. *See id.* at 107-08 (Marshall, J., concurring).

111. *See* page 41.

112. *See* page 66.

113. 111 S.Ct. 1364 (1991).

114. 111 S.Ct. 2077 (1991).

115. *See id.* at 2081-87.

116. *See id.* at 2095 (Scalia, J., dissenting); *cf. id.* at 2094 (O'Connor, J., dissenting).

117. 111 S.Ct. 1859 (1991).

118. *See id.* at 1864-68.

119. *See id.* at 1868-72.

CHAPTER 5

1. 410 U.S. 113 (1973).
2. In Roe, the Court held that state restrictions on a woman's choice to have an abortion could be justified only by a compelling state interest, either in maternal health or in the potential life of a fetus. During the first trimester of pregnancy, neither state interest could be considered compelling because an abortion posed less of a risk to maternal health than childbirth did, and because the state's interest in the potential life of the fetus could not be compelling prior to viability. During the third trimester, however, the state's interest could become compelling in light of the high likelihood of fetal viability, thereby permitting the state to prohibit third trimester abortions. See Roe, 410 U.S. at 162–66. Although the Roe rules are fairly specific, the constitutional right of privacy on which Roe was based is extremely nonspecific. See id. at 152–56 (discussing source of constitutional right to privacy); see generally G. STONE, et al., CONSTITUTIONAL LAW at 909–55 (raising numerous questions about the nature, source, and scope of the right to privacy recognized in Roe).
3. In Harris v. McRae, 448 U.S. 297 (1980), and Maher v. Roe, 432 U.S. 464 (1977), the Supreme Court held that the right to abortion recognized in Roe did not require the state to fund abortions for indigents even when the state chose to fund the medical services associated with childbirth. Because the strict scrutiny typically accorded legislative classifications that burden fundamental rights, such as the right to abortion, would not seem to tolerate the legislative differentiations that the Court upheld in Harris and Maher, the nature and scope of the right to abortion are very unclear. In recent Terms, the Court has cut back considerably on the right to abortion that was originally recognized in Roe. See, e.g., Rust v. Sullivan, 111 S.Ct 1759 (1991) (upholding restrictions on dissemination of information about abortion and abortion services by federally funded family planning organizations); Webster v. Reproductive Health Services, 429 U.S. 490 (1989) (upholding various state restrictions on right to abortion, including prohibition on abortions conducted in public medical facilities). The appointment of Justices Souter and Thomas to the Supreme Court to replace Justices Brennan and Marshall raises the possibility that Roe will be further restricted or even overruled.
4. A numerical majority of the population appears to favor the decision. According to a poll taken by Yankelovich Clancy Shulman for TIME MAGAZINE, 57 percent of those polled opposed overturning Roe v. Wade. See The Battle over Abortion, TIME, July 17, 1989, at p. 62. However, the vocal minority that opposes the decision can be viewed as an "elite" majority for present purposes. See page 22 (discussing elite nature of majority that actually makes governmental policy). Note that the "elite" majority opposed to the decision may lose its political influence in the wake of the Supreme Court's

subsequent decisions restricting the right to abortion in Rust v. Sullivan, 111 S.Ct. 1759 (1991), and Webster v. Reproductive Health Services, 429 U.S. 490 (1989). According to the same poll, 32 percent of the respondents said that they would never vote for a political candidate who advocated restricting a woman's right to obtain an abortion, while only 24 percent said they would never vote for a candidate who favored abortion. Moreover, 61 percent of those polled reported that they disagreed with the *Webster* decision. *See id.* This raises the possibility that those who support the Roe v. Wade decision will now become more active in the political arena than those who oppose it.

5. *See* Rust v. Sullivan, 111 S.Ct. 1759 (1991) (upholding restrictions on the dissemination of information about abortion services by institutions receiving federal funds); Webster v. Reproductive Health Services, 429 U.S. 490 (1989) (upholding restrictions on the availability of abortions).

6. 384 U.S. 436 (1966). The Court required that "prior to any questioning, [a suspect] must be warned that he has a right to remain silent, that any statement he does make may be used as evidence against him, and that he has the right to the presence of an attorney, either retained or appointed." *Id.* at 444. Statements obtained during custodial interrogation not preceded by this "*Miranda* warning" were deemed involuntary within the meaning of the fifth amendment privilege against self-incrimination. *See id.* at 458.

7. Cases decided shortly after *Miranda* tended to give the decision an expansive interpretation. *See, e.g.*, Orozco v. Texas, 394 U.S. 324 (1969) (questioning of suspect after four police officers entered his boarding house bedroom at 4 A.M. constituted custodial interrogation requiring *Miranda* warnings). Recent cases, however, have given the case a more restrictive reading. *See, e.g.*, Duckworth v. Eagan, 492 U.S. 195 (1989) (informing suspect that attorney would be appointed if and when defendant went to court not inadequate under *Miranda* even though defendant is not informed of right to attorney before questioning); New York v. Quarles, 467 U.S. 649 (1984) (overriding considerations of public safety create exception to need for *Miranda* warnings); Oregon v. Bradshaw, 462 U.S. 1039 (1983) (defendant's question "Well, what is going to happen to me now?" constitutes initiation of dialogue by defendant sufficient to permit inference of waiver of *Miranda* rights); Rhode Island v. Innis, 446 U.S. 291 (1980) (interrogation only includes statements made by police officer which he should have known were reasonably likely to elicit response); North Carolina v. Butler, 441 U.S. 369 (1979) (use of inculpatory statements permissible where defendant says he understands *Miranda* rights but refuses to sign written waiver of those rights); United States v. Mandujana, 425 U.S. 564 (1976) (*Miranda* warnings not required prior to compelled testimony before grand jury); Michigan v. Tucker, 417 U.S. 433 (1974) (prosecution may use testimony of witness whose identity was discovered through custodial interrogation of defendant who had not received all *Miranda* warnings).

8. *See* Seidman, *Brown and Miranda*, 80 CALIF. L. REV—(May 1992) (arguing that *Miranda* decision actually makes it easier to use coerced confessions as evidence in criminal trials).

9. *See, e.g.,* R. DWORKIN, TAKING RIGHTS SERIOUSLY 22–45 (Cambridge: Harvard University Press 1977); H. HART and A. SACKS, THE LEGAL PROCESS: BASIC PROBLEMS IN THE MAKING AND APPLICATION OF LAW 375–85 (tentative ed. 1958); Kennedy, *Form and Substance In Private Law Adjudication,* 89 HARV. L. REV. 1685, 1687–1713 (1976); Wellington, *Common Law Rules and Constitutional Double Standards,* 83 YALE L.J. 221, 222–64 (1973).

10. The jurisprudential shift from formalism to realism, and its concomitant abandonment of linguistic conceptual analysis, is described more fully in Spann, *A Critical Legal Studies Perspective On Contract Law and Practice,* 1988 ANNUAL SURVEY OF AMERICAN LAW 223, and the sources discussed therein.

11. A sophisticated yet comprehensible description of deconstructive techniques is contained in Balkin, *Deconstructive Practice and Legal Theory,* 96 YALE L.J. 743 (1987). A more elementary description, based upon Balkin's account, is contained in Spann, *Critical Legal Studies Perspective.*

12. *See* page 38 (discussing Washington v. Davis adoption of intent principle for fourteenth amendment discrimination cases).

13. *See* page 58 (discussing high level of abstraction required for legal principles).

14. *See* page 37 (discussing policy justifications for intent principle).

15. This appears to be the interpretation of the intent principle that the Supreme Court adopted in Village of Arlington Heights v. Metropolitan Housing Development Corp., 429 U.S. 252 (1977), where the Supreme Court, in upholding the denial of a rezoning permit for the construction of low- and moderate-income housing in a white residential area, was reluctant to draw an inference of discriminatory intent from the disparate impact of the official action. *Cf.* Personnel Administrator v. Feeney, 442 U.S. 256 (1979) (Supreme Court, in upholding state law establishing veterans' preference in civil service hiring, unwilling to draw inference of intent to discriminate on basis of gender despite legislature's knowledge of obvious disparate impact because there was no evidence of invidious intent).

16. This appears to be the interpretation of the intent principle that the Court adopted in Swann v. Charlotte-Mecklenburg Board of Education, 402 U.S. 1 (1971) (permitting inference of discriminatory intent in fashioning school desegregation remedy based upon school board's tolerance of known disparate impact entailed in proposed desegregation plan); *cf.* Castaneda v. Partida, 430 U.S. 482 (1977) (permitting inference of discriminatory intent in selection of jurors based upon tolerance of known disparate impact of jury selection process). *See generally* J. ELY, DEMOCRACY AND DISTRUST at 155–61; G. STONE, *et al.,* CONSTITUTIONAL LAW at 553–62.

17. *See* page 40.
18. *See* R. CHUSED, CASES, MATERIALS AND PROBLEMS IN PROPERTY at 189–95.
19. *See* Edmonson v. Leesville Concrete Co., 111 S.Ct 2077, 2082 (1991), and cases cited therein.
20. 271 U.S. 323 (1926).
21. *See id.* at 330–31 (dismissing appeal for want of substantial federal question).
22. 334 U.S. 1 (1948).
23. *See id.* at 8–9.
24. *See id.* at 18–19.
25. 346 U.S. 249 (1953).
26. *See id.* at 253–54.
27. 382 U.S. 296 (1966).
28. *See id.* at 300–02.
29. 396 U.S. 435 (1970).
30. *See id.* at 443–47.
31. *See* T. HOBBES, LEVIATHAN (New York: Dutton 1950).
32. The intractability of this problem is highlighted by the current affirmative action debate, which is discussed in Chapter 8.
33. For a general discussion of the problems posed by the state action issue and a demonstration of the difficulties inherent in various efforts to surmount it, see G. STONE, *et al.*, CONSTITUTIONAL LAW at 1488–99.
34. 347 U.S. 483 (1954).
35. 163 U.S. 537 (1896).
36. *See Brown,* 347 U.S. at 495.
37. *See, e.g.,* Korematsu v. United States, 323 U.S. 214 (1944) (upholding World War II curfews and other restrictions on Japanese-Americans after strict scrutiny); Fullilove v. Klutznick, 448 U.S. 448 (1980) (upholding affirmative action program after strict scrutiny); *cf.* Metro Broadcasting v. Federal Communications Commission, 110 S.Ct. 2997 (1990) (upholding affirmative action program after intermediate scrutiny). The affirmative action cases that permit and that prohibit racial classifications are discussed in Chapter 8.
38. *See* page 27 (discussing infiltration of legal principles by majoritarian preferences).
39. 390 U.S. 333 (1968), *affirming* Washington v. Lee, 263 F. Supp. 327 (M.D. Ala. 1966) (three-judge court).
40. *See* Washington v. Lee, 263 F. Supp. at 328–29, 331.
41. *See* Lee v. Washington, 390 U.S. at 334; Washington v. Lee, 263 F. Supp. at 331, 332.
42. *See, e.g.,* J. ELY, DEMOCRACY AND DISTRUST at 148 nn. 44 & 45.
43. Note that this is *not* the way that the Court ruled in the case. Although the Court invalidated the Alabama statute, it did so because it did not believe the state's offered justification. The Court did, however, go out of its way

to suggest that when safety and discipline concerns were genuinely at issue, limited-duration racial segregation would be permissible. *See* page 71.

44. This is the outcome that appears to correspond to the Court's actual decision. *See* page 72.

45. 347 U.S. 483 (1954) (*Brown I*) (declaring segregated public schools unconstitutional as violation of fourteenth amendment); 349 U.S. 294 (1955) (*Brown II*) (requiring desegregation of public schools "with all deliberate speed").

46. *See* Green v. County School Board, 391 U.S. 430, 435–36 (1968).

47. *See* Chapter 5, note 45 (citing *Brown* decisions).

48. *See* D. BELL, RACE, RACISM AND AMERICAN LAW at 385 ff. (Boston: Little, Brown, 2d. ed. 1980); G. STONE, *et al.*, CONSTITUTIONAL LAW at 470–75.

49. *See* Milliken v. Bradley, 418 U.S. 717, 737–38, 745–47 (1974).

50. *See* Keyes v. School District No. 1, Denver, Colorado, 413 U.S. 189, 198–205, 208–89 (1973); *citing* Swann v. Charlotte-Mecklenburg Board of Education, 402 U.S. 1, 17–18 (1971).

51. *See* cases cited in Chapter 5, note 50.

52. *See Brown I*, 347 U.S. at 486 n.1. The South Carolina, Virginia, and Delaware school systems were segregated by mandatory provisions of both state statutes and state constitutional provisions. The Topeka, Kansas, school system was segregated by a Board of Education policy that had been adopted pursuant to a Kansas statute that authorized, but did not require, segregated schools in cities whose populations exceeded 15,000. *See id.*

53. 418 U.S. 717 (1974).

54. *See Milliken*, 418 U.S. at 724, 735, 739; *id.* at 764–65 (White, J., dissenting) (citing lower court discussions of residential segregation in Detroit and surrounding suburbs).

55. *See* Chapter 5, note 52.

56. *See* page 60 (demonstrating difficulty of applying prohibition on intentional discrimination in context of racially disparate impact).

57. *See generally* D. BELL, RACE, RACISM at 402; G. STONE, *et al.*, CONSTITUTIONAL LAW at 470–75, 492–93.

58. *See* G. STONE, *et al.*, CONSTITUTIONAL LAW at 471 (discussing Cooper v. Aaron, 358 U.S. 1 (1958), in which Supreme Court denied request of Little Rock School Board to terminate desegregation order on grounds of massive public resistance).

59. *See* Dorman, *A Who's Who of Friends and Foes; Some were allies, others adversaries. All of their Lives intersected John F. Kennedy's*, NEWSDAY, Nov. 21, 1988, at p. 6 (discussing George Wallace's staunch opposition to school desegregation).

60. *See* R. FORMISANO, BOSTON AGAINST BUSING: RACE, CLASS AND ETHNICITY IN THE 1960'S AND THE 1970'S (Chapel Hill: University of North Carolina Press 1991).

61. *See* page 105 (offering majoritarian explanation for *Brown* decision).
62. *See* D. BELL, RACE, RACISM at 397–402.
63. 413 U.S. 189 (1973).
64. 418 U.S. 717 (1974).
65. *See Keyes*, 413 U.S. at 191–95, 198–213.
66. *See Milliken*, 418 U.S. at 722–36, 744–47.
67. *See Milliken*, 418 U.S. at 738–44.
68. For example, the school district involved in Green v. County School Board, 391 U.S. 430 (1968), the case in which the Supreme Court held that "freedom of choice" plans did not constitute a constitutionally sufficient desegregation remedy, contained only two schools. *See id.* at 432.
69. For example, the Detroit school district that was involved in *Milliken* contained 319 schools. *See Milliken*, 418 U.S. at 729–30 n.10.
70. This thesis and the chronology of desegregation cases upon which it rests are discussed in D. BELL, RACE, RACISM at 385–444; G. STONE, *et al.*, CONSTITUTIONAL LAW at 492, 470–495; *see also* G. GUNTHER, CONSTITUTIONAL LAW at 728–51.
71. *See* D. BELL, RACE, RACISM at 387–89; G. STONE *et al.*, CONSTITUTIONAL LAW at 492–93.
72. 391 U.S. 430 (1968).
73. 402 U.S. 1 (1971).
74. *See* page 75 (discussing *Keyes*).
75. *See* D. BELL, RACE, RACISM at 399, 402–11; G. STONE, *et al.*, CONSTITUTIONAL LAW at 492–93.
76. 425 U.S. 284 (1976).
77. 427 U.S. 424 (1976).
78. 433 U.S. 267 (1977) (*Milliken II*).
79. *See* 433 U.S. 406 (1977) (*Dayton I*) (reversing court of appeals order requiring system-wide desegregation plan); 443 U.S. 526 (1979) (*Dayton II*) (affirming court of appeals order requiring system-wide desegregation plan).
80. 443 U.S. 449 (1979).
81. *See* D. BELL, RACE, RACISM AND AMERICAN LAW SUPPLEMENT 84–86 (Boston: Little, Brown, 1984) (discussing black disenchantment with busing and desegregation in the Dallas, Texas, school system that was at issue in Tasby v. Wright, 520 F. Supp. 683 (N. D. Tex. 1981)).
82. 458 U.S. 457 (1982).
83. 458 U.S. 527 (1982).
84. *See Seattle*, 458 U.S. at 488–89 (Powell, J., dissenting).
85. 478 U.S. 385 (1986).
86. *See Green*, 391 U.S. 430 (1968).
87. 110 S.Ct. 1651 (1990).
88. Although five justices voted to uphold the authority of the district court to order a tax increase that was necessary to permit compliance with a valid

affirmative action plan, two of those justices—Justices Brennan and Marshall—are no longer on the Court, and their more conservative replacements—Justices Souter and Thomas—may choose to vote with the four justices who wished to deny district courts the power to order tax increases to pay for desegregation plans. *See Jenkins,* 110 S.Ct. at 1667 (Kennedy, J., concurring in part and concurring in the judgment, with Rehnquist, C.J., O'Connor and Scalia, JJ.). The Court also addressed a related issue in Spallone v. United States, 110 S.Ct. 625 (1990), where it upheld the authority of a district court to impose substantial civil contempt penalties against the city of Yonkers, New York, for defiance of the court's public housing desegregation orders, but reversed the imposition of such penalties against individual city officials.

89. 111 S.Ct. 630 (1991).
90. *See* Ayers v. Allain, 914 F.2d 676 (5th. Cir. 1990) (en banc), *cert. granted sub. nom.* U.S. v. Mabus, 59 L.W. 3732 (No. 90-6588, Apr. 15, 1991); Freeman v. Pitts, 887 F.2d 1438 (11th. Cir. 1989), *cert. granted,* 59 L.W. 3561 (No. 89-1290, Feb. 12, 1991).

Part II

CHAPTER 6

1. *See* J. ELY, DEMOCRACY AND DISTRUST (describing representation reinforcement theory of judicial review).
2. *See* page 12 (discussing dilution of structural safeguards during New Deal).
3. 347 U.S. 483 (1954) (*Brown I*) (abandoning separate-but-equal interpretation of fourteenth amendment); 349 U.S. 294 (1955) (*Brown II*) (requiring integration of public schools "with all deliberate speed").
4. *Butch Cassidy and the Sundance Kid* (Twentieth-Century Fox 1969).
5. *See, e.g.,* J. ELY, DEMOCRACY AND DISTRUST; *cf.* Sunstein, *Republican Revival*; Sunstein, *Interest Groups,* (both emphasizing civic republican values that can be expressed in properly operating political process).
6. *See, e.g.,* Peller, Neutral Principles *in the 1950's,* 21 MICH. J.L. REF. 561 (1988) (neutrality premise of pluralism impossible to realize); Sunstein, *Interest Groups,* 38 STAN. L. REV. at 81-85 (pluralism is normatively unattractive); Tushnet, *Darkness on the Edge of Town: The Contributions of John Hart Ely to Constitutional Theory,* 89 YALE L.J. 1073 (1980) (pluralism is descriptively inaccurate); Crenshaw, *Race, Reform, and Retrenchment: Transformation and Legitimation in Antidiscrimination Law,* 101 HARV. L. REV. 1331, 1378-79 (1988) (pluralist efforts to remedy race discrimination through colorblind antidiscrimination laws ignore racism inherent in status quo); Ehrenreich, *Pluralist Myths and Powerless Men: The Ideology of Reasonableness in Sexual Harassment Law,* 99 YALE L.J. 1177,

1190–93 (1990) (legal standard of objective reasonableness used to resolve harassment cases represents failed pluralist attempt to mediate ultimately irreconcilable conflict between divergent societal perspectives).

For general discussions of pluralist political theory, see A. BENTLEY, THE PROCESS OF GOVERNMENT (Bloomington, Ind.: Principia Press 1908); R. DAHL, A PREFACE TO DEMOCRATIC THEORY (Chicago: University of Chicago Press 1956); J. FREEDMAN, CRISIS AND LEGITIMACY (New York: Cambridge University Press 1978); T. LOWI, THE END OF LIBERALISM (New York: Norton, 2d ed. 1979); D. TRUMAN, THE GOVERNMENTAL PROCESS: POLITICAL INTERESTS AND PUBLIC OPINION (New York: Knopf 1965); THE BIAS OF PLURALISM (W. CONNELLY ed.) (New York: Atherton Press 1969); FRONTIERS OF DEMOCRATIC THEORY (H. KARIEL ed.) (New York: Random House 1970); Bourke, *The Pluralist Reading of James Madison's Tenth Federalist*, 9 PERSP. AMER. HIST. 269 (1975); Farber and Frickey, *The Jurisprudence of Public Choice*, 65 TEXAS L. REV. 873 (1987); Peltzman, *Toward a More General Theory of Regulation*, 19 J. L. & ECON. 211 (1976); Stewart, *The Reformation of American Administrative Law*, 88 HARV. L. REV. 1667 (1975); Stigler, *The Theory of Economic Regulation*, 2 BELL J. ECON. & MGMT. SCI. 3 (1971).

7. *See, e.g.,* T. PANGLE, THE SPIRIT OF MODERN REPUBLICANISM (Chicago: University of Chicago Press 1988); Appleby, *Republicanism in Old and New Contexts*, 43 WM. & MARY Q. 20 (1986); Horwitz, *Republicanism and Liberalism in American Constitutional Thought*, 29 WM. & MARY L. REV. 57 (1987); Simon, *The New Republicanism: Generosity of Spirit in Search of Something to Say*, 29 WM. & MARY L. REV. 83 (1987); Sunstein, *Republican Revival; see generally Symposium: The Republican Civic Tradition*.

8. *See, e.g.,* Michelman, *Law's Republic* 97 YALE L.J. 1493, 1529–32 (1988). Obvious problems are posed if there is no common moral theory to which the deliberating interest groups subscribe.

9. For an introduction to public choice theory see Farber and Frickey, *Jurisprudence of Public Choice*, 65 TEXAS L. REV. at 875–906 and sources cited therein. *See also* K. ARROW, SOCIAL CHOICE AND INDIVIDUAL VALUES (New Haven: Yale University Press, 2d ed. 1963); J. BUCHANAN and G. TULLOCK, THE CALCULUS OF CONSENT: LOGICAL FOUNDATIONS OF CONSTITUTIONAL DEMOCRACY (Ann Arbor: University of Michigan Press 1965); R. EPSTEIN, TAKINGS: PRIVATE PROPERTY AND THE POWER OF EMINENT DOMAIN (Cambridge: Harvard University Press 1985); W. ESKRIDGE and P. FRICKEY, CASES AND MATERIALS ON LEGISLATION: STATUTES AND THE CREATION OF PUBLIC POLICY 367–98 (St. Paul, Minn: West Publishing 1987); D. MUELLER, PUBLIC CHOICE (New York: Cambridge 1979); Kelman, *"Public Choice" and Public Spirit*, 87 PUB. INT. 80 (1987); Mueller, *Public Choice:*

A Survey, 14 J. ECON. LIT. 395 (1976); *see generally Symposium on the Theory of Public Choice,* 74 VA. L. REV. 167–518 (1988).

10. *See generally* sources cited in Chapter 6, note 9.

11. *See* U.S. CONST. amend. XIII (ratified in 1868, giving blacks right to vote); U.S. CONST. amend. XIX (ratified in 1920, giving women right to vote).

12. *See* BLACK AND WHITE CHILDREN IN AMERICA: KEY FACTS 50 (Washington, D.C.: Report of the Children's Defense Fund 1983) (supplying data indicating that in 1983, 30.1 percent of all black adults in United States lived in poverty while only 17.3 percent of white children under age of 18 lived in poverty), *based upon* CURRENT POPULATION REPORT, U.S. DEPT. OF COMMERCE, BUREAU OF CENSUS, Series P-60, No. 145 (Washington, D.C.: Government Printing Office 1983) (overall black poverty rate in 1983 was 35.7 percent compared to overall white poverty rate of 12.1 percent).

13. *See* Dred Scott v. Sandford, 60 U.S. (19 How.) 393 (1857) (holding that blacks did not have rights of citizenship, which was overruled by political process through Civil War and enactment of fourteenth amendment); Minor v. Happersett, 88 U.S. 162 (1874) (upholding constitutionality of denying women right to vote, which was overruled by political process through enactment of nineteenth amendment).

14. In the November 1989 off-year elections, several black Democratic candidates defeated white opponents by piecing together coalitions that included both black support and substantial amounts of white support. The most notable is the election of Douglas Wilder as governor of Virginia, a state whose population is 80 percent white. Wilder is the first black ever to have been elected governor of a state since Reconstruction—although Tom Bradley lost the 1982 gubernatorial election in California by a margin of 1 percent, which is roughly the same margin by which Wilder won. In both the Wilder and Bradley elections, there appears to have been a substantial "silent" racist white vote that was not reflected in the polls. In addition to Wilder, David Dinkins was elected the first black mayor of New York City (winning 91 percent of the black vote, 26 percent of the white vote and 65 percent of the Latino vote); Norman Rice was elected the first black mayor of Seattle (a City whose population is only 10 percent black); John Daniels was elected the first black mayor of New Haven, Connecticut; Chester Jenkins was elected the first black mayor of Durham, North Carolina; and Michael White defeated his black opponent in the race for mayor of Cleveland by successfully competing for the white vote. *See* Attinger, *A Nice Guy Finishes First: But Dinkins May not be Tough Enough to Cope with New York,* TIME, Nov. 21, 1989, at p. 60; Fineman, *The New Black Politics: Candidates Across the Country Win Historic Victories by Emphasizing Mainstream Values,* NEWSWEEK, Nov. 20, 1989, at p. 52; Shapiro, *Breakthrough In Virginia: In a Model of Crossover Politics, Douglas Wilder Becomes the First Elected Black Governor and Shows Others How to Crash the Color Line,* TIME,

Nov. 21, 1989, at p. 54; Toner, *Tuesday's Stakes: Black Politicians are Leaning against Some Old Barriers*, N.Y. TIMES, Week in Review, Nov. 5, 1989, at Sec. 4, p. 1.

15. In 1988 Jesse Jackson received approximately 6.6 million votes in the Democratic primaries. *See* Dionne, *Jackson Share of Votes by Whites Triples in '88*, N.Y. TIMES, June 13, 1988, at p. B7. This represented 29 percent of the overall Democratic primary vote. *See* Kondracke, *Vultures: Scenarios for the Losing and Winning Political Parties*, NEW REPUBLIC, Nov. 7, 1988, at p. 10. In 1984 Jackson received approximately 3.3 million votes, comprising 18 percent of the Democratic primary vote. *See* R. SCAMMON and A. MCGILLIVRAY, AMERICA VOTES 16, A HANDBOOK OF CONTEMPORARY AMERICAN ELECTION STATISTICS, 1984 67 (Washington, D.C.: Congressional Quarterly 1984) (supplying data on which 18 percent calculation is based).

16. 488 U.S. 469 (1989); *see* page 127 (discussing *Croson* case).

17. The presence of minority actors in television shows and commercials attests to the presence of minority purchasing power, which can be translated into political power. The success of the Montgomery, Alabama bus boycott, orchestrated by Martin Luther King, provides an example. *See* Kennedy, *Martin Luther King's Constitution: A Legal History of the Montgomery Bus Boycott*, 98 YALE L.J. 999 (1989).

18. *See* Shogan, *Seeks to Avoid Hurting the Party: Dukakis Ponders What Role He Can Offer Jackson*, L.A. TIMES, June 27, 1988, at p. 1.

19. *See* Rich, *Hispanic Population of U.S. Growing Fastest: Census Bureau Puts Total at 20.1 Million*, WASH. POST, Oct. 12, 1989, at p. A3.

20. *See* Henry, *Beyond the Melting Pot*, TIME, April 9, 1990, at p. 28, 30.

21. Creation of a lasting coalition that will, *inter alia*, benefit racial minorities was the strategy embodied in Jesse Jackson's conception of the "Rainbow Coalition." The strategy appears to have increased in effectiveness over time. In 1988, Jackson received 12 percent of the white vote, consisting of approximately 2.1 million votes. In 1984, Jackson received only 5 percent of the white vote, consisting of approximately 650,000 votes. In addition, Jackson was able to capture 92 percent of the black vote in 1988, compared to 77 percent in 1984. *See* Dionne, *Jackson's Share*. Jackson's 6.6 million votes in 1988 are roughly comparable to the 7.0 million votes received by Edward Kennedy in 1980 and the 6.8 million votes received by Walter Mondale, who captured the Democratic nomination in 1984. *See* R. SCAMMON and A. MCGILLIVRAY, AMERICA VOTES 16 at 60, 67.

22. 410 U.S. 113 (1973) (finding constitutional right to abortion); *cf.* Rust v. Sullivan, 111 S.Ct. 1759 (1991) (limiting access of indigents to information about abortion services); Webster v. Reproductive Health Services, 429 U.S. 490 (1989) (arguably limiting scope of constitutional right to abortion).

23. *See* Harris v. McRae, 448 U.S. 297 (1980) (upholding constitutionality of federal refusal to fund abortions), Maher v. Roe, 432 U.S. 464 (1977) (upholding constitutionality of state refusal to fund abortions).

24. *See* page 11 (discussing relationship between judicial review and dangers of faction).

25. *See* page 99.

26. *See* G. STONE, *et al.*, CONSTITUTIONAL LAW at 436.

27. *See* U.S. CONST. art. I, sec. 9, cl. 1.

28. *See* U.S. CONST. art. I, sec. 2, cl. 3.

29. *See* U.S. CONST. art. IV, sec. 2, cl. 3.

30. *See, e.g.,* U.S. CONST. art. I, sec. 9 (prohibiting congressional termination of slave trade until 1808); *see* G. STONE *et al.*, CONSTITUTIONAL LAW at 436-37, *quoting* D. ROBINSON, SLAVERY IN THE STRUCTURE OF AMERICAN POLITICS 1765-1820 209, 210, 244-46 (New York: Harcourt, Brace, Jovanovich 1971).

31. *See generally*; R. COVER, JUSTICE ACCUSED: ANTISLAVERY AND THE JUDICIAL PROCESS (New Haven: Yale University Press 1975); P. FINKELMAN, SLAVERY, RACE AND THE AMERICAN LEGAL SYSTEM, 1700-1872 (New York: Garland Publishing 1988); A.L. HIGGINBOTHAM, JR., IN THE MATTER OF COLOR: RACE AND THE AMERICAN LEGAL PROCESS: THE COLONIAL PERIOD (New York: Oxford University Press 1978); M. TUSHNET, THE AMERICAN LAW OF SLAVERY, 1810-1860: CONSIDERATIONS OF HUMANITY AND INTEREST (Princeton, N.J.: Princeton University Press 1981); W. WIECEK, THE SOURCES OF ANTISLAVERY CONSTITUTIONALISM IN AMERICA 1760-1848 (Ithaca, N.Y.: Cornell University Press 1977).

The precise manner in which slavery was ended varied from state to state. For example, there is debate as to precisely when slavery came to an end in Massachusetts. The state constitution, ratified in 1780, contained a clause stating, "All men are born free and equal, and have certain natural and unalienable rights; among which may be reckoned the right of enjoying and defending their lives and liberty. . . ." In 1783, a white defendant was convicted by the Supreme Judicial Court of beating and imprisoning a black man, despite the defense that the black man was the defendant's slave. In 1781, the Court reached a similar result in the case of another alleged slave. In combination, these cases helped to promote prevailing public opinion that blacks should be deemed free, thereby effectively ending slavery in Massachusetts. *See* R. COVER, JUSTICE ACCUSED at 43-50. The Massachusetts experience also dictated the status of slavery in the Territory of Maine, which did not separate from its mother state of Massachusetts until 1820. *See* WIECEK, SOURCES OF ANTISLAVERY CONSTITUTIONALISM at 51.

In Jackson v. Bulloch, 12 Conn. 38 (1837), the Connecticut Supreme Court ruled that the Connecticut Constitution, which also contained a "free and equal" provision, did not prohibit slavery. Rather, the court deferred to state emancipation statutes that freed slaves gradually. A 1774 statute prohibited the importation of slaves into Connecticut. A 1784 statute stated that no person of color born after that year could be forced to remain a slave after he or she reached the age of 25. *See Jackson,* 12 Conn. at 39; R. COVER, JUSTICE ACCUSED at 55. Similarly, in the 1845 case of State v. Post, 20 N.J.L. 368 (1845), the New Jersey Supreme Court held that the "free and equal" clause in its constitution did not apply to slaves. Therefore, the estimated 700 slaves remaining in New Jersey more than 40 years following the passage of a gradual emancipation statute in 1804 had to wait for their freedom under the Act. *See* R. COVER, JUSTICE ACCUSED at 55-60.

The Pennsylvania Act of 1780 stated that all persons born after July 4, 1780, were to be free. Slaves born before that date would remain slaves during their lifetimes. Children of these slaves-for-life would remain slaves for 28 years. *See* R. COVER, JUSTICE ACCUSED at 62-67. The Vermont Constitution contained a "free and equal" provision that was implemented through a specific prohibition on keeping a person a "servant, slave or apprentice" after age 21 for males and age 18 for females. *See id.* at 43 n.5. The Vermont Supreme Court held that this clause ended slavery in the case of Selectman v. Jacob, 2 Vt. 200 (1804). New York passed a gradual emancipation statute in 1799. Children freed by this act remained slaves until age 28 for males and 25 for females. *See* W. WIECEK, SOURCES OF ANTI-SLAVERY CONSTITUTIONALISM at 89.

Rhode Island passed a gradual emancipation statute freeing all children born after March 1, 1784. The statute declared that "all men are entitled to life, liberty, and the pursuit of happiness, and that holding mankind in a state of slavery, as private property, [i]s repugnant to this principle." In 1843, Rhode Island adopted a constitution that removed any remaining traces of slavery in the state. *See id.* at 50. Delaware, which was a slave state, had a clause in its constitution forbidding the importation of slaves. *See id.* at 48. In New Hampshire, slavery appears simply to have faded away without any specific legal cause. *See id.* at 51.

32. Act of March 6, 1820, 3 Stat. 545 (popularly known as Missouri Compromise). An amendment to the Act, which enabled Missouri to enter the Union without restrictions on slavery, was authored by Senator Jesse B. Thomas of Illinois. The Thomas Amendment was the key provision in what became known as the Missouri Compromise. The amendment stated that slavery was "forever prohibited" in the remaining portion of the Louisiana Territory, which was the area north of 36 degrees, 30 minutes latitude. There was little debate in either House of Congress over the Thomas Amendment. President Monroe signed the Act, interpreting "forever prohibited" to mean for the duration of the territorial period. It was assumed that the Compromise could be extended to any additional territories that the United States would acquire. *See* D. FEHRENBACKER, THE DRED SCOTT CASE: ITS SIGNIFICANCE IN AMERICAN LAW AND POLITICS 107-13 (New York: Oxford University Press 1978).

By 1850, with California seeking to join the Union, it became apparent that a new compromise was needed if secession by the southern states was to be avoided. Henry Clay's suggested solution to the slavery problem became the basis for the Compromise of 1850. Under this compromise, California was admitted to the Union as a free state, while the Utah and New Mexico Territories were organized without restrictions on slavery. In addition, the slave trade was prohibited in the District of Columbia. The Compromise of 1850 did not include a repeal of the Thomas Amendment because it was seen as being unrelated to that Amendment. *See id.* at 157–63.

The Kansas-Nebraska Act, which followed in 1854, did repeal the Thomas Amendment as it applied to the Kansas and Nebraska Territories. *See id.* at 108. The Act, organizing the Nebraska Territory from 36 degrees, 30 minutes to the Canadian border, was a noninterventionist compromise "not to legislate slavery into any Territory or State, nor to exclude it therefrom, but to leave the people thereof perfectly free to form and regulate their domestic institutions in their own way, subject only to the Constitution of the United States." *See id.* at 178–87.

Finally, in 1857, the greatly weakened Thomas Amendment was invalidated by the Supreme Court on constitutional grounds in Dred Scott v. Sandford, 60 U.S. (19 How.) 393 (1857).

33. The Emancipation Proclamation stated:

[A]ll persons held as slaves within any State or designated part of a State, the people whereof [are now] in rebellion against the United States, [are] [h]ence-forward, and forever free....

See J. FRANKLIN, THE EMANCIPATION PROCLAMATION 96 (Garden City, N.Y.: Doubleday 1963).

34. U.S. CONST. amend. XIII.

35. Formation of a majoritarian abolitionist coalition was attributable to four types of objections to slavery: religious and moral objections; philosophical objections; political objections; and economic objections.

The strongest objections on religious and moral grounds came from the Puritans and the Quakers. Similar objections were also raised by Congregationalists, Methodists, Baptists, and Presbyterians. Philosophically, slavery as an institution ran counter to the idea of individual liberty upon which many thought the country was founded. Slavery raised political concerns that denying liberty to some would weaken the nation as a whole. In addition, many feared retribution from slaves and wanted to diffuse what they considered to be a political timebomb.

Although there was no significant organized movement against slavery based upon economic grounds, many considered slave labor to be unprofitable. The cost of slave importation was high. Moreover, slaves were often seen as an untrustworthy labor force. In addition, it was costly to protect whites from the "undesirable" slave element of the population. Finally, there was a concern that the existence of slavery discouraged white labor. *See* M. LOCK, ANTI-SLAVERY IN AMERICA: FROM THE INTRODUCTION OF AFRICAN SLAVES TO THE PROHIBITION OF THE SLAVE TRADE (1619-1808) (Gloucester, Mass.: P. Smith 1965); *see generally* W. GODDELL, SLAVERY AND ANTI-SLAVERY: A HISTORY OF THE GREAT STRUGGLE IN BOTH HEMISPHERES: WITH A VIEW OF THE SLAVERY QUESTION IN THE UNITED STATES (New York: Negro University Press 1968) (originally published 1852); A. ZILVERSMIT, THE FIRST EMANCIPATION, THE ABOLITION OF SLAVERY IN THE NORTH (Chicago: University of Chicago Press 1967).

36. Dred Scott v. Sandford, 60 U.S. (19 How.) 393 (1857).

37. *Id.* at 404-05, 407.

38. *Id.* at 451-52.

39. *See id.* at 404-05, 407.

40. *See* O. PATTERSON, SLAVERY AND SOCIAL DEATH 94-97 (Cambridge: Harvard University Press 1982).

41. *See Dred Scott,* 60 U.S. (19 How.) at 405.

42. *See* page 94 (discussing three provisions in U.S. Constitution that recognize slavery).

43. *See* G. STONE, *et al.,* CONSTITUTIONAL LAW at 436-37, *quoting* D. ROBINSON, SLAVERY IN THE STRUCTURE OF AMERICAN POLITICS 1765-1820 at 209, 210, 244-46.

44. *See* page 95 (*Dred Scott* discussion of constitutional protections for property interests of white owners in black slaves).

45. *See* Chapter 6, note 32.

46. G. STONE, *et al.,* CONSTITUTIONAL LAW at 440.

47. *See* page 13 (discussing John Marshall's sacrifice of Marbury's right to commission as justice of peace in order to further goals of Marshall's own political party).

48. *See* G. STONE, *et al.,* CONSTITUTIONAL LAW at 444-51. The Reconstruction statutes and constitutional amendments are discussed more fully in Chapter 4. *See* page 72.

49. Civil Rights Act of 1957, Pub. L. 85-315; 71 Stat. 634 (1957) (codified as amended at 42 U.S.C. § 1971 (1982)).

50. Civil Rights Act of 1960, Pub. L. 86-449; 74 Stat. 86, 90 (1960) (codified as amended at 42 U.S.C. § 1971 (1982)).

51. Civil Rights Act of 1964, Pub. L. 88-352; 78 Stat. 241, 243 (1964) (codified at 42 U.S.C. § 2000a (1982)).

52. Civil Rights Act of 1964, Pub. L. 88-352; 78 Stat. 240 (1964) (codified at 42 U.S.C. § 2000c-6 (1982)).

53. Civil Rights Act of 1964, Pub. L. 88-352; 78 Stat. 240 (1964) (codified at 42 U.S.C. §§ 2000d to 2000d-1 (1982)).

54. Civil Rights Act of 1964, Pub. L. 88-352; 78 Stat. 241, 253 (1964) (codified as amended at 42 U.S.C. §§ 2000e to 2000e-17 (1982 & Supp. IV 1986)).

55. Voting Rights Act of 1965, Pub. L. 89-110; 79 Stat. 437 (1965) (codified as amended at 42 U.S.C. §§ 1971, 1973 to 1973bb-1 (1982)).

56. Voting Rights Act Amendments of 1970, Pub. L. 91-285; 84 Stat. 314 (1970) (codified as amended at 42 U.S.C. §§ 1973 to 1973aa-1, 1973aa-2 to 1973aa-4, 1973bb (1982)).

57. Act of Aug. 6, 1975, Pub. L. 94-73, 89 Stat. 400 (1975) (codified as amended at 42 U.S.C. §§ 1973 to 1973d, 1973h, 1973i, 1973l, 1973aa, 1973aa-1a to 1973aa-4, 1973bb (1982 & Supp. IV 1986)).

58. See G. GUNTHER, CONSTITUTIONAL LAW at 859, 929-30; G. STONE, et al., CONSTITUTIONAL LAW at 580-81.

59. Fair Housing Act of 1968, Pub. L. 90-284; 82 Stat. 73, 81 (1968) (codified as amended at 42 U.S.C. §§ 3601-3619 (1982 & Supp. IV 1986)).

60. See G. GUNTHER, CONSTITUTIONAL LAW at 916-17.

61. Public Works Employment Act of 1977, Pub. L. 95-28; 91 Stat. 116 (1977) (codified at 42 U.S.C. § 6705 (1982)).

62. See, e.g., Executive Order No. 11,246, Part II, Subpart B, 3 C.F.R. 339, 340-42 (1964-65).

63. See G. STONE, et al., CONSTITUTIONAL LAW at 474.

64. See 29 C.F.R. § 1608 (1989) (affirmative action appropriate under Title VII of Civil Rights Act of 1964, as amended); 29 C.F.R. § 1690 (1989) (procedures on interagency coordination of equal employment opportunity issuances).

65. See 24 C.F.R. §§ 106, 109-20 (1990) (fair housing administrative meetings under Title VII of Civil Rights Act of 1968).

66. 448 U.S. 448 (1980).

67. See Patterson v. McLean Credit Union, 491 U.S. 164 (1989); Runyon v. McCrary, 427 U.S. 160 (1976); Jones v. Alfred H. Mayer, 392 U.S. 409 (1968); cf. The Civil Rights Cases, 109 U.S. 3 (1883); The Slaughter-House Cases, 83 U.S. (16 Wall.) 36 (1873).

68. See page 94 (discussing Dred Scott decision).

69. 488 U.S. 469 (1989). See page 127 (discussing Croson case).

70. 491 U.S. 164 (1989).

71. See id. at 175-85.

72. See, e.g., Martin v. Wilkes, 490 U.S. 755 (1989) (constitutional challenge by nonminority firefighters to Title VII consent decree giving minority firefighters preference over nonminority firefighters for certain promotions); City of Richmond v. J.A. Croson Co., 488 U.S. 469 (1989) (constitutional challenge by nonminority contractors to minority set-aside program giving minority-owned business enterprises preference over nonminority businesses in receiving certain construction funds); Wygant v. Jackson Board of Education, 476 U.S. 267 (1986) (constitutional challenge by nonminority teachers to collective bargaining agreement giving minority school teachers layoff preference over nonminority teachers with greater seniority); Regents of the

University of California v. Bakke, 438 U.S. 265 (1978) (constitutional challenge by nonminority applicant to medical school admissions program giving preference to minority applicants over nonminority applicants for certain seats).

73. *See, e.g.,* Patterson v. McLean Credit Union, 491 U.S. 164 (1989) (minority employee sought aid of Court in using 42 U.S.C. § 1981 prohibition on discrimination in contract formation and enforcement to prevent racial harassment by employer); Wards Cove Packing Co. v. Atonio, 490 U.S. 642 (1989) (class of minority employees sought aid of Court in establishing that statistical disparities in employer use of subjective employment and promotion criteria were sufficient to prove Title VII violation); Firefighters Local Union No. 1784 v. Stotts, 467 U.S. 561 (1984) (minority class action seeking aid of Court in imposing race-conscious class-based remedy under Title VII for discriminatory hiring by municipal fire department); Guardians Association v. Civil Service Commission of the City of New York, 463 U.S. 582 (1983) (class action filed by minority police officers seeking aid of Court in enforcing antidiscrimination provisions of Title VI).

74. *See* page 23.

75. *See* W. LOCKHART, Y. KAMISAR, J. CHOPER, and S. SHIFFRIN, CONSTITUTIONAL LAW: CASES—COMMENTS—QUESTIONS App. A (St. Paul, Minn: West Publishing, 6th ed. 1986) (providing data on which statistics are based).

76. Tushnet, *The Politics of Constitutional Law,* in THE POLITICS OF LAW 219, 225-26 (D. Kairys ed.) (New York: Pantheon, rev. ed. 1990).

77. *See* U.S. CONST. art. I, sec. 2, cl. 5.

78. *See* Tushnet, *Politics of Constitutional Law,* in POLITICS OF LAW at 225.

79. *See* W. LOCKHART, *et al.,* CONSTITUTIONAL LAW at App. A (providing data on which statistic is based).

80. *See* G. STONE, *et al.,* CONSTITUTIONAL LAW at lxvi, lxxxi.

81. Justice Souter was sworn in as the 105th Justice of the Supreme Court on October 9, 1990, replacing Justice Brennan. *See* Marcus, *High Court to Review Tactic in War on Drug Trade; Justices Agree to Rule on Searches of Bus, Train Luggage as Souter Takes Oath,* WASH. POST, Oct. 10, 1990, at p. A15. Justice Thomas was sworn in as the 106th Justice of the Supreme Court on October 23, 1991, replacing Justice Marshall. *See* Savage, *Thomas Takes Oath in Secret Ceremony,* L.A. TIMES, Oct. 24, 1991, at p.26.

82. The Reagan-Bush coalition has not yet been able to secure control over the House or lasting control over the Senate, although it presently controls the Presidency and the Supreme Court. This suggests that the details of the coalition-duration model of political pluralism may need further refinement. However, the gist of the model seems to have explanatory power.

83. *See* Tushnet, *Politics of Constitutional Law,* in POLITICS OF LAW at 225.

84. *See* U.S. CONST. art. I, sec. 2, cl. 5; U.S. CONST. art. I, sec. 3, cl. 5.

85. In the history of the nation, only one Supreme Court justice has been impeached. Samuel Chase, who was one of the signers of the Declaration of Independence, was appointed to the Court by George Washington in 1796. He was impeached in 1804 for charging Thomas Jefferson with "seditious attacks on the principle of the Constitution." He was acquitted by the Senate on March 1, 1805, by only four votes. He then continued to serve on the Court until 1811. *See* A. BLAUSTEIN and R. MERSKY, THE FIRST ONE HUNDRED JUSTICES: STATISTICAL STUDIES ON THE SUPREME COURT OF THE UNITED STATES 33 n.1 (Hamden, Conn: Archon Books 1978); W. LOCKHART, *et al*, CONSTITUTIONAL LAW at App. A, p. 5. In modern times, both Chief Justice Earl Warren, *see* B. SCHWARTZ, SUPER CHIEF 280-82 (New York: New York University Press 1983), and Associate Justice William O. Douglas, *see* W. DOUGLAS, THE COURT YEARS, 1939-75: THE AUTOBIOGRAPHY OF WILLIAM O. DOUGLAS (New York: Random House 1980), have been the targets of unsuccessful impeachment campaigns.

   The fact that only one Supreme Court justice has been impeached and that no justice has been convicted can be used either to support or refute the argument that the threat of impeachment can affect judicial behavior. It may be that the apparent difficulty of securing the political support necessary to impeach and convict gives the threat of impeachment little credibility, and concomitantly, little capacity to affect judicial behavior. On the other hand, it may be that the threat of impeachment has so tempered judicial views and so prompted judicial responsiveness to majoritarian norms that the political need for impeachment rarely arises.

86. 323 U.S. 214 (1944).
87. *See, e.g.,* R. DANIELS, CONCENTRATION CAMPS; J. TEN BROEK, *et al.*, PREJUDICE, WAR AND THE CONSTITUTION.

CHAPTER 7

1. 347 U.S. 483 (1954).
2. 163 U.S. 537 (1896).
3. 347 U.S. 483 (1954).
4. *See Brown I*, 347 U.S. 483, 495 (1954).
5. *See Brown II*, 349 U.S. 294, 301 (1955).
6. 163 U.S. 537 (1896). *See Brown I*, 347 U.S. at 495.
7. *See* G. STONE, *et al.*, CONSTITUTIONAL LAW at 454-56.
8. 347 U.S. at 495.
9. *Id.* at 494.
10. *See id.* at 499, *citing* Korematsu v. United States, 323 U.S. 214, 216 (1944) ("[A]ll legal restrictions which curtail the civil rights of a single racial group are immediately suspect. That is not to say that all such restrictions are

unconstitutional. It is to say that courts must subject them to the most rigid scrutiny.").

11. *See* G. STONE, *et al.*, CONSTITUTIONAL LAW at 488–95; *see generally* D. BELL, RACE, RACISM at 385–422.

12. *See* Gayle v. Browder, 352 U.S. 903 (1956) (buses); Holmes v. City of Atlanta, 350 U.S. 879 (1955) (golf courses); Mayor of Baltimore v. Dawson, 350 U.S. 877 (1955) (beaches); *see also* G. STONE, *et al.*, CONSTITUTIONAL LAW at 465.

13. 347 U.S. 483 (1954).

14. 350 U.S. 891 (1955) (per curiam) and 350 U.S. 895 (1956) (per curiam).

15. *See Naim*, 350 U.S. at 985.

16. *See, e.g.,* G. GUNTHER, *The Subtle Vices of the "Passive Virtues"—A Comment on Principle and Expediency in Judicial Review,* 64 COLUM. L. REV. 1, 11–13 (1964); Wechsler, *Toward Neutral Principles of Constitutional Law* 73 HARV. L. REV. 1, 34 (1959) (terming dismissal of appeal "wholly without basis in the law"); *but see* A. BICKEL, LEAST DANGEROUS BRANCH at 71 & n.30, 174 (arguing that Naim v. Naim was prudent accommodation of principle and political expediency).

17. *See id.* at 174. *See generally* Hutchinson, *Unanimity and Desegregation: Decisionmaking in the Supreme Court, 1948-58,* 68 GEO. L.J. 61–67 (1979).

18. 388 U.S. 1 (1967).

19. *See id.* at 6.

20. *See* Bell, Brown *and the Interest-Convergence Dilemma,* in SHADES OF BROWN: NEW PERSPECTIVES ON SCHOOL DESEGREGATION 91–106 (D. Bell ed.) (New York: Teachers College Press, Columbia University 1980); *see also* D. BELL, RACE, RACISM at 442–44.

21. *See id.* at 96–97.

22. *See id.*

23. *Id.* at 95.

24. *See id.* at 98–102.

25. *See* page 108 (discussing decline in support for desegregation as effort moved north).

26. Dudziak, *Desegregation as a Cold War Imperative,* 41 STAN. L. REV. 61 (1988).

27. *Id.* at 65, *quoting* Brief for the United States as Amicus Curiae at 6, Brown v. Board of Education, 347 U.S. 483 (1954).

28. 347 U.S. at 495 ("Because these are class actions, because of the wide applicability of this decision, and because of the great variety of local conditions, the formulation of decrees in these cases presents problems of considerable complexity. . . . In order that we may have the full assistance of the parties in formulating decrees, the cases will be restored to the docket.").

29. *See* 349 U.S. at 301.

30. The decline in support for school desegregation that occurred as the desegregation effort moved north has been discussed more fully in Chapter 5. *See* page 78.
31. *See* Seidman, Brown *and* Miranda, 80 CALIF. L REV. (May 1992).
32. 411 U.S. 1 (1973) (upholding constitutionality of property tax based public school financing despite drastic discrepancies in funds allocated to white and minority students).
33. *See* Seidman, Brown *and* Miranda.
34. *See, e.g.,* City of Richmond v. J.A. Croson Co., 488 U.S. 469, 493–98 (1989) (invalidating minority set-aside program in construction industry because of adverse impact that program had on whites). The *Croson* case and the Supreme Court's other desegregation cases are discussed more fully in Chapter 8.
35. *See* Cooper, *Race-Based Student Aid: Practice and Policy; U.S. Providing $100 Million in Minority Scholarships While Proposing to Restrict Colleges,* WASH. POST, Dec. 26, 1991, at p. A21 (describing Bush Administration opposition to minority scholarships).
36. *See, e.g.,* S. CARMICHAEL and C. HAMILTON, BLACK POWER: THE POLITICS OF LIBERATION IN AMERICA 54–55 (New York: Vintage 1967); Bell, *A Model Alternative Desegregation Plan,* in SHADES OF BROWN at 124–39; Edmonds, *Effective Education for Minority Pupils: Brown Confounded or Confirmed,* in SHADES OF BROWN at 107–23. *See generally* D. BELL, RACE, RACISM at 424–31; Peller, *Race Consciousness,* 1990 DUKE L.J. 758, 795–802.
37. *See* Chapter 7, note 35.
38. *Cf.* Bell, *Model Alternative Desegregation Plan;* Edmonds, *Effective Education for Minority Pupils.*
39. *See* page 89 (discussing political influence of racial minorities in political process).
40. *See* page 94 (discussing minority frustrations before Supreme Court).
41. *See* page 106 (discussing failure of *Brown* to desegregate schools).
42. *See* page 78 (discussing Supreme Court failure to order effective school desegregation in northern urban centers).
43. *See, e.g.,* San Antonio Independent School District v. Rodriguez, 411 U.S. 1 (1973) (upholding constitutionality of property tax based public school financing despite drastic discrepancies in funds allocated to white and minority students).
44. *See* D. BELL, RACE, RACISM at 424–31, and authorities cited therein (discussing educational successes of all-black schools).
45. *See id.* at 424–25 (discussing problem of resegregation).
46. *See id.* at 425–27, and authorities cited therein; Peller, *Race Consciousness,* 1990 DUKE L.J. at 795–802, and authorities cited therein (both discussing burdens imposed upon minority students by desegregation).

47. *See* D. BELL, RACE, RACISM at 426, *citing*, R. RIST, THE INVISIBLE CHILDREN: SCHOOL INTEGRATION IN AMERICAN SOCIETY (Cambridge: Harvard University Press 1978) (discussing lack of minority influence in operation of desegregated schools).

48. *See* Peller, *Race Consciousness* at 795–802, and authorities cited therein (discussing loss of minority control over education of minority children that results from desegregation).

49. *See* D. BELL, RACE, RACISM at 364–68, 411–17, and authorities cited therein; H. CRUSE, PLURAL BUT EQUAL 179–203 (New York: William Morrow 1987), and authorities cited therein; Peller, *Race Consciousness*, 1990 DUKE L.J. at 783–86, 795–802, and authorities cited therein.

50. *See* D. BELL, RACE, RACISM at 364–65, 413, 424–31; H. CRUSE, PLURAL BUT EQUAL at 244–53; Peller, *Race Consciousness*, 1990 DUKE L.J. at 795–802, and authorities cited therein.

51. *See* D. BELL, RACE, RACISM at 365–66, 374–75.

52. *See id.* at 367–68.

53. *See id.* at 411–12.

54. *See* Peller, *Race Consciousness*, 1990 DUKE L.J. at 763–64, 795, *citing*, BY ANY MEANS NECESSARY: SPEECHES, INTERVIEWS AND A LETTER BY MALCOLM X 16–17 (G. Breitman ed.) (New York: Pathfinder Press 1970).

55. *See* Peller, *Race Consciousness*, 1990 DUKE L.J. at 795–802.

56. *See id.* at 795–96, *citing*, S. CARMICHAEL and C. HAMILTON, BLACK POWER at 54–55.

57. *See* Peller, *Race Consciousness*, 1990 DUKE L.J. at 783, 796, *citing*, Browne, *A Case for Separation*, in SEPARATISM OR INTEGRATION: WHICH WAY FOR AMERICA: A DIALOGUE 7–15 (R. Browne and B. Rustin eds.) (New York: A. Phillip Randolph Educational Fund 1968).

58. *See* Peller, *Race Consciousness*, 1990 DUKE L.J. at 796, *citing*, H. CRUSE, THE CRISIS OF THE NEGRO INTELLECTUAL 283 (New York: William Morrow 1967).

59. *See* Peller, *Race Consciousness*, 1990 DUKE L.J. at 796–97, *citing* Bell, *Neither Separate Schools nor Mixed Schools: The Chronicle of the Sacrificed Black Schoolchildren*, in D. BELL, AND WE ARE NOT SAVED: THE ELUSIVE QUEST FOR RACIAL JUSTICE 102–122 (New York: Basic Books 1987).

60. *See* Peller, *Race Consciousness*, 1990 DUKE L.J. at 800–01 (discussing, *inter alia*, movement for black community control of Ocean Hill-Brownsville schools in Brooklyn, New York, and seizure of student union by black students demanding autonomous Afro-American Studies Department and separate living areas at Cornell University).

61. *See* H. CRUSE, PLURAL BUT EQUAL at 379.

62. 522 F.2d 717 (5th Cir. 1975); 487 F.2d 680 (5th Cir. 1973).

63. *See* D. BELL, RACE, RACISM at 415-17 (describing dispute between national NAACP and local branch over importance of integrated schools). The Fifth Circuit ultimately upheld the compromise plan favored by the local branch. *See* Calhoun v. Cook, 522 F.2d 717 (5th Cir. 1975).

64. *See* D. BELL, RACE, RACISM at 416 n.4, *quoting* Gallagher, *Integrated Schools in the Black Cities*, 42 J. NEGRO EDUC. 336, 348 (1973).

65. *See* D. BELL, RACE, RACISM at 416 n.4, 420-22. The compromise plan was again upheld over national NAACP opposition. *See id.* at 421-22.

66. *See* Bell, *Serving Two Masters: Integration Ideals and Client Interests in School Desegregation Litigation*, 85 YALE L.J. 470 (1976).

67. *See Correspondence from Nathaniel R. Jones, General Counsel, NAACP Special Contribution Fund*, 86 YALE L.J. 378 (1976); Jones, *Is Brown Obsolete: No!*, 14 INTEGRATEDUCATION 29 (May-June 1976); *see also* D. BELL, RACE, RACISM at 412-14.

68. *See* page 108 (discussing majoritarian benefits that integration requirement has over separate-but-equal requirement).

69. *See* H. CRUSE, PLURAL BUT EQUAL at 38-41; *see generally id.* at 7-69 (criticizing choice of integration over minority control as strategy for improving minority education).

70. In the two school desegregation cases in which the Supreme Court heard argument during its 1990-91 Term, which concerned the obligation of a formerly segregated public school system to remedy the effects of resegregation through shifts in residential patterns, and the obligation of a formerly segregated state system of higher education to remedy the continuing racial imbalance that resulted from the use of standardized test scores as an admissions criterion, either the NAACP or the NAACP Legal Defense and Educational Fund filed amicus briefs urging the Court to impose continuing desegregation orders on the affected school systems. *See* Freeman v. Pitts, No. 89-1290, Brief of the NAACP, *et al.*, as Amici Curiae in Support of Respondents (public school resegregation); Ayers v. Mabus, No. 90-6588 and United States v. Mabus, No. 90-1205, Brief of NAACP Legal Defense and Educational Fund, *et al.*, as Amici Curiae in Support of Petitioners (racial imbalance in higher education due to use of standardized test scores).

71. *See* page 79 (discussing recent Supreme Court desegregation cases).

72. *See* page 114 (discussing Jones's defense of NAACP desegregation policy).

73. *See Brown I*, 347 U.S. at 494 ("To separate [black children] from others of similar age and qualifications solely because of their race generates a feeling of inferiority as to their status in the community that may affect their hearts and minds in a way unlikely ever to be undone.").

74. 411 U.S. 1, 35 (1973) ("Education, of course, is not among the rights afforded explicit protection under our Federal Constitution. Nor do we find any basis for saying it is implicitly so protected.").

75. *See* page 109 (discussing constitutionality of disproportionate funding).

76. *See* page 105 (discussing *Brown* invalidation of *Plessy* separate-but-equal doctrine).
77. *See* Chapter 7, note 73.
78. *See* Peller, *Race Consciousness*, 1990 DUKE L.J. at 764, *quoting* BY ANY MEANS NECESSARY at 16–17.
79. *See* page 89 (discussing minority influence in pluralist politics).
80. *See* Bell, *The Racial Limitation on Black Voting Power: The Chronicle of the Ultimate Voting Rights Act*, in D. BELL, AND WE ARE NOT SAVED at 75–101 (discussing benefits to minorities of proportional representation).
81. The problem of minority participation in white-dominated political action is discussed more fully in Chapter 8. *See* page 134.
82. *See* Introduction, note 4 (describing political environment surrounding proposed Civil Rights Acts of 1990 and 1991).
83. *See* Chapter 6, note 14 (discussing success of minority political candidates in white election districts).

CHAPTER 8

1. 488 U.S. 469 (1989).
2. 110 S.Ct. 2997 (1990).
3. *Cf.* Sullivan, *Sins of Discrimination: Last Term's Affirmative Action Cases*, 100 HARV. L. REV. 78 (1986) (arguing that validity of affirmative action should be determined on basis of prospective benefit, and that affirmative action should not be viewed as "penance" for past discrimination, as Supreme Court has viewed it).
4. *See* A COMMON DESTINY: BLACKS AND AMERICAN SOCIETY 14 (G. Jaynes & R. Williams, Jr. eds.) (Washington, D.C.: National Academy Press 1989) (discussing minority population).
5. *See id.* at 274, 279 (poverty).
6. *See id.* at 274, 292, 302 (income and net worth). For a systematic discussion of the economic disadvantages confronting blacks in each socioeconomic class, see R. BROOKS, RETHINKING THE AMERICAN RACE PROBLEM (Berkeley: University of California Press 1990).
7. *See id.* at 415, 419 (homicide).
8. *See id.* at 398 (infant mortality). Infant mortality is defined as the rate at which children die before they reach their first birthdays. *See id.* at 397.
9. *See id.* at 464 (crime victims). The term "serious crimes" includes robbery, vehicle theft, and aggravated assault. *See id.*
10. *See id.* at 238, 240 (black elected officials). Although over 400 candidates are elected to the House of Representatives every two years, during the time period between 1941 and 1985, in total, only 72 blacks were elected to the House of Representatives. *See id.*
11. *See* Chapter 2, note 2 (Justices Marshall and Thomas only two blacks ever appointed to Supreme Court).

12. *See* Introduction, note 4 (discussing Civil Rights Acts of 1990 and 1991).
13. *See* T. EDSALL, with M. EDSALL, CHAIN REACTION; Morley, *Bush & the Blacks* (both discussing racially divisive political strategies of President Bush); *see generally* Introduction, note 4 (discussing Civil Rights Acts of 1990 and 1991).
14. A measure of the disingenuousness of President Bush's position is provided by the supplemental justification that he offered for his opposition to the proposed Civil Rights Act of 1991 after he was accused of incorporating racially polarizing tactics into his initial opposition. The President stated that his new reason for opposition to the bill was that it undermined the value of education in the United States. According to the President, if employers were prohibited from utilizing educational degrees as employment requirements, even when the jobs they were filling did not require such degrees, the prohibition would provide a disincentive for students to remain in school. Even moderate Republicans have suggested that the President's stated objection masks a deeper hostility to civil rights. *See* Eaton, *Bush Rejects Civil Rights Compromise by Moderates*, L.A. TIMES, Aug. 2, 1991, at p. A20.
15. *See, e.g.,* United Jewish Organizations v. Carey, 430 U.S. 144 (1977) (upholding New York redistricting plan designed to enhance black voting strength in order to comply with 1965 Voting Rights Act).
16. *See, e.g.,* City of Richmond v. J.A. Croson Co., 488 U.S. 469, 486–506 (1989) (invalidating municipal affirmative action plan due, *inter alia*, to lack of evidence of prior racial discrimination).
17. *See* Brest, *Forward: In Defense of the Antidiscrimination Principle*, 90 HARV. L. REV. 1, 48–52 (1976); Perry, *The Principle of Equal Protection*, 32 HASTINGS L.J. 1133, 1145–48 (1981) (both arguing that discrimination, and consequently discrimination remedies, should be viewed as individual phenomena).
18. *See* Fiss, *Groups and the Equal Protection Clause*, 5 J. PHIL. & PUB. AFF. 107, 147–77 (1976) (arguing that discrimination, and consequently discrimination remedies, should be viewed as group phenomena).
19. *See, e.g., Croson*, 488 U.S. at 493 (opinion of O'Connor, J., joined by Rehnquist, C.J., White and Kennedy, JJ., arguing that equal protection rights created by fourteenth amendment are personal rights).
20. *See* Metro Broadcasting v. Federal Communications Commission, 110 S.Ct. 2997, 3009–11 (1990) (upholding F.C.C. affirmative action plan because of plan's ability to increase prospective broadcast diversity).
21. 410 U.S. 113 (1973) (recognizing constitutional right to abortion).
22. Dred Scott v. Sandford, 60 U.S. (19 How.) 393 (1857) (holding that black slaves were not citizens within meaning of Constitution).
23. *See* City of Richmond v. J.A. Croson Co., 488 U.S. 469, 497–98 (1989) (discussing and rejecting role model justification for affirmative action).
24. For examples of such favorable press coverage see Brodie, *Politics Beckons the Hero General*, DAILY TELEGRAPH, Mar. 1, 1991, at p. 4; Morganthau,

The Military's New Image, NEWSWEEK, Mar. 11, 1991, at p. 50; Walte, *Powell to Head Joint Chiefs for 2 More Years*, USA TODAY, May 24, 1991, at p. 4A.

25. For discussions of the legal restrictions, distrust, and practical difficulties that have historically confronted blacks seeking to become doctors or medical professionals, see A.L. HIGGINBOTHAM, JR., IN THE MATTER OF COLOR at 198–99; C. MANGUM, THE LEGAL STATUS OF THE NEGRO 72–74 (Chapel Hill: University of North Carolina Press 1939); G. MYRDAL, AN AMERICAN DILEMMA: THE NEGRO PROBLEM AND MODERN DEMOCRACY 322–25 (New York: Harper & Row 1962).

26. For discussions of the legal restrictions, distrust, and practical difficulties that have historically confronted blacks seeking to become lawyers, see C. MANGUM, LEGAL STATUS OF THE NEGRO at 72–74; G. MYRDAL, AMERICAN DILEMMA at 325–26; G. STEPHENSON, RACE DISTINCTIONS IN AMERICAN LAW 239–41 (Miami Fla: Mnemosyne Publishing 1969).

27. *See* Kirkpatrick, *The Night They Drove Old Dixie Down*, SPORTS ILLUSTRATED, Apr. 1, 1991, at p. 70 (discussing startled white reaction when all-black basketball team first beat all-white team for NCAA Title in 1966).

28. *See* Chapter 8, note 24.

29. *See, e.g.,* page 123 (discussing individual v. group basis of affirmative action).

30. For example, in City of Richmond v. J.A. Croson Co., 488 U.S. 469 (1989), the Supreme Court treated remediation of past discrimination as the only appropriate justification for affirmative action. *See id.* at 498–506. However, in Metro Broadcasting v. Federal Communications Commission, 110 S.Ct. 2997 (1990), the Court treated prospective diversity as an adequate justification. *See id.* at 3009–27.

31. *See* page 121.

32. *See* page 94. *See generally* G. STONE *et al.,* CONSTITUTIONAL LAW at 436–37.

33. *See* page 42 (discussing adoption of Reconstruction amendments after Civil War).

34. U.S. CONST. amend. XIV.

35. *See id.* at sec. 5.

36. Some of these statutes are discussed at page 97.

37. A constitutional amendment requires adoption by a two-thirds vote in both the House of Representatives and the Senate, and ratification by three-fourths of the states. *See* U.S. CONST. art. V.

38. *See* page 42 (discussing Reconstruction Amendments and Reconstruction civil rights legislation). *See generally* G. STONE, *et al.,* CONSTITUTIONAL LAW at 444–51.

39. *See, e.g.,* The Slaughter-House Cases, 83 U.S. (16 Wall.) 36 (1873) (adopting narrow construction of fourteenth amendment privileges and immunities clause, closely limiting clause to problems related to racial discrimination).

40. *See, e.g.,* The Civil Rights Cases, 109 U.S. 3 (1883) (invalidating public accommodations provisions of Civil Rights Act of 1875 on federalism grounds).

41. *See* page 97 (discussing modern civil rights legislation).

42. *See* Brown v. Board of Education, 347 U.S. 483 (1954) *(Brown I)* (abandoning separate-but-equal interpretation of fourteenth amendment); 349 U.S. 294 (1955) *(Brown II)* (requiring integration of public schools "with all deliberate speed"); *see also* North Carolina State Board of Education v. Swann, 402 U.S. 43, 45–46 (1971) (effectively requiring race-based pupil assignment when necessary to remedy prior school segregation).

43. *See generally* G. STONE, *et al.,* CONSTITUTIONAL LAW at 578–79.

44. *See* page 108.

45. 416 U.S. 312 (1974).

46. 430 U.S. 144 (1977).

47. 438 U.S. 265 (1978).

48. *See id.* at 272–75.

49. *See id.* at 412–21 (Stevens, J., concurring in the judgment in part and dissenting in part, joined by Burger, C.J., Stewart and Rehnquist, JJ.); *id.* at 305–20 (opinion of Powell, J.).

50. *See id.* at 355–62 (opinion of Brennan, J., concurring in the judgment in part and dissenting in part, joined by White, Marshall, and Blackmun, JJ.); *id.* at 287–320 (opinion of Powell, J.).

51. *See id.* at 307–10 (opinion of Powell, J.).

52. *See id.* at 324–26 (Brennan, J., concurring in the judgment in part and dissenting in part).

53. 448 U.S. 448 (1980).

54. *See id.* at 482–84 (opinion of Burger, C.J., joined by White and Powell, JJ.); *id.* at 517–19 (Marshall, J., concurring in the judgment, joined by Brennan and Blackmun, JJ.); *id.* at 548 (Stevens, J., dissenting). This observation is made in *The Supreme Court, 1979 Term,* 94 HARV. L. REV. 75, 128 (1980).

55. Three members of the Court thought that the quota component of the set-aside program defeated the constitutional narrowness requirement. *See Fullilove,* 448 U.S. at 530 n.12 (Stewart, J., dissenting, joined by Rehnquist, J.); *id.* at 535–36, 540, 549 n.25, 552 n.30 (Stevens J., dissenting). However, Justice Stevens' opposition was based on procedural rather than substantive grounds. *See id.* at 552.

56. 476 U.S. 267 (1986).

57. *See id.* at 270–73 (opinion of Powell, J.).

58. *See id.* at 278–84 (opinion of Powell, J.); *id.* at 294–95 (White, J., concurring in the judgment).

59. *See id.* at 273–74 (opinion of Powell, J., arguing for strict scrutiny); *id.* at 301–03 (Marshall, J., dissenting, arguing for intermediate scrutiny); *id.* at 313 (Stevens, J., dissenting, apparently arguing for minimal scrutiny).

60. 478 U.S. 421 (1986).

61. 480 U.S. 92 (1987).
62. 488 U.S. 469 (1989).
63. *See Croson*, 488 U.S. at 477–86.
64. 110 S.Ct. 2997 (1990).
65. *See id.* at 3003–05.
66. *See Metro Broadcasting*, 110 S.Ct. at 3008–90.
67. *See Croson*, 488 U.S. at 493–98 (opinion of O'Connor, J., joined by Rehnquist, C.J., White and Kennedy, JJ.) Although Justice Scalia did not sign the portion of Justice O'Connor's opinion that called for strict scrutiny, Justice Scalia's own opinion favored strict scrutiny, thereby providing a fifth vote for this holding. *See id.* at 520–21 (Scalia, J., concurring in the judgment).
68. *See Croson*, 488 U.S. at 486–511, 717–30 (demonstrating difficulty of surviving strict scrutiny). Although it is extremely rare for the Supreme Court to uphold a racial classification in the face of strict scrutiny, it does happen on occasion. *See, e.g.,* Korematsu v. United States, 323 U.S. 214 (1944) (upholding certain restrictions on travel of Japanese-American citizens during World War II); Hirabayshi v. United States, 320 U.S. 81 (1943) (upholding constitutionality of military curfew on Japanese-American citizens during World War II); *cf.* Lee v. Washington, 390 U.S. 333 (1968) (stating in dicta that racial segregation of prisoners could be constitutional when necessary to prevent prison violence). *Korematsu* is discussed more fully in Chapter 3. *See* page 32. Lee v. Washington is discussed more fully in Chapter 5. *See* page 71.
69. *See* Wygant v. Jackson Board of Education, 476 U.S. 267, 273–74 (1986) (opinion of Powell, J.); *see also* Korematsu v. United States, 323 U.S. 214; 216 (1944); *cf. Croson*, 488 U.S. at 486–93 (suggesting that only state interest in providing remedy for past discrimination could be sufficiently compelling). Strict scrutiny is also discussed in Chapter 3. *See* page 31.
70. *See Metro Broadcasting*, 110 S.Ct. at 3008–09.
71. *See id.*
72. *See Croson*, 488 U.S. at 486–93.
73. *See Metro Broadcasting*, 110 S.Ct. at 3008–09.
74. *See Carey*, 430 U.S. at 165–68 (opinion of White, J., joined by Stevens and Rehnquist, JJ.).
75. *See Fullilove*, 448 U.S. at 453 (opinion of Burger, C.J., joined by White and Powell, JJ.); *Bakke* 438 U.S. at 324 (opinion of Brennan, J., concurring in the judgment in part and dissenting in part, joined by White, Marshall, and Blackmun, JJ.); *Carey*, 430 U.S. at 147 (opinion of White, J.); *DeFunis*, 416 U.S. at 348 (Brennan, J., dissenting, joined by Douglas, White, and Marshall, JJ.). Although Justice White's vote in *DeFunis* was only a vote to decide the case on the merits rather than to dismiss it as moot, his subsequent vote to uphold a similar affirmative action plan in *Bakke* suggests that he would have voted to uphold the *DeFunis* plan if the Court had reached the merits.

76. *See Croson*, 488 U.S. at 475-76 (opinion of the Court, joined by White, J.); *Paradise*, 480 U.S. at 196 (White, J., dissenting); *Sheet Metal Workers*, 478 U.S. at 499 (White, J., dissenting); *Wygant*, 476 U.S. at 294 (White, J., concurring in the judgment).

77. *See Fullilove*, 448 U.S. at 539, 541-42 (Stevens, J., dissenting). Justice Stevens also viewed the *Fullilove* plan as having suffered from inadequate congressional consideration. *See id.* at 545, 548-54.

78. *See* Varat, *Justice White and the Breadth and Allocation of Federal Authority*, 58 COLORADO L. REV. 371, 373-408 (1987) (discussing Justice White's belief in desirability of broad federal powers).

79. *See Croson*, 488 U.S. at 511 (Stevens, J., concurring in part and concurring in the judgment).

80. *See Fullilove*, 448 U.S. at 532 (Stevens, J., dissenting).

81. *See Metro Broadcasting*, 110 S.Ct. at 3002-05.

82. *See* Mincberg, *Furtive and Unproductive Souter Falls Right In*, CONN. LAW TRIBUNE, July 9, 1991, at p. A2; Riccio, *School's Daze: Free Speech v. Freedom from Fear*, N.J. LAW J., Oct. 10, 1991, at p. 15; *cf.* Fein, *Souter's Judicial Soul Facing an Early Test*, WASH. TIMES, Sept. 14, 1990, at p. F1 (all commenting on willingness of present Supreme Court and new justices to overrule recent precedents).

83. *See* page 121 (discussing present allocation of societal resources).

84. *See* R. POSNER, ECONOMIC ANALYSIS OF LAW 3-10 (Boston: Little, Brown, 3d ed. 1986); *see also* M. KELMAN, A GUIDE TO CRITICAL LEGAL STUDIES 115-26 (Cambridge: Harvard University Press 1987) (both describing rational wealth maximization assumption of neoclassical law and economics movement).

85. *See* M. KELMAN, CRITICAL LEGAL STUDIES at 119; R. POSNER, ECONOMIC ANALYSIS OF LAW at 129-30.

86. Professor Kelman has articulated a strong objection to the rational wealth-maximization and efficiency assumptions of neoclassical economics. In addition to arguing that these assumptions are normatively unattractive, *see* M. KELMAN, CRITICAL LEGAL STUDIES at 151-85, Kelman argues that the assumptions are simply meaningless. Dual incoherences in the concepts of individual preference and efficiency render the neoclassical assumptions about law and economics untenable. *See id.* at 126-50. My utilization of the neoclassical model should not in any sense be viewed as a rejection of the Kelman criticisms, but rather as a recognition that the neoclassical account has sufficient utility to the white majority to make it the model that must be accommodated in order for racial minorities to secure meaningful concessions from whites. Moreover, neoclassical law and economics connotes a certain vulgarity that is consonant with the crass political pluralism that I am advocating in the present book.

87. *See* Witt, *Deferred Dreams: Mandela, DeKlerk Find Old Ways Die Hard in "New South Africa,"* CHICAGO TRIB., Apr. 29, 1990, at sec. Perspective,

p. 1; Wren, *Rumblings on the Right*, N.Y. TIMES, Oct. 7, 1990, at sec. Magazine, p. 32; Yalowitz & Jones, *South Africa's Unstoppable March Toward Multiracial Rule*, U.S. NEWS & WORLD REPT., Feb. 25, 1991, at p. 44 (all describing instability of current South African regime).

88. Slavery provides an extreme but obvious example. *See* page 92 (discussing self-interested reasons for which white slave owners would make resource concessions to black slaves).

89. Whites, of course, derive substantial financial benefits from the services of minority athletic and entertainment celebrities. Not only do white owners derive revenue from their investments in production companies and athletic franchises that feature black celebrities, but white-owned companies also derive substantial revenue from the commercial endorsement of their products by black celebrities. In many respects, these profits are generated through the exploitation of the black celebrities who generate them. Indeed, such exploitation in the context of amateur and professional athletics persists despite more than twenty years of documentation and criticism. *See, e.g.,* Johnson, *The Black Athlete Revisited: How Far Have We Come?*, SPORTS ILLUSTRATED, Aug. 5, 1991, at p. 38.

90. For example, Charles Drew, a famous black physician, discovered a process for isolating and storing blood plasma in a way that facilitated lifesaving blood transfusions during World War II. He went on to coordinate the establishment of the American Red Cross Blood Bank based upon the technique that he developed. A widely circulated myth has arisen concerning the circumstances surrounding Dr. Drew's death in 1950. According to the myth, Dr. Drew died from injuries suffered in an automobile accident after a segregated hospital in North Carolina refused to give him medical care or blood transfusions because he was black. In fact, it appears that the hospital made vigorous efforts to save Dr. Drew's life, including giving Dr. Drew the necessary blood transfusions. However, an irony that is not mythical is that the Red Cross Blood Bank—at the insistence of the then-segregated military—segregated by race the blood that was donated for storage in accordance with Dr. Drew's process. *See* R. MAHONE-LONESOME, CHARLES DREW 76–83, 95–103 (New York: Chelsea House 1990).

91. *See* Chapter 6, note 35.

92. *See* page 105.

93. *See* page 99 (discussing inherent conservatism of Supreme Court).

94. This theory of judicial review is described at page 31.

95. Some of the most significant political advances that racial minorities have been able to secure have resulted from economic boycotts and urban riots. Martin Luther King's famed Montgomery Bus Boycott ended segregated seating in the Montgomery, Alabama, public transportation system. *See* Kennedy, *Martin Luther King's Constitution: A Legal History of the Montgomery Bus Boycott*, 98 YALE L.J. 999 (1989). In addition, the urban riots that resulted during the late 1960s contributed significantly to passage of the

fair housing provisions of the Civil Rights Act of 1968. *See* McCormack, *Business Necessity in Title VIII: Incorporating an Employment Discrimination Doctrine into the Fair Housing Act,* 54 FORDHAM L. REV. 563, 582 (1986); Note, *The Legality of Integration Maintenance Quotas: Fair Housing or Forced Housing,* 55 BROOKLYN L. REV. 197, 211 n.49 (1989). In addition, peaceful civil rights protests and demonstrations have also contributed significantly to the enactment of civil rights legislation. *See* Bernstine, *Book Review of Hearts and Minds: The Anatomy of Racism From Roosevelt to Reagan* by Harry S. Ashmore, 1982 WIS. L. REV. 1157, 1161.

96. The Supreme Court invalidated the affirmative action programs at issue in *Croson,* 488 U.S. 469 (1989); *Wygant,* 476 U.S. 267 (1986); and *Bakke,* 438 U.S. 265 (1978). The Court upheld the programs at issue in *Metro Broadcasting,* 110 S.Ct. 2997 (1990); *Paradise,* 480 U.S. 92 (1987); *Sheet Metal Workers,* 478 U.S. 421 (1986); *Fullilove,* 448 U.S. 448 (1980); and *Carey,* 430 U.S. 144 (1977). The Court did not reach the merits in *DeFunis,* 416 U.S. 312 (1974), which it dismissed on mootness grounds. These cases are discussed at page 126.

97. *See Croson,* 488 U.S. at 477–81, 495–96. Although blacks held five of the nine seats on the Richmond City Council, the vote in favor of the minority set-aside was 6–3. *See* J.A. Croson Co. v. City of Richmond, 822 F.2d 1355, 1362–64 (4th Cir. 1987) (Sprouse, J., dissenting).

98. *See* Chapter 8, note 4.

99. *See* page 97 (discussing federal civil rights statutes).

100. *See* page 126 (discussing affirmative action cases including *Metro Broadcasting* and *Fullilove*).

101. These proposed statutes sought simply to restore certain antidiscrimination laws to the status that they had prior to a series of Supreme Court decisions that cut back on the scope of civil rights protections. Although the Civil Rights Act of 1991 was ultimately enacted after President Bush abruptly abandoned his opposition, racial minorities are now in the position of having expended an enormous amount of political capital not to advance their interests but merely to reestablish an earlier status quo. *See* page 1 (discussing efforts to obtain legislative reversal of Supreme Court decisions).

102. The abortion funding experience in the District of Columbia provides a stark example. Repeatedly during the last decade, the District of Columbia City Council adopted budgets that provided for the District to fund abortions for indigent women, but the abortion funding provisions were repeatedly eliminated from the District's budget by Congress, often in response to the threat of a presidential veto. *See* Raskin, *Liberate the District; Washington, D.C.,* NATION, Mar. 25, 1991, at p. 371.

103. *See* page 121 (discussing disproportionate income distribution between whites and racial minorities).

104. *See* Bell, *Racial Limitation on Black Voting Power,* in D. BELL, AND WE ARE NOT SAVED (discussing proportional representation).

105. *See* Molotsky, *N.A.A.C.P. Urges Souter's Defeat, Citing Earlier Statements on Race*, N.Y. TIMES, Sept. 21, 1990, at sec. 1, p. 7.
106. *See* Chapter 2, note 6 (discussing past and present political views of Justice Thomas).
107. The relationship between universalism, rational objectivity, and race neutrality is developed in Peller, *Race Consciousness*.
108. *See id.* at 763–83.
109. The relationship between parochialism, irrational subjectivity, and racial bias is also developed by Professor Peller. *See id.*
110. *See id.*
111. *See, e.g., Croson*, 488 U.S. at 494, 495, 505–06 (discussing ultimate need for race-neutral, colorblind society as reason for invalidating affirmative action set-aside program).
112. *See, e.g., Fullilove*, 448 U.S. at 516 (Powell, J., concurring) (discussing ultimate need for race-neutral, colorblind society as reason for upholding affirmative action set-aside program).
113. The observation that colorblind race neutrality no longer makes sense as a strategy for resolving our current racial conflicts, but rather perpetuates majoritarian exploitation of minority interests, is being made by an increasingly large number of legal commentators who seem to share the view that it is time to stop playing racial charades. *See, e.g.,* P. WILLIAMS, THE ALCHEMY OF RACE AND RIGHTS (Cambridge: Harvard University Press 1991); Aleinikoff, *A Case for Race Consciousness*, 91 COLUM. L. REV. 1060 (1991); Bell, *Forward: The Final Civil Rights Act*, 79 CALIF. L. REV. 597 (1991); Bell, *Neither Separate Schools nor Mixed Schools*, in D. BELL, AND WE ARE NOT SAVED; Cook, *Beyond Critical Legal Studies: The Reconstructive Theology of Dr. Martin Luther King, Jr.*, 103 HARV. L. REV. 985 (1990); Crenshaw, *Race, Reform, and Retrenchment*; Culp, *Toward a Black Legal Scholarship: Race and Original Understanding*, 1991 DUKE L.J. 39; Delgado, *Affirmative Action as a Majoritarian Device: Or Do You Really Want To Be a Role Model?*, 89 MICH. L. REV. 1222 (1991); Delgado, *Recasting the American Race Problem*, 79 CALIF. L. REV. 1389 (1991) (book review of R. BROOKS, RETHINKING THE AMERICAN RACE PROBLEM); Kennedy, *Frontier of Legal Thought III: A Cultural Pluralist Case for Affirmative Action in Legal Academia*, 1990 DUKE L.J. 705; Matsuda, *Voices of America: Accent, Antidiscrimination Law, and a Jurisprudence for the Last Reconstruction* 100 YALE L.J. 1329 (1991); Peller, *Race Consciousness*; *cf.* R. BROOKS, RETHINKING THE AMERICAN RACE PROBLEM (still liberal but poised to make the leap); Strauss, *The Law and Economics of Racial Discrimination in Employment: The Case for Numerical Standards*, 79 GEO L.J. 1619 (1991) (same); Strauss, *The Myth of Colorblindness*, 1986 SUP. CT. REV. 99 (same).
114. Because racial minorities such as blacks are disproportionately represented among the poor and disproportionately unrepresented among the middle

class and the upper-middle class, *see* page 121, the degree to which our income tax structure is progressive or regressive determines the degree to which societal resources will be allocated to racial minorities or to the white majority.

115. Defense spending and spending for social programs have traditionally been viewed as inversely related in the federal budgetary process. Because racial minorities benefit more from social programs than from defense-related spending, the traditional "guns or butter" debate also resonates along racial lines. The issue has acquired renewed interest in connection with the size and shape of the "peace dividend" that may or may not flow from the break-up of the Soviet Union and the collapse of many Eastern European communist regimes. *See, e.g.,* McAllister, *Proportion Of Blacks in South Rises; Census Cites Reversal Of Trend Since 1900,* WASH. POST, Jan. 10, 1990, at p. A1; Moore, *After the Marching,* NATIONAL JOURNAL, June 23, 1990, at p. 1525.

116. In recent decades, black military casualties have been disproportionately high because black representation in the Army has been disproportionately high. *See* A COMMON DESTINY at 71–74.

117. Capital punishment has persisted despite our fifty-year recognition of the fact that racial minority group members will be executed in disproportionate numbers as compared to whites. *See id.* at 488–89.

118. Not only are black capital defendants executed in disproportionate numbers as compared to whites, but black defendants charged with killing white victims are also executed in disproportionate numbers as compared to black defendants charged with killing black victims. This means that any deterrent benefits that capital punishment may have to offer are disproportionately accorded to white potential victims as compared to black potential victims. *See id.* Professor Kennedy has characterized this more subtle form of racial discrimination as the placement by the majority of a higher value on white lives than on minority lives. *See* Kennedy, *McCleskey v. Kemp* at 1390–95.

119. Because blacks have both higher abortion rates than whites, *see* A COMMON DESTINY at 513, and lower access to health care than whites, *see id.* at 35, abortion and abortion-funding policies will have a disproportionate impact on minorities as compared to whites.

120. *See* Linmark Associates v. Township of Willingboro, 431 U.S. 85 (1977) (invalidating ordinance that prohibited display of "for sale" signs in order to prevent white "panic selling" from turning racially integrated residential neighborhood into predominantly minority neighborhood).

121. *See generally* Schrag, *The Future of District of Columbia Home Rule,* 39 CATH. L. REV. 311 (1990); Seidman, *The Preconditions for Home Rule,* 39 CATH. L. REV. 373 (1990) (discussing complexities entailed in home-rule debate).

122. *See* page 60 (deconstructing competing principles of discriminatory intent and discriminatory effects).

123. *See* page 62 (discussing how tolerating known ignorance about disparate impact can constitute discriminatory intent).
124. *See* Peller, *Espousing a Positive Vision of Affirmative-Action Policies,* CHRON. HIGHER EDUC. Dec. 18, 1991, at p. B1.
125. Although the racial preference controversy has arisen on many campuses, one particular incident at the Georgetown University Law Center, where the Dean disciplined a student who wrote a school newspaper article that was critical of the school's minority preference program, attracted national attention. *See id.; see also* Escobar, *At GU Law Center, Silence Speaks in Protest; Green Ribbons, Placards Replace Angry Words as Author of Race Article Receives Degree,* WASH. POST, May 28, 1991, at p. B3; McCall, *Reprimand 'Vindicates Me,' Georgetown Law Student Says,* WASH. POST, May 22, 1991, at p. C3; Torry, *GU Reprimands Law Student; Permission to Graduate Angers Blacks,* WASH. POST, May 21, 1991, at p. B1.
126. *See, e.g.,* Areen, *Affirmative Action: The Benefits of Diversity,* WASH. POST, May 26, 1991, at p. D7.
127. *See* page 123 (discussing majoritarian justifications for affirmative action).
128. *See generally* Dawson, *The Law School Admission Test Battery: A Different Selection Concept for the 1980's and Beyond,* 34 J. LEGAL EDUC. 388 (1984). The correlation between undergraduate grades and law school success is not as high as one might at first expect because different undergraduate institutions use different formal and operational grading scales. In addition, some empirical findings have been counterintuitive, such as the slight negative correlation that exists between a student's increasing undergraduate grade point trend and his or her subsequent law school grades. *See id.* at 390 n.7, 396 n.39. It is because of these deficiencies in the predictive value of undergraduate grades alone that the LSAT was developed. The LSAT has always been designed explicitly to correlate with academic success during the first year of law school. *See id.* at 391 n.10, 393 n.24. Changes in the format and scoring for the LSAT have been made from time to time, and the most recent change was made in 1991. Such changes, however, have not resulted in large gains in the predictive power of the test. *See id.* at 400 n.51.
129. *See* Dawson, *Law School Admission Test Battery,* 34 J. LEGAL EDUC. at 389–95; *see also* Simien, *The Law School Admission Test as a Barrier to Almost Twenty Years of Affirmative Action,* 12 T. MARSHALL L.J. 359, 370–78 (1987) (arguing that admissions committees place heaviest weight on LSAT scores and noting that LSAT scores correlate with race and wealth).
130. *See* Chapter 8, note 128.
131. Prior to 1982, the LSAT contained a math section that was formally entitled "Quantitative Comparison/Data Interpretation." *See* J. BOBROW, BARRON'S GUIDE TO THE "NEW" LAW SCHOOL ADMISSION TEST: LSAT viii, 352–73 (Woodbury N.Y.: Barron's Educational Series, 2d ed. 1982); C. NEUBERT & J. WITHIAM, JR., THE LAW SCHOOL GAME 16 (New York: Drake, rev. ed. 1980). Currently, the LSAT tests for proficiency in

solving complex logic puzzles in its section entitled "Analytical Reasoning."
See INFORMATION BOOK 1991–92: REGISTRATION INFORMATION
AND MATERIALS FOR LAW SCHOOL ADMISSION TEST 42–49 (Law
School Admissions Service 1991).

132. *See* Larew, *Why Are Droves of Unqualified, Unprepared Kids Getting into
Our Top Colleges?: Because their Dads Are Alumni*, WASHINGTON
MONTHLY, June 1991, at p. 10.

133. *See* Peller, *Race Consciousness*, 1990 DUKE L.J. at 763–83.

134. *See id.*

135. *See id.*

136. *See id.*

137. *See* page 105 (discussing frustrated promise of *Brown* as device to promote
racial equality).

138. *See* T. EDSALL with M. EDSALL, CHAIN REACTION; Morley, *Bush &
the Blacks*.

139. *See id.* President Bush appears to have abandoned his opposition to civil
rights reform only when the appearance of David Duke on the Republican
political scene made Bush's opposition cease to be politically expedient. *See*
Raspberry, *Bush, Civil Rights and the Specter of David Duke*.

140. *See* page 132 (discussing doctrinal difficulty in using fourteenth amendment
as basis for invalidating voluntary affirmative action).

141. *See* page 59 (describing deconstruction and inversion of hierarchies).

142. *See* Cooper & Walsh, *Riding the Victory Train*, U.S. NEWS & WORLD
REPT., Mar 25, 1991, at p. 24 (suggesting that Bush plans to characterize
Desert Storm victory as establishing correctness of traditional American values that are inconsistent with civil rights bill); *see also Merit, Heart, Will—
And Affirmative Action*, NEWSDAY, June 4, 1991, at p. 56 (commenting
on Bush opposition to civil rights bill as inconsistent with American ideal
of merit).

143. *See* Layne, *Why the Gulf War was Not in the National Interest*, ATLANTIC,
July 1991, at p. 55 (discussing and rejecting three national interests offered
by Bush Administration to justify Gulf War: need to protect American interest
in continued flow of oil; need to protect American security interests by
countering Iraqi biological and nuclear threat; and need to secure peace and
stability for American friends in Middle East); *see also* Cooper & Walsh,
Riding the Victory Train, U.S. NEWS & WORLD REPT., Mar 25, 1991,
at p. 24 (suggesting that Bush plans to characterize Desert Storm victory as
establishing correctness of traditional American values on which many of his
political programs are based).

144. *See, e.g.* Layne, *Why the Gulf War was Not in the National Interest* (arguing
that Bush actually believed that Gulf War was necessary to establish preem-
inence of United States in securing new world order after end of cold war).

145. *See* page 32 (discussing World War II internment of Japanese Americans).

146. President Truman's decision to drop two atomic bombs on Japan has always been controversial. Although a consensus of Americans supported the decision at the time, revisionist understandings of the decision to drop the bombs are more critical, suggesting that there were neither military nor political considerations that justified Truman's actions. *See generally* THE ATOMIC BOMB: THE CRITICAL ISSUES (Boston: Little, Brown 1976); G. HERKEN, THE WINNING WEAPON: THE ATOMIC BOMB IN THE COLD WAR, 1945–1950 (New York: Knopf 1980).

147. *See* Barber, *Ethnic Struggles Test New Republics: Tony Barber Assesses the Growing Threat of Violence as the Empire Breaks Up into its Constituent Parts*, THE INDEPENDENT, Dec. 22, 1991, at p. 10; *Freedom's Year: Hope—and Chaos—Fill Gorbachev's Final Days*, MACLEAN'S, Dec. 23, 1991, at p. 22; Gray, *Hate of Ages: Nationalist Violence Is Spreading*, MACLEAN'S, Dec. 23, 1991, at p. 27 (discussing outbreak of nationalistic violence that accompanied disintegration of Soviet empire).

148. *See* Fidelman, *Film Captures Depth of Hatred in Middle East; Documentary Crew Tried to Get the Full Story Behind the News*, GAZETTE (Montreal), Nov. 28, 1991, at p. H15; Fisk, *Peace through Coercion, US Style; Robert Fisk, in Beirut, Accuses America of Basking in Glory for Arranging Middle East Talks, while Planning to Punish Palestinians for their Stance in the Gulf War*, INDEPENDENT, Oct. 23, 1991, at p. 21; Wright, *Gulf War Forced Washington to Tackle Arab-Israeli Conflict*, REUTER LIBRARY REPT., July 30, 1991 (discussing nationalist motivations in Middle East conflict).

149. For discussions of the nationalistic underpinnings of the long-standing political and religious conflict in Northern Ireland, see R. ROSE, GOVERNING WITHOUT CONSENSUS: AN IRISH PERSPECTIVE (London: Farber and Farber 1971); V. RYAN, IRELAND RESTORED: THE NEW SELF-DETERMINATION (New York: Freedom House 1991).

150. *See* Ellis, *Another Deadly Day as the ANC Signs for Peace*, SUNDAY TIMES, Sept. 15, 1991, at sec. Overseas News; Waldmeir, *S African Cauldron of Tribalism and Politics*, FINANCIAL TIMES, Nov. 28, 1991, at p. 4; Waldmeir, *Why Murder Ended in Mpumalanga*, FINANCIAL TIMES, Sept. 18, 1991, at p. 4; Waldmeir, *South Africa 3: Where the Central Fact is Violence*, FINANCIAL TIMES, May 7, 1991, at p. 3 (discussing tribal violence among blacks in South Africa).

CHAPTER 9

1. *See* Chapter 6, note 14 (discussing election of minority political candidates in white electoral districts).

2. For a general discussion of the phenomenon of legitimation, on which the present discussion is heavily dependent, see M. KELMAN, CRITICAL LE-

GAL STUDIES at 262–95. Professor Kelman develops a model of legitimation that is more elaborate than is necessary for present purposes, but is nevertheless quite provocative. For a more skeptical discussion, suggesting that the legitimation phenomenon may not be as well-founded as many commentators seem to believe, see Hyde, *The Concept of Legitimation in the Sociology of Law*, 1983 WIS. L. REV. 379. The Kelman discussion also offers responses to Professor Hyde's reservations. *See* M. KELMAN, CRITICAL LEGAL STUDIES at 262–68.

3. For a demonstration of such scrutiny and a taste of the skepticism that it can generate, see Kelman, *Interpretive Construction in the Substantive Criminal Law*, 33 STAN. L. REV. 591 (1981), which is discussed in M. KELMAN, CRITICAL LEGAL STUDIES 286–90.

4. *See* A. DWORKIN, RIGHT-WING WOMEN 77–80, 85–87 (New York: Coward-McCann 1983); MacKinnon, *Feminism, Marxism, Method, and the State: Toward Feminist Jurisprudence*, 8 SIGNS 635, 638–39, 643–44, 647–51 (1983); MacKinnon, *Feminism, Marxism, Method, and the State: An Agenda for Theory*, 7 SIGNS 515 (1982). This thesis is also discussed in M. KELMAN, CRITICAL LEGAL STUDIES at 285.

5. Husbands are completely immune from rape prosecution in at least nine states, while ten states impose no restrictions on the ability of a wife to prosecute her husband for rape. In the remaining 31 states, rape prosecutions against husbands are permitted in only a limited number of circumstances, such as when the husband and wife are living separately under court order, or when divorce papers have been filed. *See* S. ESTRICH, REAL RAPE: HOW THE LEGAL SYSTEM VICTIMIZES WOMEN WHO SAY NO 4 n.3 (Cambridge: Harvard University Press 1987).

6. A mid-1960s study showed that a jury was four times more likely to convict a rape defendant in cases that involved extrinsic violence—*i.e.*, guns, knives, or beatings—multiple assailants, or no previous relationship between the victim and the assailant than in cases in which those factors were absent. *See id.* at 4–5, *citing* H. KALVEN and H. ZEISEL, THE AMERICAN JURY (Chicago: University of Chicago Press 1966). Professor Estrich has concluded that the relationship between the victim and the defendant and the circumstances surrounding the initial encounter dictate the outcome in most rape cases. A review of New York City district attorney files indicated that, although 67 percent of reported rape cases involved acquaintances, only 7 percent of those cases resulted in the issuance of indictments. *See id.* at 18 n.42, citing H. KALVEN and H. ZEISEL, AMERICAN JURY. In addition, juries appear to be prejudiced against the prosecution in rape cases, but will strain to be lenient toward defendants if there is any suggestion of "contributory behavior" on the part of the victim, which includes hitchhiking, dating, or talking to men at parties. *See id.* at 19, citing H. KALVEN and H. ZEISEL, AMERICAN JURY at 249–54.

7. *See* Chapter 5 (discussing indeterminacy of legal doctrine).

8. This simplistic version is developed and rejected in M. KELMAN, CRITICAL LEGAL STUDIES at 262–63.

9. This characterization too is developed and rejected by Professor Kelman. *See id.* at 262–63.

10. Professor Kelman has developed an elaborate "cognitive" model of legitimation. *See id.* at 269–95.

11. For a discussion of legitimation addressed specifically to antidiscrimination laws, see Freeman, *Legitimizing Racial Discrimination through Antidiscrimination Law: A Critical Review of Supreme Court Doctrine*, 62 MINN. L. REV. 1049 (1978); *see also* Freeman, *Antidiscrimination Law: The View From 1989*, in THE POLITICS OF LAW 121–50 (D. Kairys ed., rev. ed. 1990). For a discussion of how race itself can serve a legitimating function, see Crenshaw, *Race, Reform, and Retrenchment*, 101 HARV. L. REV. at 1370–81.

12. Of course, democracy too legitimates a set of assumptions that scrutiny might render unacceptable.

13. *See* Tushnet, *An Essay On Rights*, 62 TEXAS L. REV. 1363, 1363–94 (1984); Crenshaw, *Race, Reform and Retrenchment*, 101 HARV. L. REV. at 1350–56; Delgado, *The Ethereal Scholar: Does Critical Legal Studies Have What Minorities Want?*, 22 HARV. C.R.-C.L. L. REV. 301, 302–07 (1987). *See generally Symposium: A Critique of Rights*, 62 TEXAS L. REV. 1363–1599 (1984). For a sample of the skepticism that this critique has produced concerning the continued utility of the concept of rights, see Tushnet, *An Essay in Informal Political Theory*, 17 POLS. & SOC. 403 (1989).

14. *See* Carrington, *Of Law and the River*, 34 J. LEGAL EDUC. 222, 227 (1984) (suggesting that members of the critical legal studies movement should leave legal academics).

15. *See* Martin, *"Of Law and the River," and Of Nihilism and Academic Freedom*, 37 J. LEGAL EDUC. 1–24 (1984) (responses to Professor Carrington's suggestion).

16. *See* commentators cited in Chapter 9, note 19.

17. *See* page 94 (discussing history of minority frustrations before Supreme Court).

18. *See, e.g.,* Bell, *Brown and the Interest-Convergence Dilemma*, in SHADES OF BROWN. I interpret Professor Bell's recent advocacy of proportional representation as a preference for political over judicial solutions to race-related problems. *See* Bell, *Racial Limitation on Black Voting Power*, in D. BELL, AND WE ARE NOT SAVED at 75–101; *cf.* Cook, *Beyond Critical Legal Studies* (using critique of rights as springboard for theological reconstruction of social hierarchy).

19. *See, e.g.,* Bracamonte, *Minority Critiques of the Critical Legal Studies Movement: Forward*, 22 HARV. C.R.-C.L. L. REV. 297 (1987); Crenshaw, *Race, Reform, and Retrenchment*, 101 HARV. L. REV. at 1356–69, 1381–84; Dalton, *The Clouded Prism*, 22 HARV. C.R.-C.L. L. REV. 435 (1987); Del-

gado, *The Ethereal Scholar: Does Critical Legal Studies Have What Minorities Want?*, 22 HARV. C.R.-C.L. L. REV. 301 (1987); Williams, *Alchemical Notes: Reconstructing Ideals from Deconstructed Rights*, 22 HARV. C.R.-C.L. L. REV. 401 (1987); Williams, *Taking Rights Aggressively: The Perils and Promise of Critical Legal Theory for Peoples of Color*, 5 LAW & INEQUALITY 103 (1987).

20. *See, e.g.*, T. SOWELL, CIVIL RIGHTS: RHETORIC OR REALITY (New York: William Morrow 1984) (criticizing contemporary civil rights movement for attempting to supplant goal of equal opportunity with goal of equal political outcomes, which politicizes and thereby undermines neutral rule of law); *cf.* Kennedy, *Racial Critiques of Legal Academia*, 102 HARV. L. REV. 1745 (1989) (rejecting argument that criteria used to judge legal scholarship are race dependent, and arguing that neutral criteria do in fact exist—something that implicitly accepts substantive rights assumption by endorsing belief in determinate standards necessary for existence of such rights); *see also* S. CARTER, REFLECTIONS OF AN AFFIRMATIVE ACTION BABY 13, 65–69 (New York: Basic Books 1991) (agreeing with Kennedy and arguing that blacks should attempt to satisfy traditional criteria of merit rather than press for racial preferences).

21. The framers envisioned such political enforcement. *See* page 10.

22. *See* page 99 (discussing inherent conservatism of the Supreme Court).

23. *See* page 13 (discussing Supreme Court failure to protect legal right to commission as justice of peace in *Marbury*).

24. *See* page 94 (discussing Supreme Court denial of citizenship to blacks in *Dred Scott*).

25. *See, e.g.*, T. SOWELL, CIVIL RIGHTS; *cf.* S. CARTER, REFLECTIONS OF AN AFFIRMATIVE ACTION BABY; Kennedy, *Racial Critiques of Legal Academia*.

26. *See* G. STONE, *et al.*, CONSTITUTIONAL LAW at 444–51.

27. The danger of minority dependence on the Supreme Court is discussed more fully in Chapter 7.

28. *See* S. CARTER, REFLECTIONS OF AN AFFIRMATIVE ACTION BABY.

29. *See* D. D'SOUZA, ILLIBERAL EDUCATION: THE POLITICS OF RACE AND SEX ON CAMPUS (New York: Free Press 1991).

30. *See* Kennedy, *Racial Critiques of Legal Academia*.

31. *See* Loury, *Who Speaks for American Blacks*, COMMENTARY, Jan. 1987, at p. 34.

32. *See* T. SOWELL, PREFERENTIAL POLICIES: AN INTERNATIONAL PERSPECTIVE (New York: William Morrow 1990); T. SOWELL, CIVIL RIGHTS.

33. *See* S. STEELE, THE CONTENT OF OUR CHARACTER: A NEW VISION OF RACE IN AMERICA (New York: St. Martin's Press 1990).

34. *See* page 21 (discussing conservative philosophy of Justice Thomas).

35. *See* Delgado, *Enormous Anomaly: Left-Right Parallels in Recent Writing About Race*, 91 COLUM. L. REV. 1547 (1991) (comparative book review of D. BELL, AND WE ARE NOT SAVED; S. CARTER, REFLECTIONS OF AN AFFIRMATIVE ACTION BABY; S. STEELE, THE CONTENT OF OUR CHARACTER; P. WILLIAMS, THE ALCHEMY OF RACE AND RIGHTS).

36. *See id.* at 1554–55.

37. *See id.* at 1555–56.

CHAPTER 10

1. *See* page 16 (discussing Supreme Court refusal to protect Cherokee sovereignty in face of defiance of Supreme Court authority by President Andrew Jackson).

2. *See* page 94 (discussing *Dred Scott* decision).

3. *See* page 44 (discussing *Civil Rights Cases*).

4. *See* page 105 (discussing separate-but-equal requirement of *Plessy v. Ferguson*).

5. *See* page 105 (discussing majoritarianism inherent in *Brown* decision).

Bibliography

Aleinikoff, *A Case for Race Consciousness*, 91 COLUM. L. REV. 1060 (1991).

Alfred and Knowlton, *Civil Rights Act Will Encourage Federal Claims: The Civil Rights Act Of 1991*, MASSACHUSETTS LAWYERS WEEKLY, Dec. 9, 1991, at p. 5.

Apple, *The Thomas Confirmation; Senate Confirms Thomas, 52–48, Ending Week of Bitter Battle; 'Time for Healing,' Judge Says*, N.Y. TIMES, Oct. 16, 1991, at p. A1.

Appleby, *Republicanism in Old and New Contexts*, 43 WM. & MARY Q. 20 (1986).

Areen, *Affirmative Action: The Benefits of Diversity*, WASH. POST, May 26, 1991, at p. D7.

K. ARROW, SOCIAL CHOICE AND INDIVIDUAL VALUES (New Haven: Yale University Press, 2d ed. 1963).

THE ATOMIC BOMB: THE CRITICAL ISSUES (B. Bernstein ed.) (Boston: Little, Brown 1976).

Attinger, *A Nice Guy Finishes First: But Dinkins May not be Tough Enough to Cope with New York*, TIME, Nov. 21, 1989, at p. 60.

Balkin, *Deconstructive Practice and Legal Theory*, 96 YALE L.J. 743 (1987).

Balkin, *The Footnote*, 83 NW. UNIV. L. REV. 275 (1989).

Barber, *Ethnic Struggles Test New Republics: Tony Barber Assesses the Growing Threat of Violence as the Empire Breaks Up into its Constituent Parts*, THE INDEPENDENT, Dec. 22, 1991, at p. 10.

P. BATOR, D. MELTZER, P. MISHKIN, and D. SHAPIRO, HART AND WECHSLER'S THE FEDERAL COURTS AND THE FEDERAL SYSTEM (Mineola, N.Y.: Foundation Press, 3d ed. 1988).

The Battle over Abortion, TIME, July 17, 1989, at p. 62.

D. BELL, AND WE ARE NOT SAVED: THE ELUSIVE QUEST FOR RACIAL JUSTICE (New York: Basic Books 1987).

Bell, Brown *and the Interest-Convergence Dilemma*, in SHADES OF BROWN: NEW PERSPECTIVES ON SCHOOL DESEGREGATION (D. Bell ed.) (New York: Teachers College Press, Columbia University 1980).

Bell, *Forward: The Final Civil Rights Act*, 79 CALIF. L. REV. 597 (1991).

Bell, *A Model Alternative Desegregation Plan*, in SHADES OF BROWN: NEW PERSPECTIVES ON SCHOOL DESEGREGATION (D. Bell ed.) (New York: Teachers College Press, Columbia University 1980).

Bell, *Neither Separate Schools nor Mixed Schools: The Chronicle of the Sacrificed Black Schoolchildren*, in D. BELL, AND WE ARE NOT SAVED: THE ELUSIVE QUEST FOR RACIAL JUSTICE (New York: Basic Books 1987).

D. BELL, RACE, RACISM AND AMERICAN LAW (Boston: Little, Brown, 2d. ed. 1980).

D. BELL, RACE, RACISM AND AMERICAN LAW SUPPLEMENT (Boston: Little, Brown 1984).

Bell, *The Racial Limitation on Black Voting Power: The Chronicle of the Ultimate Voting Rights Act*, in D. BELL, AND WE ARE NOT SAVED: THE ELUSIVE QUEST FOR RACIAL JUSTICE (New York: Basic Books 1987).

Bell, *Serving Two Masters: Integration Ideals and Client Interests in School Desegregation Litigation*, 85 YALE L.J. 470 (1976).

Bennett, *Constitutional Interpretation and Judicial Self-Restraint*, 39 MICH. L. REV. 213 (1940).

A. BENTLEY, THE PROCESS OF GOVERNMENT (Bloomington, Ind.: Principia Press 1908).

Bernstine, *Book Review of Hearts and Minds: The Anatomy of Racism From Roosevelt to Reagan* by Harry S. Ashmore, 1982 WIS. L. REV. 1161.

THE BIAS OF PLURALISM (W. Connelly ed.) (New York: Atherton Press 1969).

A. BICKEL, THE LEAST DANGEROUS BRANCH: THE SUPREME COURT AT THE BAR OF POLITICS (New Haven: Yale University Press 1962).

BLACK AND WHITE CHILDREN IN AMERICA: KEY FACTS (Washington, D.C.: Report of the Children's Defense Fund 1983).

A. BLAUSTEIN and R. MERSKY, THE FIRST ONE HUNDRED JUSTICES: STATISTICAL STUDIES ON THE SUPREME COURT OF THE UNITED STATES (Hamden, Conn: Archon Books 1978).

J. BOBROW, BARRON'S GUIDE TO THE "NEW" LAW SCHOOL ADMISSION TEST: LSAT (Woodbury N.Y.: Barron's Educational Series, 2d ed. 1982).

Bourke, *The Pluralist Reading of James Madison's Tenth Federalist*, 9 PERSP. AMER. HIST. 269 (1975).

Bracamonte, *Minority Critiques of the Critical Legal Studies Movement: Forward*, 22 HARV. C.R.-C.L. L. REV. 297 (1987).

Brest, *Forward: In Defense of the Antidiscrimination Principle*, 90 HARV. L. REV. 1 (1976).

Broder, *Bush's Favorite Victim*, WASH. POST, June 9, 1991, at p. D7.

Brodie, *Politics Beckons the Hero General*, DAILY TELEGRAPH, Mar. 1, 1991, at p. 4.

R. BROOKS, RETHINKING THE AMERICAN RACE PROBLEM (Berkeley: University of California Press 1990).

Browne, *A Case for Separation*, in SEPARATISM OR INTEGRATION: WHICH WAY FOR AMERICA: A DIALOGUE (R. Browne and B. Rustin eds. 1968).

J. BUCHANAN and G. TULLOCK, THE CALCULUS OF CONSENT: LOGICAL FOUNDATIONS OF CONSTITUTIONAL DEMOCRACY (Ann Arbor: University of Michigan Press 1965).

Burke, *The Cherokee Cases: A Study in Law, Politics and Morality*, 21 STAN. L. REV. 500 (1969).

Butch Cassidy and the Sundance Kid (Twentieth-Century Fox 1969).

BY ANY MEANS NECESSARY: SPEECHES, INTERVIEWS AND A LETTER BY MALCOLM X (G. Breitman ed.) (New York: Pathfinder Press 1970).

B. CARDOZO, THE NATURE OF THE JUDICIAL PROCESS (New Haven: Yale University Press 1921).

S. CARMICHAEL and C. HAMILTON, BLACK POWER: THE POLITICS OF LIBERATION IN AMERICA (New York: Vintage 1967).

Carrington, *Of Law and the River*, 34 J. LEGAL EDUC. 222 (1984).

S. CARTER, REFLECTIONS OF AN AFFIRMATIVE ACTION BABY (New York: Basic Books 1991).

R. CHUSED, CASES, MATERIALS AND PROBLEMS IN PROPERTY (New York: Matthew Bender 1988).

A COMMON DESTINY: BLACKS AND AMERICAN SOCIETY 14 (G. Jaynes & R. Williams, Jr. eds.) (Washington, D.C.: National Academy Press 1989).

CONGRESS RECONSIDERED (L. Dodd and B. Oppenheimer, eds.) (New York: Praeger Publishers 1977).

Cook, *Beyond Critical Legal Studies: The Reconstructive Theology of Dr. Martin Luther King, Jr.*, 103 HARV. L. REV. 985 (1990).

Cooper, *Race-Based Student Aid: Practice and Policy; U.S. Providing $100 Million in Minority Scholarships While Proposing to Restrict Colleges*, WASH. POST, Dec. 26, 1991, at p. A21.

Cooper and Walsh, *Riding the Victory Train*, U.S. NEWS & WORLD REPORT, Mar 25, 1991, at p. 24.

Correspondence from Nathaniel R. Jones, General Counsel, NAACP Special Contribution Fund, 86 YALE L.J. 378 (1976).

R. COVER, JUSTICE ACCUSED: ANTISLAVERY AND THE JUDICIAL PROCESS (New Haven: Yale University Press 1975).

Cover and Mayhew, *Congressional Dynamics and the Decline of Competitive Congressional Elections*, in CONGRESS RECONSIDERED (L. Dodd and B. Oppenheimer, eds.) (New York: Praeger Publishers 1977).

Crenshaw, *Race, Reform, and Retrenchment: Transformation and Legitimation in Antidiscrimination Law*, 101 HARV. L. REV. 1331 (1988).

H. CRUSE, THE CRISIS OF THE NEGRO INTELLECTUAL (New York: William Morrow 1967).

H. CRUSE, PLURAL BUT EQUAL (New York: William Morrow 1987).

Culp, *Toward a Black Legal Scholarship: Race and Original Understanding*, 1991 DUKE L.J. 39.

CURRENT POPULATION REPORT, U.S. DEPT. OF COMMERCE, BUREAU OF CENSUS, Series P-60, No. 145 (Washington, D.C.: Government Printing Office 1983).

Currie, *The Constitution in the Supreme Court: The New Deal, 1931–1940*, 59 U. CHI. L. REV. 504 (1987).

D. D'SOUZA, ILLIBERAL EDUCATION: THE POLITICS OF RACE AND SEX ON CAMPUS (New York: Free Press 1991).

R. DAHL, A PREFACE TO DEMOCRATIC THEORY (Chicago: University of Chicago Press 1956).

Dalton, *The Clouded Prism*, 22 HARV. C.R.-C.L. L. REV. 435 (1987).

R. DANIELS, CONCENTRATION CAMPS, NORTH AMERICA: JAPANESE IN THE UNITED STATES AND CANADA DURING WORLD WAR II (Malabar, Fla.: R.E. Krieger Publishing, rev. ed. 1981).

Dawson, *The Law School Admission Test Battery: A Different Selection Concept for the 1980's and Beyond*, 34 J. LEGAL EDUC. 388 (1984).

Delgado, *Affirmative Action as a Majoritarian Device: Or Do You Really Want To Be a Role Model?*, 89 MICH. L. REV. 1222 (1991).

Delgado, *Enormous Anomaly: Left-Right Parallels in Recent Writing About Race*, 91 COLUM. L. REV. 1547 (1991) (comparative book review of D. BELL, AND WE ARE NOT SAVED; S. CARTER, REFLECTIONS OF AN AFFIRMATIVE ACTION BABY; S. STEELE, THE CONTENT OF OUR CHARACTER; P. WILLIAMS, THE ALCHEMY OF RACE AND RIGHTS).

Delgado, *The Ethereal Scholar: Does Critical Legal Studies Have What Minorities Want?*, 22 HARV. C.R.-C.L. L. REV. 301 (1987).

Delgado, *Recasting the American Race Problem*, 79 CALIF. L. REV. 1389 (1991) (book review of R. BROOKS, RETHINKING THE AMERICAN RACE PROBLEM).

Delgado, Dunn, Brown, Lee, and Hubbert, *Fairness and Formality: Minimizing the Risk of Prejudice in Alternative Dispute Resolution*, 1985 WIS. L. REV. 1359.

Dionne, *Jackson Share of Votes by Whites Triples in '88*, N.Y. TIMES, June 13, 1988, at p. B7.

Dorman, *A Who's Who of Friends and Foes; Some were allies, others adversaries. All of their Lives intersected John F. Kennedy's*, NEWSDAY, Nov. 21, 1988, at p.6.

W. DOUGLAS, THE COURT YEARS, 1939–75: THE AUTOBIOGRAPHY OF WILLIAM O. DOUGLAS (New York: Random House 1980).

Dudziak, *Desegregation as a Cold War Imperative*, 41 STAN. L. REV. 61 (1988).

A. DWORKIN, RIGHT-WING WOMEN (New York: Coward-McCann 1983).

R. DWORKIN, TAKING RIGHTS SERIOUSLY (Cambridge: Harvard University Press 1977).

Eaton, *Bush Rejects Civil Rights Compromise by Moderates*, L.A. TIMES, Aug. 2, 1991, at p. A20.

Edmonds, *Effective Education for Minority Pupils:* Brown *Confounded or Confirmed*, in SHADES OF BROWN: NEW PERSPECTIVES ON SCHOOL DESEGREGATION (D. Bell ed.) (New York: Teachers College Press, Columbia University 1980).

T. EDSALL, with M. EDSALL, CHAIN REACTION: THE IMPACT OF RACE, RIGHTS, AND TAXES ON AMERICAN POLITICS (New York: Norton 1991).

Ehrenreich, *Pluralist Myths and Powerless Men: The Ideology of Reasonableness in Sexual Harassment Law*, 99 YALE L.J. 1177 (1990).

Ellis, *Another Deadly Day as the ANC Signs for Peace*, SUNDAY TIMES, Sept. 15, 1991, at sec. Overseas News.

J. ELY, DEMOCRACY AND DISTRUST: A THEORY OF JUDICIAL REVIEW (Cambridge: Harvard University Press 1980).

R. EPSTEIN, TAKINGS: PRIVATE PROPERTY AND THE POWER OF EMINENT DOMAIN (Cambridge: Harvard University Press 1985).

Escobar, *At GU Law Center, Silence Speaks in Protest; Green Ribbons, Placards Replace Angry Words as Author of Race Article Receives Degree*, WASH. POST, May 28, 1991, at p. B3.

Eskridge, *Politics Without Romance: Implications of Public Choice Theory for Statutory Interpretation*, 74 VA. L. REV. 275 (1988).

Eskridge, *Reneging on History? Playing the Court/Congress/President Civil Rights Game*, 79 CALIF. L. REV. 613 (1991).

W. ESKRIDGE and P. FRICKEY, CASES AND MATERIALS ON LEGISLATION: STATUTES AND THE CREATION OF PUBLIC POLICY 367–98 (St. Paul, Minn: West Publishing 1987).

S. ESTRICH, REAL RAPE: HOW THE LEGAL SYSTEM VICTIMIZES WOMEN WHO SAY NO (Cambridge: Harvard University Press 1987).

Farber and Frickey, *The Jurisprudence of Public Choice*, 65 TEXAS L. REV. 873 (1987).

THE FEDERALIST (H. Lodge ed.) (New York: G.P. Putnam's Sons 1888).

D. FEHRENBACKER, THE DRED SCOTT CASE: ITS SIGNIFICANCE IN AMERICAN LAW AND POLITICS (New York: Oxford University Press 1978).

Fein, *Souter's Judicial Soul Facing an Early Test*, WASH. TIMES, Sept. 14, 1990, at p. F1.

Fidelman, *Film Captures Depth of Hatred in Middle East; Documentary Crew Tried to Get the Full Story Behind the News*, GAZETTE (Montreal), Nov. 28, 1991, at p. H15.

Fineman, *The New Black Politics: Candidates Across the Country Win Historic Victories by Emphasizing Mainstream Values*, NEWSWEEK, Nov. 20, 1989, at p. 52.

H. FINK and M. TUSHNET, FEDERAL JURISDICTION: POLICY AND PRACTICE (Charlottesville, Va.: Michie 1984).

P. FINKELMAN, SLAVERY, RACE AND THE AMERICAN LEGAL SYSTEM, 1700–1872 (New York: Garland Publishing 1988).

M. FIORINA, CONGRESS: KEYSTONE OF THE WASHINGTON ESTABLISHMENT (New Haven: Yale University Press 1977).

Fisk, *Peace through Coercion, US Style; Robert Fisk, in Beirut, Accuses America of Basking in Glory for Arranging Middle East Talks, while Planning to Punish Palestinians for their Stance in the Gulf War*, INDEPENDENT, Oct. 23, 1991, at p. 21.

Fiss, *Groups and the Equal Protection Clause*, 5 J. PHIL. & PUB. AFF. 107 (1976).

R. FORMISANO, BOSTON AGAINST BUSING: RACE, CLASS AND ETHNICITY IN THE 1960'S AND THE 1970'S (Chapel Hill: University of North Carolina Press 1991).

THE FOUNDERS' CONSTITUTION, VOL. 4 (P. Kurland and R. Lerner eds.) (Chicago: University of Chicago Press 1987).

J. FRANKLIN, THE EMANCIPATION PROCLAMATION 96 (Garden City, N.Y.: Doubleday 1963).

J. FREEDMAN, CRISIS AND LEGITIMACY (New York: Cambridge University Press 1978).

Freedom's Year: Hope-and Chaos-Fill Gorbachev's Final Days, MACLEAN'S, Dec. 23, 1991, at p. 22.

Freeman, *Antidiscrimination Law: The View From 1989*, in THE POLITICS OF LAW (D. Kairys ed., rev. ed. 1990).

Freeman, *Legitimizing Racial Discrimination through Antidiscrimination Law: A Critical Review of Supreme Court Doctrine*, 62 MINN. L. REV. 1049 (1978).

FRONTIERS OF DEMOCRATIC THEORY (H. Kariel ed.) (New York: Random House 1970).

Gallagher, *Integrated Schools in the Black Cities*, 42 J. NEGRO EDUC. 336 (1973).

W. GODDELL, SLAVERY AND ANTI-SLAVERY: A HISTORY OF THE GREAT STRUGGLE IN BOTH HEMISPHERES: WITH A VIEW OF THE SLAVERY QUESTION IN THE UNITED STATES (New York: Negro University Press 1968) (originally published 1852).

Gray, *Hate of Ages: Nationalist Violence Is Spreading*, MACLEAN'S, Dec. 23, 1991, at p. 27.

Greenhouse, *Bork's Nomination is Rejected, 58-42; Reagan "Saddened,"* N.Y. TIMES, Oct. 24, 1987 at p. 1.

G. GUNTHER, CONSTITUTIONAL LAW (Mineola, N.Y.: Foundation Press, 11th ed. 1985).

G. Gunther, *The Subtle Vices of the "Passive Virtues"—A Comment on Principle and Expediency in Judicial Review*, 64 COLUM. L. REV. 1 (1964).

H. HART and A. SACKS, THE LEGAL PROCESS: BASIC PROBLEMS IN THE MAKING AND APPLICATION OF LAW (tentative ed. 1958).

Henry, *Beyond the Melting Pot*, TIME, April 9, 1990, at p. 28, 30.

G. HERKEN, THE WINNING WEAPON: THE ATOMIC BOMB IN THE COLD WAR, 1945–1950 (New York: Knopf 1980).

A.L. HIGGINBOTHAM, JR., IN THE MATTER OF COLOR: RACE AND THE AMERICAN LEGAL PROCESS: THE COLONIAL PERIOD (New York: Oxford University Press 1978).

T. HOBBES, LEVIATHAN (New York: Dutton 1950).

Horwitz, *Republicanism and Liberalism in American Constitutional Thought*, 29 WM. & MARY L. REV. 57 (1987).

Hutchinson, *Unanimity and Desegregation: Decisionmaking in the Supreme Court, 1948-58*, 68 GEO. L.J. (1979).

Hyde, *The Concept of Legitimation in the Sociology of Law*, 1983 WIS. L. REV. 379.

INFORMATION BOOK 1991-92: REGISTRATION INFORMATION AND MATERIALS FOR LAW SCHOOL ADMISSION TEST (Law School Admissions Service 1991).

Jackson, *The Supreme Court, the Eleventh Amendment, and State Sovereignty*, 98 YALE L.J. 1 (1988).

Johnson, *The Black Athlete Revisited: How Far Have We Come?*, SPORTS IL-LUSTRATED, Aug. 5, 1991, at p. 38.

Jones, *Is* Brown *Obsolete: No!*, 14 INTEGRATEDUCATION 29 (May-June 1976).

H. KALVEN and H. ZEISEL, THE AMERICAN JURY (Chicago: University of Chicago Press 1966).

M. KELMAN, A GUIDE TO CRITICAL LEGAL STUDIES (Cambridge: Harvard University Press 1987).

Kelman, *Interpretive Construction in the Substantive Criminal Law*, 33 STAN. L. REV. 591 (1981).

Kelman, *"Public Choice" and Public Spirit*, 87 PUB. INT. 80 (1987).

Kennedy, *Form and Substance in Private Law Adjudication*, 89 HARV. L. REV. 1685 (1976).

Kennedy, *Frontier of Legal Thought III: A Cultural Pluralist Case for Affirmative Action in Legal Academia*, 1990 DUKE L.J. 705.

Kennedy, *Martin Luther King's Constitution: A Legal History of the Montgomery Bus Boycott*, 98 YALE L.J. 999 (1989).

Kennedy, McCleskey v. Kemp: *Race, Capital Punishment, and the Supreme Court*, 101 HARV. L. REV. 1388 (1988).

Kennedy, *Racial Critiques of Legal Academia*, 102 HARV. L. REV. 1745 (1989).

Kirkpatrick, *The Night They Drove Old Dixie Down*, SPORTS ILLUSTRATED, Apr. 1, 1991, at p. 70.

R. KLUGER, SIMPLE JUSTICE: THE HISTORY OF *BROWN V. BOARD OF EDUCATION* AND BLACK AMERICA'S STRUGGLE FOR EQUALITY (New York: Knopf 1976).

Kondracke, *Vultures: Scenarios for the Losing and Winning Political Parties*, NEW REPUBLIC, Nov. 7, 1988, at p. 10.

Labaton, *Thomas Smoked Marijuana But Retains Bush Support*, N.Y. TIMES, July 11, 1991, at p. A17.

LaFraniere, *Despite Achievement, Thomas Felt Isolated; Rebuffs Stung Emerging Conservative*, WASH. POST, Sept. 9, 1991, at p. A1.

Lancaster and LaFraniere, *Thomas: Growing Up Black in a White World*, WASH. POST, Sept. 8, 1991, at p. A1.

Larew, *Why Are Droves of Unqualified, Unprepared Kids Getting into Our Top Colleges?: Because their Dads Are Alumni*, WASHINGTON MONTHLY, June 1991, at p. 10.

Lawrence, *The Id, the Ego, and Equal Protection: Reckoning with Unconscious Racism*, 39 STAN. L. REV. 317 (1987).

Layne, *Why the Gulf War was Not in the National Interest*, ATLANTIC, July 1991, at p. 55.

Leuchtenberg, *The Origins of Franklin D. Roosevelt's "Court- Packing" Plan*, 1966 SUP. CT. REV. 347.

M. LOCK, ANTI-SLAVERY IN AMERICA: FROM THE INTRODUCTION OF AFRICAN SLAVES TO THE PROHIBITION OF THE SLAVE TRADE (1619–1808) (Gloucester, Mass: P. Smith 1965).

W. LOCKHART, Y. KAMISAR, J. CHOPER, and S. SHIFFRIN, CONSTITU-TIONAL LAW: CASES—COMMENTS—QUESTIONS App. A (St. Paul, Minn: West Publishing, 6th ed. 1986).

Loury, *Who Speaks for American Blacks*, COMMENTARY, Jan. 1987, at p. 34.

T. LOWI, THE END OF LIBERALISM (New York: Norton, 2d ed. 1979).

MacKinnon, *Feminism, Marxism, Method, and the State: An Agenda for Theory*, 7 SIGNS 515 (1982).

MacKinnon, *Feminism, Marxism, Method, and the State: Toward Feminist Juris-prudence*, 8 SIGNS 635 (1983).

R. MAHONE-LONESOME, CHARLES DREW (New York: Chelsea House 1990).

C. MANGUM, THE LEGAL STATUS OF THE NEGRO (Chapel Hill: University of North Carolina Press 1939).

Marcus, *High Court to Review Tactic in War on Drug Trade; Justices Agree to Rule on Searches of Bus, Train Luggage as Souter Takes Oath*, WASH. POST, Oct. 10, 1990, at p. A15.

Margolick, *In Land of Death Penalty, Accusations of Racial Bias*, N.Y. TIMES, July 10, 1991, at p. A1.

Martin, *"Of Law and the River," and Of Nihilism and Academic Freedom*, 37 J. LEGAL EDUC. 1 (1984).

Matsuda, *Voices of America: Accent, Antidiscrimination Law, and a Jurisprudence for the Last Reconstruction*, 100 YALE L.J. 1329 (1991).

McAllister, *Proportion Of Blacks in South Rises; Census Cites Reversal Of Trend Since 1900*, WASH. POST, Jan. 10, 1990, at p. A1.

McCall, *Reprimand 'Vindicates Me,' Georgetown Law Student Says*, WASH. POST, May 22, 1991, at p. C3.

McCormack, *Business Necessity in Title VIII: Incorporating an Employment Dis-crimination Doctrine into the Fair Housing Act*, 54 FORDHAM L. REV. 563 (1986).

Merit, Heart, Will-And Affirmative Action, NEWSDAY, June 4, 1991, at p. 56.

Michelman, *Law's Republic*, 97 YALE L.J. 1493 (1988).

Mincberg, *Furtive and Unproductive Souter Falls Right In*, CONN. LAW TRIBUNE, July 9, 1991, at p. A2.

Molotsky, *N.A.A.C.P. Urges Souter's Defeat, Citing Earlier Statements on Race*, N.Y. TIMES, Sept. 21, 1990, at sec. 1, p. 7.

Moore, *After the Marching*, NATIONAL JOURNAL, June 23, 1990, at p. 1525.

Morganthau, *The Military's New Image*, NEWSWEEK, Mar. 11, 1991, at p. 50.

Morley, *Bush & the Blacks: An Unknown Story*, N.Y. REVIEW OF BOOKS, Jan. 16, 1991, at p. 19.

D. MUELLER, PUBLIC CHOICE (New York: Cambridge University Press 1979).

Mueller, *Public Choice: A Survey*, 14 J. ECON. LIT. 395 (1976).

Mydans, *Seven Minutes in Los Angeles—A Special Report; Videotaped Beating by Officers Puts Full Glare on Brutality Issue*, N.Y. TIMES, Mar. 18, 1991, at p. A1.

G. MYRDAL, AN AMERICAN DILEMMA: THE NEGRO PROBLEM AND MODERN DEMOCRACY (New York: Harper & Row 1962).

C. NEUBERT and J. WITHIAM, JR., THE LAW SCHOOL GAME (New York: Drake, rev. ed. 1980).

Note, *The Bounds of Legislative Specification: A Suggested Approach to the Bill of Attainder Clause*, 72 YALE L.J. 330, (1962).

Note, *The Legality of Integration Maintenance Quotas: Fair Housing or Forced Housing*, 55 BROOKLYN L. REV. 197 (1989).

T. PANGLE, THE SPIRIT OF MODERN REPUBLICANISM (Chicago: University of Chicago Press 1988).

O. PATTERSON, SLAVERY AND SOCIAL DEATH (Cambridge: Harvard University Press 1982).

Peller, *Espousing a Positive Vision of Affirmative-Action Policies*, CHRON. HIGHER EDUC. Dec. 18, 1991, at p. B1.

Peller, *Neutral Principles in the 1950's*, 21 MICH. J.L. REF. 561 (1988).

Peller, *Race Consciousness*, 1990 DUKE L.J. 758.

Peltzman, *Toward a More General Theory of Regulation*, 19 J. L. & ECON. 211 (1976).

Perry, *The Principle of Equal Protection*, 32 HASTINGS L.J. 1133 (1981).

THE POLITICS OF LAW: A PROGRESSIVE CRITIQUE (D. Kairys ed.) (New York: Pantheon, rev. ed. 1990).

R. POSNER, ECONOMIC ANALYSIS OF LAW (Boston: Little, Brown, 3d ed. 1986).

Race Is On for 152 New Judgeships, U.S. NEWS & WORLD REPORT, Oct. 9, 1978, at p. 54.

Raskin, *Liberate the District; Washington, D.C.*, NATION, Mar. 25, 1991, at p. 371.

Raspberry, *Bush, Civil Rights and the Specter of David Duke*, WASH. POST, Oct. 30, 1991, at p. A23.

Review of Supreme Court's Term: Labor and Employment Law, 58 LW 3065 (Aug. 8, 1989).

Riccio, *School's Daze: Free Speech v. Freedom from Fear,* N.J. LAW J., Oct. 10, 1991, at p. 15.

Rich, *Hispanic Population of U.S. Growing Fastest: Census Bureau Puts Total at 20.1 Million,* WASH. POST, Oct. 12, 1989, at p. A3.

R. RIST, THE INVISIBLE CHILDREN: SCHOOL INTEGRATION IN AMERICAN SOCIETY (Cambridge: Harvard University Press 1978).

Roberts, *Ginsburg withdraws Name as Supreme Court Nominee, Citing Marijuana "Clamor,"* N.Y. TIMES, Nov. 8, 1987 at p. 1.

D. ROBINSON, SLAVERY IN THE STRUCTURE OF AMERICAN POLITICS 1765–1820 (New York: Harcourt, Brace, Jovanovich 1971).

R. ROSE, GOVERNING WITHOUT CONSENSUS: AN IRISH PERSPECTIVE (London: Farber and Farber 1971).

V. RYAN, IRELAND RESTORED: THE NEW SELF-DETERMINATION (New York: Freedom House 1991).

Savage, *Thomas Takes Oath in Secret Ceremony,* L.A. TIMES, Oct. 24, 1991, at p. 26.

R. SCAMMON and A. MCGILLIVRAY, AMERICA VOTES 16, A HANDBOOK OF CONTEMPORARY AMERICAN ELECTION STATISTICS, 1984 67 (Washington, D.C.: Congressional Quarterly 1985).

Schauer, *Formalism,* 97 YALE L.J. 509 (1988).

Schneider, *For Danforth & Co., An Uncivil Snub,* NATIONAL JOURNAL, July 6, 1991, at p. 1716.

Schrag, *The Future of District of Columbia Home Rule,* 39 CATH. L. REV. 311 (1990).

B. SCHWARTZ, SUPER CHIEF (New York: New York University Press 1983).

Seidman, *Brown and Miranda,* 80 CALIF. L. REV.— (May 1992).

Seidman, *The Preconditions for Home Rule,* 39 CATH. L. REV. 373 (1990).

SEPARATISM OR INTEGRATION: WHICH WAY FOR AMERICA: A DIALOGUE (R. Browne & B. Rustin eds.) (New York: A. Phillip Randolph Educational Fund 1968).

SHADES OF BROWN: NEW PERSPECTIVES ON SCHOOL DESEGREGATION (D. Bell ed.) (New York: Teachers College Press, Columbia University 1980).

Shapiro, *Breakthrough In Virginia: In a Model of Crossover Politics, Douglas Wilder Becomes the First Elected Black Governor and Shows Others How to Crash the Color Line,* TIME, Nov. 21, 1989, at p. 54.

Shogan, *Seeks to Avoid Hurting the Party: Dukakis Ponders What Role He Can Offer Jackson,* L.A. TIMES, June 27, 1988, at p. 1.

Simien, *The Law School Admission Test as a Barrier to Almost Twenty Years of Affirmative Action,* 12 T. MARSHALL L.J. 359 (1987).

Simon, *The New Republicanism: Generosity of Spirit in Search of Something to Say,* 29 WM. & MARY L. REV. 83 (1987).

T. SOWELL, CIVIL RIGHTS: RHETORIC OR REALITY (New York: William Morrow 1984).

T. SOWELL, PREFERENTIAL POLICIES: AN INTERNATIONAL PERSPECTIVE (New York: William Morrow 1990).

Spann, *A Critical Legal Studies Perspective On Contract Law and Practice*, 1988 ANNUAL SURVEY OF AMERICAN LAW 223.

S. STEELE, THE CONTENT OF OUR CHARACTER: A NEW VISION OF RACE IN AMERICA (New York: St. Martin's Press 1990).

G. STEPHENSON, RACE DISTINCTIONS IN AMERICAN LAW (Miami Fla.: Mnemosyne Publishing 1969).

Stewart, *The Reformation of American Administrative Law*, 88 HARV. L. REV. 1667 (1975).

Stigler, *The Theory of Economic Regulation*, 2 BELL J. ECON. & MGMT. SCI. 3 (1971).

G. STONE, L. SEIDMAN, C. SUNSTEIN, and M. TUSHNET, CONSTITUTIONAL LAW (Boston: Little, Brown 1986).

Strauss, *The Law and Economics of Racial Discrimination in Employment: The Case for Numerical Standards*, 79 GEO L.J. 1619 (1991).

Strauss, *The Myth of Colorblindness*, 1986 SUP. CT. REV. 99.

Sullivan, *Sins of Discrimination: Last Term's Affirmative Action Cases*, 100 HARV. L. REV. 78 (1986).

Sunstein, *Beyond the Republican Revival*, 97 YALE L.J. 1539 (1988).

Sunstein, *Constitutionalism after the New Deal*, 101 HARV. L. REV. 421 (1987).

Sunstein, *Interest Groups in American Public Law*, 38 STAN. L. REV. 29, (1985).

The Supreme Court, 1979 Term, 94 HARV. L. REV. 75 (1980).

Symposium: A Critique of Rights, 62 TEXAS L. REV. 1363–1599 (1984).

Symposium on the Theory of Public Choice, 74 VA. L. REV. 167–518 (1988).

Symposium: The Republican Civic Tradition, 97 YALE L.J. 1493–1851 (1988).

J. TEN BROEK, E. BARNHART, and F. MATSON, PREJUDICE, WAR AND THE CONSTITUTION (Berkeley: University of California Press 1954).

Toner, *Tuesday's Stakes: Black Politicians are Leaning against Some Old Barriers*, N.Y. TIMES, Week in Review, Nov. 5, 1989, at Sec. 4, p. 1, col. 1.

Torry, *GU Reprimands Law Student; Permission to Graduate Angers Blacks*, WASH. POST, May 21, 1991, at p. B1.

L. TRIBE, AMERICAN CONSTITUTIONAL LAW (Mineola, N.Y.: Foundation Press, 2d ed. 1988).

D. TRUMAN, THE GOVERNMENTAL PROCESS: POLITICAL INTERESTS AND PUBLIC OPINION (New York: Knopf 1965).

M. TUSHNET, THE AMERICAN LAW OF SLAVERY, 1810–1860: CONSIDERATIONS OF HUMANITY AND INTEREST (Princeton, N.J.: Princeton University Press 1981).

Tushnet, *Darkness on the Edge of Town: The Contributions of John Hart Ely to Constitutional Theory*, 89 YALE L.J. 1073 (1980).

Tushnet, *An Essay in Informal Political Theory*, 17 POLS. & SOC. 403 (1989).

Tushnet, *An Essay On Rights*, 62 TEXAS L. REV. 1363 (1984).

M. TUSHNET, THE NAACP'S LEGAL STRATEGY AGAINST SEGREGATED EDUCATION, 1925-1950 (Chapel Hill: University of North Carolina Press 1987).

Tushnet, *The New Law of Standing: A Plea for Abandonment*, 62 CORNELL L. REV. 663 (1977).

Tushnet, *The Politics of Constitutional Law*, in THE POLITICS OF LAW (D. Kairys ed., rev. ed. 1990).

Tushnet, Kovner, and Schneider, *Judicial Review and Congressional Tenure: A Research Note*, 66 TEXAS L. REV. 967 (1988).

Varat, *Justice White and the Breadth and Allocation of Federal Authority*, 58 COLORADO L. REV. 371 (1987).

Waldmeir, *S African Cauldron of Tribalism and Politics*, FINANCIAL TIMES, Nov. 28, 1991, at p. 4.

Waldmeir, *South Africa 3: Where the Central Fact is Violence*, FINANCIAL TIMES, May 7, 1991, at p. 3.

Waldmeir, *Why Murder Ended in Mpumalanga*, FINANCIAL TIMES, Sept. 18, 1991, at p. 4.

Walte, *Powell to Head Joint Chiefs for 2 More Years*, USA TODAY, May 24, 1991, at p. 4A.

Wechsler, *Toward Neutral Principles of Constitutional Law*, 73 HARV. L. REV. 1 (1959).

Wellington, *Common Law Rules and Constitutional Double Standards*, 83 YALE L.J. 221 (1973).

G. WHITE, TORT LAW IN AMERICA (New York: Oxford University Press 1980).

W. WIECEK, THE SOURCES OF ANTISLAVERY CONSTITUTIONALISM IN AMERICA 1760-1848 (Ithaca, N.Y.: Cornell University Press 1977).

Williams, *Alchemical Notes: Reconstructing Ideals from Deconstructed Rights*, 22 HARV. C.R.-C.L. L. REV. 401 (1987).

P. WILLIAMS, THE ALCHEMY OF RACE AND RIGHTS (Cambridge: Harvard University Press 1991).

Williams, *A Question of Fairness; Clarence Thomas, a Black, is Ronald Reagan's Chairman of the Equal Employment Opportunity Commission*, ATLANTIC, Feb. 1987, at p. 70.

Williams, *Taking Rights Aggressively: The Perils and Promise of Critical Legal Theory for Peoples of Color*, 5 LAW & INEQUALITY 103 (1987).

Witt, *Deferred Dreams: Mandela, DeKlerk Find Old Ways Die Hard in "New South Africa,"* CHICAGO TRIB., Apr. 29, 1990, at sec. Perspective, p. 1.

Wren, *Rumblings on the Right*, N.Y. TIMES, Oct. 7, 1990, at sec. Magazine, p. 32.

Wright, *Gulf War Forced Washington to Tackle Arab-Israeli Conflict*, REUTER LIBRARY REPT., July 30, 1991.

Yalowitz & Jones, *South Africa's Unstoppable March Toward Multiracial Rule*, U.S. NEWS & WORLD REPORT, Feb. 25, 1991, at p. 44.

A. ZILVERSMIT, THE FIRST EMANCIPATION, THE ABOLITION OF SLAVERY IN THE NORTH (Chicago: University of Chicago Press 1967).

Table of Legal Authorities

Home Building & Loan Association v. Blaisdell, 290 U.S. 398 (1934).
Humphrey's Executor v. United States, 295 U.S. 602 (1935).
Hunter v. Underwood, 471 U.S. 222 (1985).
Independent Federation of Flight Attendants v. Zipes, 491 U.S. 754 (1989).
INS v. Chadha, 462 U.S. 919 (1983).
J.A. Croson Co. v. City of Richmond, 488 U.S. 469 (1989).
J.A. Croson Co. v. City of Richmond, 822 F.2d 1355 (4th Cir. 1987).
Jackson v. Bulloch, 12 Conn. 38 (1837).
Jackson v. Metropolitan Edison, 419 U.S. 345 (1974).
Jett v. Dallas Independent School District, 491 U.S. 701 (1989).
Jones v. Alfred H. Mayer, 392 U.S. 409 (1968).
Katzenbach v. McClung, 379 U.S. 294 (1964).
Keyes v. School District No. 1, Denver, Colorado, 413 U.S. 189 (1973).
Korematsu v. United States, 323 U.S. 214 (1944).
Lee v. Washington, 390 U.S. 333 (1968), aff'g Washington v. Lee, 263 F. Supp.
327 (M.D. Ala. 1966) (three-judge court).
Linmark Associates v. Township of Willingboro, 431 U.S. 85 (1977).
Local 28, Sheet Metal Workers International Association v. Equal Employment
Opportunity Commission, 478 U.S. 421 (1986).
Logan v. United States, 144 U.S. 263 (1892).
Londoner v. Denver, 210 U.S. 373 (1908).
Lorance v. AT&T Technologies, 490 U.S. 900 (1989).
Loving v. Virginia, 388 U.S. 1 (1967).
Lugar v. Edmondson Oil Co., 457 U.S. 922 (1982).
Lynch v. Household Finance Corp., 405 U.S. 538 (1972).
Maher v. Roe, 432 U.S. 464 (1977).
Marbury v. Madison, 5 U.S. (1 Cranch.) 137 (1803).
Martin v. Wilkes, 490 U.S. 755 (1989).
Mayor of Baltimore v. Dawson, 350 U.S. 877 (1955).
McCleskey v. Kemp, 481 U.S. 279 (1987), *rehearing denied*, 482 U.S. 920
(1987).
McClure v. Carter, 513 F. Supp. 265 (D. Idaho) (three-judge court), *aff'd mem.*,
454 U.S. 1025 (1981).
Metro Broadcasting v. Federal Communications Commission, 110 S.Ct. 2997
(1990).
Metropolitan Washington Airports Authority v. Citizens for the Abatement of
Aircraft Noise, 111 S.Ct. 2298 (1991).
Michigan v. Tucker, 417 U.S. 433 (1974).
Milliken v. Bradley, 418 U.S. 717 (1974) *(Milliken I)*.
Milliken v. Bradley, 433 U.S. 267 (1977) *(Milliken II)*.
Minor v. Happersett, 88 U.S. 162 (1874).
Miranda v. Arizona, 384 U.S. 436 (1966).
Missouri v. Jenkins, 110 S.Ct. 1651 (1990).
Mistretta v. United States, 488 U.S. 361 (1989).

Monell v. New York Department of Social Services, 438 U.S. 658 (1978).
Monroe v. Pape, 365 U.S. 167 (1961).
Morrison v. Olson, 487 U.S. 654 (1988).
Naim v. Naim, 350 U.S. 891 (1955) (per curiam) and 350 U.S. 895 (1956) (per curiam).
New Orleans v. Dukes, 427 U.S. 297 (1976).
New York v. Quarles, 467 U.S. 649 (1984).
Norris v. Alabama, 294 U.S. 587 (1935).
North Carolina State Board of Education v. Swann, 402 U.S. 43 (1971).
North Carolina v. Butler, 441 U.S. 369 (1979).
O'Shea v. Littleton, 414 U.S. 488 (1974).
Oregon v. Bradshaw, 462 U.S. 1039 (1983).
Orozco v. Texas, 394 U.S. 324 (1969).
Pasadena Board of Education v. Spangler, 427 U.S. 424 (1976).
Patsy v. Board of Regents of Florida, 457 U.S. 496, 503 (1982).
Patterson v. McLean Credit Union, 485 U.S. 617 (1988).
Patterson v. McLean Credit Union, 491 U.S. 164 (1989).
Penry v. Lynaugh, 492 U.S. 302 (1989).
Personnel Administrator v. Feeney, 442 U.S. 256 (1979).
Plessy v. Ferguson, 163 U.S. 537 (1896).
Plyler v. Doe, 457 U.S. 202 (1982).
Powell v. McCormack, 395 U.S. 486 (1969).
Powers v. Ohio, 111 S.Ct. 1364 (1991).
Price Waterhouse v. Hopkins, 490 U.S. 228 (1989).
Quern v. Jordan, 440 U.S. 332 (1979).
Regents of the University of California v. Bakke, 438 U.S. 265 (1978).
Rhode Island v. Innis, 446 U.S. 291 (1980).
Rizzo v. Goode, 423 U.S. 362 (1976).
Roe v. Wade, 410 U.S. 113 (1973).
Roth v. United States, 354 U.S. 476 (1957).
Runyon v. McCrary, 427 U.S. 160 (1976).
Rust v. Sullivan, 111 S.Ct. 1759 (1991).
San Antonio Independent School District v. Rodriguez, 411 U.S. 1 (1973).
Schlesinger v. Reservists Committee to Stop the War, 418 U.S. 208 (1974).
Selectman v. Jacob, 2 Vt. 200 (1804).
Shelley v. Kraemer, 334 U.S. 1 (1948).
The Slaughter-House Cases, 83 U.S. (16 Wall.) 36 (1873).
Spallone v. United States, 110 S.Ct. 625 (1990).
Spomer v. Littleton, 414 U.S. 514 (1974).
State v. Post, 20 N.J.L. 368 (1845).
Strauder v. West Virginia, 100 U.S. 303 (1880).
Sturges v. Crowninshield, 17 U.S. (4 Wheat.) 122 (1918).
Supreme Court of New Hampshire v. Piper, 470 U.S. 274 (1985).
Swain v. Alabama, 380 U.S. 202 (1965).

Swain v. State, 275 Ala. 508; 156 So. 2d 368 (1963).
Swann v. Charlotte-Mecklenburg Board of Education, 402 U.S. 1 (1971).
Tasby v. Wright, 520 F. Supp. 683 (N. D. Tex. 1981).
Toomer v. Witsell, 334 U.S. 385 (1948).
United Building & Construction Trades Council v. Mayor of Camden, 465 U.S. 208 (1984).
United Jewish Organizations v. Carey, 430 U.S. 144 (1977).
United States Trust Co. v. New Jersey, 431 U.S. 1 (1977).
United States v. Butler, 297 U.S. 1 (1936).
United States v. Carolene Products, 304 U.S. 144 (1938).
United States v. Cruikshank, 92 U.S. 542 (1875).
United States v. Curtiss-Wright, 299 U.S. 304 (1936).
United States v. Harris, 106 U.S. 629 (1882).
United States v. Leslie, 783 F.2d 541 (5th Cir. 1986) (en banc).
United States v. Mabus, 59 L.W. 3732 (No. 90–6588, Apr. 15, 1991).
United States v. Mandujana, 425 U.S. 564 (1976).
United States v. Nixon, 418 U.S. 683 (1973).
United States v. Paradise, 480 U.S. 92 (1987).
Village of Arlington Heights v. Metropolitan Housing Development Corp., 429 U.S. 252 (1977).
Wards Cove Packing Co. v. Atonio, 490 U.S. 642 (1989).
Warth v. Seldin, 422 U.S. 490 (1975).
Washington v. Davis, 426 U.S. 229 (1976).
Washington v. Lee, 263 F. Supp. 327 (M.D. Ala. 1966) (three-judge court).
Washington v. Seattle School District No. 1, 458 U.S. 457 (1982).
Watson v. Fort Worth Bank & Trust, 487 U.S. 977 (1988).
Webster v. Reproductive Health Services, 429 U.S. 490 (1989).
Weiner v. United States, 357 U.S. 349 (1958).
Wickard v. Filburn, 317 U.S. 11 (1942).
Will v. Michigan Department of State Police, 491 U.S. 58 (1989).
Wygant v. Jackson Board of Education, 476 U.S. 267 (1986).

CONSTITUTIONAL PROVISIONS

U.S. CONST. art. I, sec. 2, cl. 3.
U.S. CONST. art. I, sec. 2, cl. 5.
U.S. CONST. art. I, sec. 3, cl. 5.
U.S. CONST. art. I, sec. 6, cl. 2.
U.S. CONST. art. I, sec. 8, cl. 1.
U.S. CONST. art. I, sec. 8, cl. 3.
U.S. CONST. art. I, sec. 9.
U.S. CONST. art. I, sec. 9, cl. 1.
U.S. CONST. art. I, sec. 9, cl. 3.

U.S. CONST. art. I, sec. 10, cl. 1.
U.S. CONST. art. III, sec. 1.
U.S. CONST. art. III, sec. 2.
U.S. CONST. art. III, sec. 2, cl. 2.
U.S. CONST. art. IV, sec. 2.
U.S. CONST. art. IV, sec. 2, cl. 3.
U.S. CONST. art. V.
U.S. CONST. amend. II.
U.S. CONST. amend. IX.
U.S. CONST. amend. XI.
U.S. CONST. amend. XIII.
U.S. CONST. amend. XIV.
U.S. CONST. amend. XV.
U.S. CONST. amend. XIX.

STATUTES

Act of April 9, 1866, 14 Stat. 27.
Act of May 31, 1870, 16 Stat. 140, 144.
Act of Aug. 6, 1975, Pub. L. 94-73, 89 Stat. 400 (1975) (codified as amended at 42 U.S.C. §§ 1973 to 1973d, 1973h, 1973i, 1973l, 1973aa, 1973aa-1a to 1973aa-4, 1973bb (1982 & Supp. IV 1986)).
Civil Rights Act of 1866, Act of April 9, 1866, 14 Stat. 27.
Civil Rights Act of 1957, Pub. L. 85-315; 71 Stat. 634 (1957) (codified as amended at 42 U.S.C. § 1971 (1982)).
Civil Rights Act of 1960, Pub. L. 86-449; 74 Stat. 86, 90 (1960) (codified as amended at 42 U.S.C. § 1971 (1982)).
Civil Rights Act of 1964, Pub. L. 88-352; 78 Stat. 241, 243 (1964) (codified at 42 U.S.C. § 2000a (1982)).
Civil Rights Act of 1964, Pub. L. 88-352; 78 Stat. 240 (1964) (codified at 42 U.S.C. § 2000c-6 (1982)).
Civil Rights Act of 1964, Pub. L. 88-352; 78 Stat. 240 (1964) (codified at 42 U.S.C. §§ 2000d to 2000d-1 (1982)).
Civil Rights Act of 1964, Pub. L. 88-352; 78 Stat. 241, 253 (1964) (codified as amended at 42 U.S.C. §§ 2000e to 2000e-17 (1982 & Supp. IV 1986)).
Civil Rights Act of 1991, Pub. L. 102-166; 105 Stat. 1071 (1991) (to be codified).
Enforcement Act of 1870, Act of May 31, 1870, 16 Stat. 140, 144.
Fair Housing Act of 1968, Pub. L. 90-284; 82 Stat. 73, 81 (1968) (codified as amended at 42 U.S.C. §§ 3601-3619 (1982 & Supp. IV 1986)).
Public Works Employment Act of 1977, Pub. L. 95-28; 91 Stat. 116 (1977) (codified at 42 U.S.C. § 6705 (1982)).

Voting Rights Act of 1965, Pub. L. 89–110; 79 Stat. 437 (1965) (codified as amended at 42 U.S.C. §§ 1971, 1973 to 1973bb-1 (1982)).

Voting Rights Act Amendments of 1970, Pub. L. 91–285; 84 Stat. 314 (1970) (codified as amended at 42 U.S.C. §§ 1973 to 1973aa-1, 1973aa-2 to 1973aa-4, 1973bb (1982)).

28 U.S.C. § 1343(3).

42 U.S.C. § 1981.

42 U.S.C. § 1983.

42 U.S.C. §§ 2000e-2000e-15.

42 U.S.C. § 2000e-2.

EXECUTIVE ORDERS AND REGULATIONS

Executive Order No. 11,246, Part II, Subpart B, 3 C.F.R. 339, 340–42 (1964–65).

24 C.F.R. §§ 106, 109–20 (1990).

29 C.F.R. § 1608 (1989).

29 C.F.R. § 1690 (1989).

Index

of minority political resources to Supreme Court, 105; and failure to desegregate schools, 104, 166; and foreign policy, 104, 107–08, 166; holding
of, 73, 199 n.2; as icon of judicial sensitivity to minority interests, 3; as impediment to equal treatment, 109; as
impediment to minority acquisition of
political power, 3; and integrationism,
145; invalidation of separate-but-equal
public facilities, 71, 105–10, 166; and
liberals, 75; as majoritarian decision,
104, 105–10, 161; massive resistance
to, 104, 105, 166; and minority-controlled schools, 110–18, 167; and minority dependence upon Supreme
Court, 3, 7, 103, 104–18, 159, 166,
167, 170; minority disillusionment
with, 110; and miscegenation, 106–07;
and "mongrelization of the race," 107;
and political model of Supreme Court,
105–10, 159; as product of veiled majoritarianism, 86, 161; rhetorical success of, 106. See also Busing; School
desegregation
Browne, Robert, 113
Bush, George: appointment of Clarence
Thomas to Supreme Court, 21; conservative Supreme Court appointments
of, 101, 130, 135; opposition to affirmative action, 147; opposition to civil
rights legislation, 1, 122, 145, 174 n.4,
215 n.14; and opposition to minority
scholarships, 109–10; and racial divisiveness, 1, 174 n.4; and Willie Horton, 145
Busing, 75, 78, 79–80, 105. See also School
desegregation
Butch Cassidy and the Sundance Kid, 86

Calhoun v. Cook, 113
Capital punishment, 28–31; statistical evi-
dence of racial disparities in applica-
tion of, 28–29
Carmichael, Stokely, 113
Carrington, Paul, 155
Carter, Stephen, 158–59

Catholic-Protestant conflict in Northern
Ireland, 148
Centralization, connotations of, 136–38,
144–49. See also Affirmative action
Characterization of case, 50–57, 164
Chase, Samuel, 209 n.85
Cherokee Indian Tribe, 16, 161
Cherokee Nation v. State of Georgia, 16,
161
City of Cleburne v. Cleburne Living Cen-
ter, 182 n.13, 182 n.16
City of Richmond v. J.A. Croson Co., 91,
98, 119, 120, 127–30, 132, 134,
173 n.2
Civic republicanism, 90
Civic virtue, 90
Civil Rights Act of 1866, 43, 47
Civil Rights Act of 1957, 97
Civil Rights Act of 1960, 97
Civil Rights Act of 1964, 46, 97; Title II
of, 97; Title IV of, 97; Title VI of, 97,
98; Title VII of, 37–41, 97, 98,
173 n.2
Civil Rights Act of 1968, 46, 98
Civil Rights Act of 1990, 117, 122, 134,
173 n.2, 174 n.4, 221 n.101
Civil Rights Act of 1991, 1, 117, 122, 134,
173 n.2, 174 n.4, 221 n.101
Civil Rights Cases, 45, 161
Civil War, 13, 42, 48, 94, 97, 124, 131, 137
Colorblind principle. See Race neutrality
Columbus Board of Education v. Penick,
79
Commerce power. See Congress
Congress: and absence of principled decision making, 17; and affirmative action, 1, 119, 127, 128; and commerce
power, 46; and determination of federalism restrictions, 28; intent of, with
respect to "person" requirement under
§ 1983, 49; and job security, 23; and
means for circumventing formal safeguards for judicial independence, 15,
23, 163; and opposition to busing, 78;
and power to enforce fourteenth
amendment, 43, 128; and power to